THE THUMPING

J. S. LAU

XEMPLI PTY LTD

Published by Xempli Pty Ltd (Australia) ACN 618420063

Edited Dr Jocelyn Rikard-Bell

To Jocelyn

My love, my dream, my universe.

CONTENTS

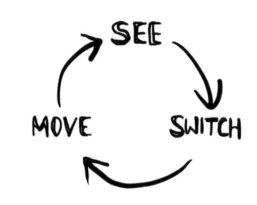

PART I

INTRODUCTION

THE HIDDEN FORCE THAT HOLDS US BACK

Fear shapes our lives, affects our biggest decisions and defines who we are. Here's a story to give you a feel for what is to come.

You want to write a book, but you don't.

You're twenty-three years old. You're afraid you're too young. *Do I have anything original worth saying? Does the world really need yet another book?* You're afraid that you won't be good enough, afraid of wasting time, so you put aside this fancy.

Ten years go by. During this time, you build a career in the aviation industry, travel and see the world, meet someone and start a family. The ambition to write a book remains lurking in the back of your mind, but you do nothing about it because of the fear that you won't have time to do it justice. You're afraid that it is a selfish pursuit – it would take you away from your obligations.

Another ten years go by. You work hard, rise through the

ranks, break through the glass ceiling, buy a house, renovate it, and raise your family. You're far too busy to write a book. It remains an unfulfilled ambition. A part of you wishes you started earlier when you were younger. *I had so much time back then. Why didn't I make a start?*

Then one day, unexpectedly, you get retrenched. You struggle to find work. It's a terrifying feeling. Fear and uncertainty occupies you: fear of not knowing if you will get a job again, of letting your partner down, of being stuck with full-time domestic duties, of not fulfilling your potential in the eyes of your parents, and that others will think less of you.

You decide to write a book. It's a fear driven decision: fear that your life will amount to nothing; fear of facing the big great void now that you don't have a job; fear of not knowing what to say when strangers at parties ask, "What do you do?"

The trouble is, you're not sure what to write about. You're afraid your current set of ideas for a book aren't interesting. You're afraid of wasting time on an unworthy topic. You've never done this before, and you're afraid you can't write as well as Tolstoy or Hemmingway. Of course, you don't say any of this out loud, or even admit it to yourself. It sounds too cowardly. It's an unconscious fear. The fear manifests as procrastination.

In the first few months, you are easily distracted. You redecorate the house; plan a holiday; cook amazing meals for your family; help a friend move – anything to make yourself feel useful. Then eventually, you settle on a topic that gives you a kernel of enthusiasm. It helps you overcome your fears and you finally make a start.

It's joyous to create, to be creative, and you really get into it. You don't just write at your desk, you're forming lines in your head all the time: during walks, in the car, and when you're cooking and shopping.

A few weeks into the venture, fear creeps into your mind: *Is this any good? What is the point I am making? Am I being long-winded? Maybe I haven't got what it takes to be a writer? Maybe I should do something else? What if I do all this work and nobody cares? Am I wasting my time?*

You're in desperate need of validation, but you can't ask for an opinion. Not yet. Not until you have a polished version that is worthy of the world to see.

You take weeks to rework sentences and paragraphs, but after a few weeks you're still unhappy to show it to anyone. You spend a few more weeks polishing, re-writing, restructuring and embellishing. Weeks turn into months. The delay is driven by the fear of being judged, of putting your reputation at risk, and your fear of not being good enough.

Finally, you share your writing with a few people you trust. Although they say encouraging things, you're not sure if they are just being polite. You need more evidence that you're not wasting your time. Your fears cause you to need a higher threshold of affirmation.

You send some of your writing to a short list of publishers, but you don't hear from them. *Are they too busy or is my work not good enough?*

You post some of your writing on social media. Although you get a few likes from friends, you doubt that they actually read all of the material.

You're not getting the clear signal you need. Meanwhile, there is much chatter in your head: *Should I back myself and keep going? After all, I've done so much already. On the other hand, am I ignoring the signs that I am wasting my time? Am I falling for the sunk-cost trap?*[1] *Do I need to face the truth that I'm not good enough?*

The dilemma torments you because you lack information to help you decide what to do. And you don't know who to ask.

You're afraid of being a failure even before you have failed.

Not wanting to be the kind of person who appears weak to others, you keep all this mental chatter to yourself. It consumes a lot of mental energy, and distracts you from your writing. If you could be free from it, you'd get into a 'flow' state more often, stay there longer, be more productive, more creative, and importantly, you'd enjoy the process. Unfortunately, you don't realise this. You're not alone. So many of us are blind to it.

You keep going anyway because you are not the kind of person who gives up easily.[2] After all, you're out of work, and you need to be doing something.

You pump yourself up with optimism and press on. For the moment, you ignore your fears. This can be a dangerous thing to do because a fear buried is a fear brewing. There's also the risk of false optimism.

After a few months, you stop writing altogether. Tired of the self-doubt, uncertainty, anxiety and isolation, you give up. You send out your resume and get a job. You archive the half-written book. *Maybe I'll come back to it one day.*

To save face, you tell others that a headhunter offered you a position that is too good to miss out on. *It's a great company, a great team, their mission is so inspiring...*

"What about the book?" they ask.

"It will have to wait. This is too important."

"Good for you," they say.

For several years, when you turn on your computer and see the file that contains your half-written book, you are reminded of your abandoned project, the failure to see things through, the daily grind of that era, the uncertainty and self-doubt.

Then one day, sick of being triggered into having these bad feelings, you erase the file that is your half-written book. *I need to put that stage of my life behind me. It's time to let go of my childish dreams. I am a professional now with a serious career. I've* broken through the glass ceiling in the aviation industry, and I have family responsibilities. I need to think positive, and remove any negativity in my mind.

Over time, this mindset defines you. You don't allow yourself any creative time or time to write; you dismiss ideas that come into your head, and kill the hopes of anyone around you who dares to dream of a career in the arts. It's not because you don't want to give false hope, it's the fear and bitter experience deep within you that speaks on your behalf.

We never lose our fears, we only learn to live with them

This story is for dreamers, big and small. Whether you're wanting to change the world or just your backyard; to become a rock-star or start a scrapbook; to build a start-up or make a career change – take heed:

Fear exists at the very beginning of every journey. We can fail even before we start because we're afraid of leaving the shores of safety.

Fear is with us throughout the journey. It slows us down, takes us off course and makes us feel lost at sea. We don't look out the window and enjoy the journey as much as we otherwise would. We play it safe, take the cautious road rather than the right road and waste time going around in circles looking for validation that doesn't exist.

Fear stays with us years after our journey's end and haunts us even when we've had raging success. "Was I actually that good?

Did I do enough? Should I have done it differently? Did I really make a difference? What was it all for?"

Whilst fear can be a ten tonne load of baggage that we carry around with us, it can also be a great thing, and maybe the best of things. It is a powerful motivator that helps us get out of bed on time and work till the wee hours. And thanks to our fears, we listen, get in touch, change tack, push the envelope and press on to overcome the odds. Fear keeps us safe, helps us avoid lifelong mistakes – a healthy sense of caution is essential to staying alive.

The great challenge is to tell the difference between fears that are warranted versus the baseless ones, rational versus irrational. Our aim is to harness fear, rather than be harnessed by it, and become resilient in the face of it, rather than being blindly optimistic in the face of real dangers.

We'll get to this.

THE WAKE-UP CALL

A few years ago, I found myself in hospital waiting for an operation. It would be the second in two weeks.

I shared the room with three patients: a twenty year-old man with cystic fibrosis, living on borrowed time, who was told at birth he'd have a life expectancy of only twenty-one years; a man in his seventies who didn't speak a word because he physically wasn't able to produce a sound; and a man in his sixties who had difficulty breathing and needed air tanks just to leave the hospital for a couple of hours.

Lying there in a hospital bed, with the endless beeping of machines around me, I asked myself: "I'm a fit and healthy forty-four-year-old, how did I get here?"

The answer was obvious to everyone but me: stress. The same worries and thoughts went around and around in my head. I was crabby all the time, slept only four to five hours each night, typically less. I thought I was super productive, but in hindsight, I was spinning my wheels. One of my clients took me aside one day and asked, "Don't take this the wrong way, James, but are you OK?" I've always thought of myself as being tougher than the rest, and so I laboured on ignoring the signs. I put positive thinking into overdrive. The assumption was that everything would be OK once this and that fell into place.

The only thing that fell was my health.

When I got out of hospital, I was determined to beat the stress, so I read widely on the topic, sought advice from experts, created a short-list of strategies, came up with a few original ideas of my own, put them to the test, dismissed the bad ones and nurtured the promising ones. This book is a product of over six years of research, analysis, and experimentation.

One of the first things I discovered was that we can't beat stress by trying to avoid stressful situations, telling ourselves to "relax", assuming that everything will be OK or forcing ourselves to think positive. We can live in the lap of luxury in a villa in Tuscany, have all our hopes and dreams come true, with millions of adoring fans and a room full of trophies; we can be relatively free from life's big problems; we can have family, close friends, and a devoted spouse, and STILL be anxious, obnoxious and thankless for all that we have if we aren't able to master our fears.

As many writers will attest, writing a book is a journey punctuated by loneliness, self-doubt, and bouts of insecurity. Stephen King describes it as "crossing the Atlantic Ocean in a bathtub.[1]*" Scarcely a week goes by without my feeling that I should give up this project and do something more "worthwhile".*

So what sustained me during these moments of self-doubt?

My driving motivation was the belief that we can and need to rise above our irrational fears, make ourselves impervious to fear-mongering, and avoid unnecessary worry, anxiety, and conflict.

We are living in a pandemic of fear. People are unnecessarily anxious, some to the point of mental illness, because of a plethora of fears, such as the fear of not being good enough, fear of being lied to or taken advantage of, fear of the world going mad and fear of loss of control. It robs us of our happiness and our well-being. We lose sleep, micromanage, nag, yell, lie, cheat, bully and torment others because of it. We give up before we start, and harbour self-doubt even when there is no justification for it. Fear causes us to overwork, overeat, overexercise and obsess over how we appear, what we should eat, where we are in life, and what others should or should not be doing. Marketers tap into our fears to make us buy products we don't need, such as oversized vehicles and premium petrol. We get trapped into the cycle of feeling like we need more money, so that we can buy things we don't need. Politicians, extremists, media and social media use fear-mongering to incite outrage over things we can't control, such as shifts in the geopolitical power balance. Over-exposure to these sources results in widespread chronic worrying, anxiety or apathy towards issues that actually warrant attention and action (such as global warming or public school funding). When we're afraid, we lose our sense of generosity and powers of empathy, and instead become egotistical, self-centric, territorial and, at times, brutal. It causes us to accept ludicrous ideas (such as the flat-earth fallacy), become hostile to anyone who doesn't see our point of view, and at the most extreme, incite bigotry, discrimination and violence.

I set out on a self-help journey and ended up with a help-others book. For while the benefit of mastering our own fears is huge, the benefit of mastering the fears of others dwarfs it. Imagine having X-Ray vision to see what troubles everyone: to have the empathy to understand their true feelings, acknowledge and address them, furnish them with a sense of control, and give them the confidence to take on life's greatest challenges. Take parenting as an example: to succumb to our fears is to be overbearing parents, dragging our children through the mud pit of our fears, burdening them with our issues, potentially for life. To master our fears is to free them of this torment and be the parent we all dream of being. To master their fears and role model fear mastery is to give our children a gift for life.

I used to say things like "think positive" or "stop worrying" to my mother, who was prone to episodes of negativity and fear-driven anxiety. I realise now that it was both naïve and cruel to ask her to change her mindset, because fear isn't something that is easily switched off. I know this because I later experienced the same bouts of negativity myself. The slightly wiser me knows that fear is an emotion, not something easily countered with logic and deduction. You can't end someone's worry by telling them to stop worrying, in the same way you can't stop a child from crying by telling them to stop crying. Thus, you won't find "think positive", "relax", "be courageous" and other such platitudes in this book. I won't be prescribing herbal tea or telling you to take time out. These things might help, but at the height of stress and anxiety fueled by palpable fear, it would be like trying to quell a house fire with tiny squirts of a water pistol. Trust me, I know, I've tried it all.

What is the Thumping?

The Thumping is the feeling we have in our body when fears take hold of us. It's the heart palpitations, the nervous, toxic energy throbbing in our veins, the noises in our head, and the inability to get back to sleep at 4am.

It can happen when we are kept in the dark about what is going on at work; when people say yes, but go behind our back to work against us; when we feel our children are out of control; when news stories makes it seem like the world has gone mad; when we are stuck in a rut and lose confidence in ourselves; and when the loss of a family member shatters our sense of normal.

The Thumping defines us – it causes us to be overly cautious or dangerously reckless; be all things to all people or nothing to anyone; over-work and burn out or to give up too easily and miss opportuni-

ties; to waste money on things we don't need or be too miserly at our own detriment.

Left unchecked causes us to surrender our happiness, fill our lives with unnecessary stress, and age before our time.

Who is this for?

This book is for people who want to live life to the maximum, and believe that there's got to be more to beating stress than scented candles, stress balls and breathing exercises. This period of our lives when we're depended on professionally and in our home lives is the point at which we face the most noise, and when the actions and decisions of today affect us for decades to come. It's arguably the point at which we have the most impact on our families, our colleagues and the world.

What you'll get from this book

Domestic bliss. *Fear lies behind every unfulfilled need, every grudge, and every argument. It's not just about being a better person to live with, it's about being the best version of ourselves. We owe this to our relationships. This book offers couples a common language and framework to help each other throughout life's difficult moments, from making better financial decisions to dealing with sexlessness and infidelity.*

Better parenting. *Author Mitch Albom wrote: "All parents damage their children. It cannot be helped. Youth, like pristine glass, absorbs the prints of its handlers. Some parents smudge, others crack, a few shatter childhoods completely into jagged little pieces.[2]" We give our children the best start in life when we avoid projecting our irrational fears on them. This book hopes to give parents the mental fortitude to worry less, to stop barking at their kids, and* instead enjoy the important job of creating competent, confident, kind and responsible humans.

Life and career fulfilment. To be a puppet to our fears is to overwork, chase someone else's dreams, and miss out on opportunities. When we are free from the noise and distraction of a fearful mind, we are in a better position to grow, be more creative and productive, and focus on what matters most.

Empathy and influence. When someone is boastful, they're expressing a fear of not being relevant; when someone is obstructive, they're expressing a fear of being out of control. The ability to see, understand and acknowledge the fears of others is a precursor to building trust. We get to choose what to do with this trust.

Better decision making and resilience. This book aims to provide a framework to discern rational from irrational fear. With practice, we can immunise ourselves against manipulators, including politicians, the media and salespeople. Mastery of fear over the long term gives us the stoicism to handle life's most difficult moments with poise and resilience.

I think back to the three weeks I spent in the hospital. Lying in bed, with the endless beeping of machines in the background. I thought about how my wife had to fend for herself, how my children had to put up with my crabbiness, how the stress affected my work and my professional reputation. I felt selfish to have not addressed fears in my life before it came to all this. This book is about me doing something about it.

LIMITATIONS OF THIS BOOK

Not Phobias. *This book isn't about phobias such as fear of flying, spiders or public speaking.*

Not medical advice. *The ideas, concepts, and strategies in this book do not constitute medical or psychological advice. Treatment of serious mental illness such as chronic anxiety, depression and other psychological disorders is well outside the scope of this book. I have written the stories without the benefit of knowing your context, your history and the circumstances you face.*

I have no medical or psychological qualification. *This is liberating in a sense because the book is void of jargon, footnotes and references. It doesn't formulate one-size-fits all theories from data samples, or assume that everyone will regress to the mean. I am unperturbed by the possibility of being ostracised by academic circles, being proven wrong, or whether what I say in public will affect my medical practice. This said, I am guilty of assuming that naivety is an advantage. In most cases, it isn't. Thus, I've gone to great lengths to* avoid sounding like a guru, to tell you what to do or how you should live. I've reworked the voice, the tone, the language many times over in this book, so that readers get to decide for themselves what resonates. It's important to me you know this. I only meant the ideas and stories in the book to trigger self-reflection: no more, no less.

Story-telling is a dangerous device. The book comprises a series of short stories, employing story-telling tricks from Leo Tolstoy to Dan Harmon. I chose the story form because change is hard. Facts and knowledge aren't enough for change to come about. If it were, then losing weight and giving up smoking would be a breeze. Stories take us on a journey, make us feel something, and open us up to deeper empathy and insight. The danger of a well-told story, however, is that it can fool us into accepting flimsy evidence as being universal truths. Readers who identify with the stories should be wary of this vulnerability and always treat the ideas as hypotheses and conjecture. The stories are works of fiction where I get to play God and decide the fate of the characters to support my case. It's also potentially manipulative. I invite you to read the stories in this book critically, and disagree with me if my conclusions don't fit with your own experience.

Oversimplification. The book is an exercise in looking at human behaviour through the lens of fear. This oversimplification is a limitation because human motivation is highly complicated, affected by a broad range of emotions, not just fear. We do things out of love, joy, generosity, jealousy, a sense of pride, and a sense of justice. We're creatures of routines and habits. Our genetic disposition, cultural context, upbringing, tribal loyalties, and values all affect us. Our identity, the image we have of ourselves, is a powerful driver of our thoughts and actions. For example, people who run 100km in the snow, pushing the limits of human endurance, aren't necessarily driven by fear (such as fear of being mediocre). They might do it because it feels good to them.

I've used the term "fear" in place of a range of terms such as "worry", "concern", "trepidation" and "caution". The differences between these words are not subtle. The condensation of complexity into simple is intentional for two reasons:

One. It makes it a lot easier to see the fear within us and around us. To understand ourselves, we only have to ask one question: "What am I afraid of here?" In order to understand why people behave the way they do, we only have to ask one question: "What are people afraid of?" To become immune to manipulation of advertisers, politicians, and salespeople, we only need to ask: "What fears are they seeking to tap into here?" The simplicity is important because often we don't have the luxury of time for deeper analysis and reflection in the heat of the moment. For example, when a colleague in a business meeting talks over us, we're likely to get frustrated and retaliate by cutting off their sentences. If in that moment we can ask ourselves: "What is the fear driving this behaviour?" we might arrive at answers such as "fear of being irrelevant in the meeting; fear of not being good enough". The insight empowers us with the empathy we need to better deal with the situation. Cutting off this colleague only exacerbates their fears, perpetuating the problem. Whereas a compliment, or an acknowledgement of our colleague's importance in the meeting, would put them at ease and reduce their need to dominate the room.

Two. Some people wear "worrying" and "cautiousness" as a badge of honour. For example, some of us say things like, "The only reason you don't have to worry is *because people like me do all the worrying." And we regard worrying as a show of love, e.g. "Of course I worry, I am your mother." By contrast, fear isn't something we consider desirable, and therefore we're more likely to give it the attention it deserves. Consider this example: you nag at your daughter for eating too much. Your daughter is not overweight now, but you are weary that she could get fat. This seems to be a reasonable thing to do as a parent – we feel our worrying and over-caution is justified because of love and care for our children. Let's consider for a moment what fears you might harbour here. To what extent are you afraid that she will become grossly obese, suffer poor health, and become a social outcast at school? To what extent are you motivated by the fear of being judged as a bad parent? Are these fears warranted given she isn't over-weight now? Is the nagging more about you, rather than her? By recognising our own fears, and not hiding it under the guise of love, we give ourselves a chance of not projecting our fears on our children. This allows us to act rationally, put good practices into place that are actually beneficial, such as keeping junk food out of the house, serving nutritious meals, avoiding fast food advertising, and setting an example of body positivity. People use love to justify their nagging, and in the process cause shame, set their children up to have an unhealthy relationship with food, and strip from their children the precursor for healthy living: self-love.*

Not a cure. *It would be a lie to promise that this book will help us rid ourselves of our fears. Nothing can do this (not for very long, anyway). Some of our greatest fears will stay with us for life. We may conquer it momentarily with insight and resolution, but they* *almost always return, usually at our most vulnerable moments. Even the most adept fear masters have to keep working to stay above their fears, in the same way top athletes have to work to stay conditioned. The good news is that with time and practice, it gets easier and easier to see ourselves, stop ourselves from making mistakes we would later regret, and to dig ourselves out of a mess.*

OUTLINE

The chapters of this book follows the four steps of the Fear Mastery model. I will cover each step in greater detail in the book. For now, here is a high level summary:

See. The first step to being in control of our lives is to see the fear that is affecting us, as well as those around us – ideally as it is happening as opposed to afterwards. A good habit to get into is to address the fear, not the words people utter. Our aim should therefore not be fearlessness, but mastery of fear, to gain the superpower to discern rational from irrational fear.

Switch. Whilst the first challenge to mastering fear is to see it in real time, the second challenge is to "unsee" it, to be free from its often suffocating grip, and make room for a deeper, more complete, and balanced view of the world.

Move. In the end, what counts is our actions, not just our thoughts. Pre-decision-making is the practice of deciding ahead of time so that when we encounter 'moments of truth', we can fall back on prior thinking, one that is more complete, free from fatigue and away from the heat of the moment. To truly master our fears, it helps to formally list fear-driven actions (behaviours we often fall *back on and want to avoid) and fear-mastery actions (behaviours that help us be the better version of ourselves in those moments).*

*   **Quell.** *Fear is an emotional experience. We can't always expect to master our emotions with reasoning and knowledge. It's as futile as trying to control what dreams we have at night. Quelling fears requires a consistent, lifelong approach, which we will explore later in this book – chapter 6 will show the perils of not dealing with chronic fear adequately, and chapters 7 and 8 shows how we can tackle the deepest scars caused by fear.*

3.BLIND

PART II

BLIND

Why everything we do is driven by fear, and why we can't afford to be blind to it.

WHAT PROGRESSIVES AND CONSERVATIVES HAVE IN COMMON

People on both sides of the political fence share one thing in common: fear. Here's a story to illustrate this.

You love your brother, but the two of you can't agree on anything. You think he is an imbecile.

You believe vaccination is harmful – a conspiracy to line the pockets of pharmaceutical companies. He believes the risk posed to the individual is justified because it serves the greater good. *What a load of baloney!*

You believe tighter border security and lower immigration rates are necessary to protect your nation's limited resources from being squandered. He believes we should welcome refugees because it is the humanitarian thing to do. If it were up to him, borders would be open to the diseased, the mentally unstable, the welfare cheats, the criminals and the terrorists. It's impossible to have a conversation with him about this topic without being accused of being a racist.

You believe humanity is too insignificant to affect earth's climate. Every time there is a wintry day, or a flood somewhere on earth, he says, "You see? It's climate change." The only thing you see is confirmation bias.

You don't trust governments – they are the enemy against civil liberty and hopeless at getting anything done except waste taxpayer's money. He believes people are stupid, and capitalism is prone to greed and market failure. If it were up to him, he'd let governments decide what we eat, where we live and what thoughts we're allowed to have.

You're flabbergasted that someone who shares the same genes, upbringing and education can have such a distorted view of the world.

Family gatherings in the past were civil. Although you might disagree on certain issues, back then the differences were able to coexist amicably. These days, the two of you can't seem to have a rational conversation without getting emotional.

One night, the two of you are out with a group of friends. He makes snide remarks all night long at your expense. At a Mexican food truck, he says, "I see you're still happy to eat foreign food even though you don't welcome foreigners."

"Why don't you shut up?"

Your friends say nothing.

"Am I not speaking the truth?" he asks.

"You're so blind to the truth, you wouldn't know it if it hit you in the face," you say.

"Well at least I'm not a redneck."

You say, "Why don't you go and find your own friends to be with?"

"Hey look," you continue, "there's a group of immigrants over there, maybe they'll take you in."

No one says anything. Your brother takes off. Jackie, your

friend, goes after him, but returns alone. As usual, your brother isn't open to reason. *Why is he like this? Why does he get so worked up? Why do intelligent people fall for fake news?*

After this incident, the two of you stop speaking to each other. Months go by, and you spend a lot of time in your head. You miss him. It's the regular things you do together that you miss most, like movie-night Wednesdays.

The empty feeling comes out as frustration and anger.

"What's the point of saying sorry if we can't see eye to eye on anything?" you say to your friend Jackie over coffee. "Am I to suppress my opinions just to keep the peace?"

"We are all living in a pandemic of fear, conservatives and progressives," says Jackie. "Fear that evil will take place if we do nothing. Fear that our future and the wellbeing of our clan are under threat. Neither side can understand why perfectly normal, seemingly intelligent people can hold a distorted view of the world. We see bad things happening on TV and on social media every day, and we feel helpless to do anything about it." This is one of Jackie's pet rants. You let Jackie continue. "News is commercially driven to perpetuate fears because that which we find threatening, we find irresistible. It's how they get eyeballs, it's how they get us hooked. The consequence is that it keeps us at a constant state of simmer, ready to boil over at the slightest provocation."

"Like my brother," you mutter under your breath.

"It's not just your brother. We're all in the same slaughter house. If you watch the news, it's impossible not to be outraged. I stay away from it altogether."

"But how do you stay in touch with what is going on? Isn't apathy corrosive to democracy?" You crinkle your brow. "Don't we need everyone to stay informed to keep governments in check? Did you know that the Immigration Department blew its budget by more than $25 billion last year? And 80% of the $1 trillion so-called economic stimulus went straight into the trust funds of the rich?[1] How can we afford to stay blind and silent?"

You're seething, thus proving Jackie's point. Being too gracious to say so, Jackie takes a sip of coffee and feigns interest in what you're saying, as if you're saying it for the first time. You stop yourself from continuing your rant, aspiring to be as gracious as Jackie, and instead pick up the menu to study it.

You think to yourself: *What good has come of the fighting and the stand-off between me and my brother? Has it made a material difference to the political issues I care so much about? Have either of us won an argument or changed each other's minds over the past decade? Given this record, how likely am I to change my brother's mind?*

As if reading your mind, Jackie says, "Time is the ultimate finite resource. How much lost time can the two of you afford?"

"What's the point of making peace if he persists with the bickering and personal attacks? You know what it's like, you were there the other night."

"Personal attacks are just an expression of fear."

"Am I to suppress my opinions and swallow my feelings? Freud said, 'Unexpressed emotions will never die. They are buried alive and will come forth later in uglier ways.'"

"That's your fear speaking."

"Fear of what?"

"Fear of not being able to control a family member, fear of being humiliated again, fear of getting into an argument, fear of immigrants destroying our community, taking our jobs and squandering our resources."

"No, that's not it. You're saying I'm blind to my fears, yet you're going through life with blinkers on, you don't watch the news, have no idea what is going on. Don't you see the irony in that?" The words came out harsher than you expected.

"Ah yes. You've always been good at keeping me grounded!" says Jackie.

You resist the urge to press your point, realising that you're directing your frustration at Jackie unnecessarily. Giving Jackie the benefit of the doubt, you say, "Let's just say you're right, I *am* affected by fear."

"I am too. We all are."

"What if the fear is justified? How do we separate genuine threats from imagined ones? How do we know what the truth is, and therefore how to act, if, as you say, the news is designed to outrage rather than inform?"

"I don't know, but it's one of the greatest challenges of our time. I admit that having my head in the sand isn't the answer, it is itself an act of fear – a fear of being lied to, tainted, manipulated, getting hooked and emotionally destabilised. Staying in the dark is my way of coping with the lies and hyperbole. Apathy is toxic to democracy. You're right."

"I'm sorry I got loud. The stand-off is eating away at me."

"Fear is behind every argument, conflict and feeling of guilt. The trick is to see the fear, rather than react to the words people say. I think of the film, The Matrix, when I say this. You know the bit I'm talking about? At the end, Keanu Reeves can see the code, the 1s and 0s, and therefore bend reality. The best way to deal with conflict is like that, to be able to see the surrounding fear, work out which threats are real, and avoid being affected by those that aren't."

"Are you trying to tell me I'll be able to dodge the bullets my brother aims at me?"

"No, I'm telling you that when you're ready, you won't have to dodge bullets."

After coffee, a strong need occupies you. You need your

brother, and he needs you. You worry he might not answer your call, or worse, he could be cold, and expect you to grovel.

Self-talk: *See his insults and bickering as fear. He is in pain. Ignore the personal attacks. Don't be afraid if he is cold.*

Check what day of the week it is. Wednesday. Call him. He picks up.

"Hi."

"Movie tonight?" you ask.

"Sure, what do you want to watch?" he replies.

"How about an action thriller?"

"Action thriller?" he asks sceptically. "What's it called?"

"Carbon Neutraliser. It's about an action hero that vanquishes evil carbon villains. Plenty of romance. Layers of complexity. You'd love it."

"Are you joking?"

"Yes."

"Ha ha."

"How about you pick the movie?"

"Alright. Same time?" he asks.

"Yep."

"Nice to hear from you," he says.

"Yeah, it's been too long."

∾

Why does family make us furious?

It's curious why people in our family can upset us so easily. We often treat them with a fraction of the courtesy, kindness and profession- alism we reserve for friends and peers at work. Often we don't realise this until they are gone.

We know it ought to be the other way around. We ought to be more generous and tolerant with the ones closest to us, but this is easier said than done. Why is that? Is it because our family members know us too well and therefore know which buttons to push? Because we regress to being our teenage selves? Carry baggage of misdeeds that we haven't fully forgiven? Do we expect more of them? Or is it because they're just small-minded and infuriating?

These explanations are all plausible. Looking at it from the lens of fear, I'd add that it's got to do with a sense of control. If we can't control those closest to us, then what control do we have at all?

Anthropologists might have another take: for most of human history, we lived in small tribes. An opposing view within the group can endanger the survival of our tribe. There is a lot at stake if, for example, someone in our tribe believes it is safe to cross a bridge or invade the neighbouring people, but we don't. In modern times we are less dependent on our families, so differences in opinion, especially political ones, have little to no impact on our survival. It's curious that we still behave as if it does. Is it a form of primal fear, no different from our discomfort with rats and spiders (a legacy of human evolution)? We can only hypothesise.

WHY WE ARE HARD ON OUR CHILDREN

All children want is a stable, loving family, and all parents aim to be stable and loving. That's the plan until fear comes into the equation...

You have three children. One of them is challenging.

Your eldest is a model child. She is conscientious, does her chores without your asking, and everyone regards her highly, including her teachers.

Your second child is the opposite. He is uncooperative, lazy, whines when there is work to be done, throws tantrums, slams doors, claims that you favour his siblings, and acts entitled. It's difficult to have a conversation with your son. Even the slightest hint of disappointment will precipitate self-loathing, "I'm bad, I know I'm bad." This upsets you because you've read that children with low self-esteem are less resilient. You love him, hate to see him this way, and worry that the negativity and hopelessness is becoming a permanent part of his character.

To deal with this, you praise everything he does, remind him not to compare himself with his siblings, avoid giving feedback, and give him a lot of slack when he slacks off. You even avoid praising your eldest daughter in front of him.

One day, you hear the children screaming at each other in the living room. You rush over to see what the commotion is about. It appears your eldest child has hit your second child. You don't condone violence, but you suspect he must have deserved it. Conscious to not take sides, in your calmest tone, you ask them what happened. Your eldest child is hysterical. "He has been sneaking up to me, doing silent farts, then denying it. He cut up my eraser into tiny pieces with his new pocket knife; hid my trolls around the house; and put sand on my bed. I told him to stop, but he denied it. And this is the last straw: he put sand down the back of my underpants."

Your son chuckles.

"It's not funny!" shouts your daughter.

"She stole my eraser, it's my eraser so I can cut it up if I want to," says your son.

Your daughter screams profanity at this.

"And what about the farts and the sand?" you ask.

"Why are you taking her side? You always take her side!"

You hate being accused of being biassed; look to your partner for support, but your partner says nothing. You gather your calm and say: "I'm not taking sides. I just want to know what happened. Let me hear your side of the story: what have you got to say about the farts and the sand?"

Despite your effort to stay impartial, he responds as if he's being interrogated. With a wobble in his voice he says: "What's the point of arguing? You're going to be on her side, even though she hit me!"

"Just try to stay calm, buddy. I'm just gathering facts here."

"She's not calm. She's yelling at me, she swore, and she hit me. And now you're shouting at me."

"I'm not shouting."

Tears well up in his eyes. He describes your "process" with profanity, then takes off. Stomp, stomp, stomp, up the stairs, and you hear his door slam loudly.

Your eldest child asks, "So you're just going to let him get away with it?"

You feel awful, angry, and hopeless all at once. Your partner gives you a look of disappointment. This really gets under your skin.

After having a few words with your eldest child, you go to your son's room to remedy the situation. You reassure him of your love, that you're on his side, but he needs to stop provoking his sister. You ask him why he's doing all the things he did.

He says he is sorry, but it doesn't sound sincere.

"You can't just say sorry to make me go away."

"Sorry."

"Don't say sorry. I want to understand what's going on."

"Sorry. I said I'm sorry. What more do you want?" he cries.

"I just want to understand."

With great strain, he says, "I already said I am sorry. Will you go away, please!"

You leave his room fuming because he isn't sorry. You've failed to get through to him, didn't get the chance to explain right from wrong, got accused of being a biased parent, and worst of all, you've made him feel bad about himself. It feels like a total failure.

At night, you have a big row with your partner. You are furious because it feels like you are doing this parenting thing alone, but instead of getting an apology, your partner thinks you should stop picking on your son.

"Pick on him?! What do you mean by that?! I give him more love, attention and slack than anyone else."

"Well, congratulations on that front. You've completely crushed any sense of self-worth left in him."

Who's at fault here – the adult or the child?

At the core of sibling rivalry lies the fear that we're not as talented, good looking, strong or well-liked as our siblings, and that our parents don't favour us. It's about living up to expectations (real or imagined) and getting our fair share of a parent's love and attention, which in the eyes of children may be perceived as scarce resources.

Where do these insecurities come from? In short, they come from us, the parents. We forge our own fears in our childhood, then unwittingly, and with the best of intentions, project our fears onto the next generation.

What fears do we have as parents? Concern for our children's safety is natural, and necessary. But it also causes us to be over-protective, to fuss, shout, nag, suffocate, spy and lose sleep. As parents, we fear our children might lack confidence and people will tread over them. We compensate for this by giving too much praise, or by praising talent rather than effort. It is easy for parents to inadvertently create unhealthy competition between siblings and, in doing so, foster jealousy and ill will. If we fear our children might become weak as adults and lack resilience, some of us feel the need to dish out tough love, set impossible standards, and put our children through tests. The tests are about satisfying our own fears and do little to help the child. The fears can be self-fulfilling in that the child loses confidence every time they fail an impossible standard. We fear our children will become ungrateful and ill-mannered. This causes us to be afraid of what people think of us as parents. We fear our children won't embody our values and culture, afraid that they will be lazy or dishonest, and end up at the bottom of the social heap, or worse, become criminals. Driven by these fears, but under the guise of "it's for their own good", we do too much coaching, shouting, punishing, bullying, spying, we're harsher than we need to be, less patient, we overreact to minor issues, over project short-term behaviour, jam-pack our children's week with extra-curricular activities, and show disappointment unnecessarily.

We overlook the fact that values, diligence and conscience take time to develop, often not until adulthood. We ought to recognise that it is healthy for children to goof off, rebel or test the boundaries we set them.

If we have more than one child, we're afraid that the conduct of one will influence the others, which causes us to feel justified in being especially harsh. Teachers will relate to this situation, where they find themselves being hard on 'troublemakers' in their class-room, for fear of losing control of the entire class.

No matter how much we try to hide our fears, the reality is that we wear our fears on the outside. Kids can read our body language and interpret our actions. They can sense our delight when their siblings gain our approval.

Parents cast long shadows. It's rare to find individuals who aren't affected by the fears of their own parents.

Although our parent's fears might haunt us our entire lives, it doesn't mean we have to act on them. We can't choose our parents, we can't go back in time to erase their hang-ups, but we can recognise them, and with practice, free ourselves of these deeply ingrained responses that shape our own behaviour.

Chapter 2 is about helping us "See" and therefore become conscious of our fears.

The Parent-Child Fear Trap

Parent projects
fear

Parent puts child
through tests
"You can do it"

Parent's concerns
exacerbated

Child doesn't fully
allay parent's fear

Child loses
confidence and
rebels

Parent shows
disappointment

PASSIVE AGGRESSIVE

Fear undermines trust, innovation, collaboration and a sense of ownership at a workplace. It explains territorial and obstructive behaviour, gossiping, risk avoidance, sabotage, and so much more.

You are working on a project in Japan that is going well, except you are struggling to get a meeting with the executive considered most important to the project, Yamada-san, the Head of Sales.

At first you don't make a big fuss because Yamada is very senior in the organisation. Getting into his diary is understandably difficult. You don't realise this, but your reluctance to be more assertive stems from your fear of authority (which stems from your upbringing).

When you finally meet Yamada-san, you're a little nervous. You are worried about not knowing what to say to someone in an important role, or of saying the wrong thing.

Your demeanour when interacting with Yamada-san

comes across as respectful bordering on subservient. The executive appreciates this, but immediately takes you for granted. You don't get the respect you deserve.

The executive appears supportive of the project and assigns a senior manager to work with you. It's a tremendous relief.

The trouble is, the senior manager isn't particularly helpful. Like his boss, he rarely shows up to meetings.

You'd raise your concerns if you could, but it's hard to gain quick access to Yamada-san in person, and it's not the sort of thing you document in emails because you're afraid it might come back to bite you.

You book weeks in advance to get a meeting, only to get a call on the day of the meeting from the executive's assistant, "Have to cancel... very sorry... unforeseen circumstances."

More than a month has passed. By this point, you have had to write an interim report without input from Yamada-san. This is disastrous because without Yamada-san's input, the report will lack credibility.

You call the assistant, conveying your urgency. "I must meet Yamada-san tomorrow".

"Yamada-san is leaving in the morning for an overseas trip".

"Really? When will Yamada-san return?"

"In two weeks."

"Two weeks!"

You can't afford a two-week delay. Think fast: *persistence is an admired virtue in Japan.* Offer: "Can I offer to drive Yamada-san to the airport?"

The assistant says, "I'll ask".

The cultural knowledge and persistence pays off. The assistant offers dinner with Yamada-san.

"When?"

"Tonight."

"Tonight? Great."

Yamada-san is a gracious host. You find yourself in a restaurant with lush private booths and crisp white linen. The waiter serves you an amuse-bouche that looks like the texture of the innards of a sea creature. You overcome your fear of putting foreign slimy things in your mouth, and much to your surprise and delight it tastes like salmon and buttered popcorn. The texture isn't so great.

Yamada-san praises your work, and admires your cultural sensitivity.

You are careful not to embarrass the executive so you don't say anything about the lack of support to date for fear of upsetting people.

"It's vital we have your input, Yamada-san. You have the expertise and the full respect of the executive committee. In a few weeks, the project will end, and we will depend on your help to execute the plans."

Yamada-san promises to read the report on the flight, and to provide input upon the plane touching down. You'd like to go through the document now, but you're afraid that it would ruin the pleasant moment you're experiencing with Yamada-san, and being assertive now implies distrust.

Yamada-san orders dessert and refills your tea cup when it is empty – it's an enormous honour for a senior person in Japan to do this.

Unfortunately, things don't improve. Yamada-san does not respond to your follow-up emails, and is unreachable.

You decide to plough on without Yamada-san. There's no choice. You feel that you can't complain to a higher authority because it would make you look incompetent (i.e. you'd look like you lack influencing and stakeholder management skills). You're afraid of speaking up at this late stage.

You make a presentation to the executive committee, including Yamada-san, the CEO and executives from the regional office. Yamada-san doesn't say much. People raise questions about the practicality of your recommendations. Only Yamada-san can speak to this, but Yamada-san only offers nods as if in deep thought, neither agreeing with nor disagreeing. Other Japanese executives sense this, and suddenly the room turns against you. One after another they express doubt, nitpick or flat out criticise the recommendations. At the end of the meeting, Yamada-san praises you for your hard work, sounding magnanimous in doing so.

The project ends, you leave Japan. You learn later that the recommendations are being ignored. The optics are bad: it looks like you've failed to achieve anything despite having Yamada-san's support. They do not invite you back to the company, you never hear from any of the people you worked closely with. *I worked so hard, displayed much cultural sensitivity, treated Yamada-san with respect, bent over backwards to help – all for what? Nothing but a black mark on my record.*

You blame Yamada-san, and form a loathing for the client organisation. *They're all so insular, closed minded and political. It drives me crazy. I'll never work there again, or if I do, the gloves will be off. I will not let them treat me the way they did.* This is a fear of bad things in the past repeating itself.

It's easier to blame others than to admit that you missed something.

At the heart of passive aggressive behaviour is fear

Have you encountered passive aggressive behaviour like the example given above, if not at work, then at home? Your spouse agreeing to something but not following through? A child sabotaging your plans by feigning illness? Your adult siblings not carrying their weight?

Would scenarios like the one in this story have a different ending if the protagonist were less blind to Yamada-san's fears? What are these fears? An obvious one is the fear of outside intervention, which comprises a subset of fears such as fear of losing control (e.g. we're forced to do something we don't agree with or people force change upon us without our say); fear of loss of power and respect (i.e. people listen to others but ignore you); fear that someone else will undo the work we've done; fear that someone else will get the credit for our past work; fear of confrontation; fear of wasting time; and fear of loss (e.g. wasting money). These fears manifest in distrust, territorial behaviour, stonewalling, duplicity and passive aggression.

For those working in matrix organisational structures, this is useful knowledge because we're often required to work with and influence people who don't answer to us, and we can't always rely on a higher authority (such as the CEO) to put his or her weight behind every need in the business.

Project and change management disciplines say that we should seek to understand "stakeholder objectives". Would we be better off addressing "stakeholder fears" instead if we want to get our way more often? For example, to pitch "increase sales" might align with the objectives of a Head of Sales, but it wouldn't address any of the underlying fears, such as those mentioned above. Experienced managers who are good at getting others to cooperate already know this instinctively. They spend as much time allaying fears as they do searching for common objectives.

WHY WE OVERWORK, OVEREAT AND OVEREXERCISE

How can we make the most of our short lives without the stress and anxiety that often comes with it?

You work four days a week, but on your days off you check emails and tinker with reports. You resent these extra unpaid hours of work, but you believe that if you don't do this, you might miss an important email, or let down your team. This behaviour is driven by fear: fear of letting people down, of not making progress, not being good enough, fear of what people will say behind your back if you are not 110% on top of your game (especially given you work part time).

Conventional wisdom says that we get a small dopamine hit when we check our emails. The hit feels more like relief than a high, relief that there is nothing left outstanding or that you have met your obligations to your colleagues or clients. The act of checking your emails several times a day, sometimes within the hour, gives you a sense of progress. The question is: progress towards what?

You pride yourself on your work ethic. Everything you do has to serve a purpose. Whilst these are good virtues, they are in part motivated by fear: fear of wasting time and your life amounting to nothing. You have a low tolerance for small talk and time wasters around the office, but you engage in small talk anyway because you don't want to be seen as being arrogant for fear of not fitting in.

Your work ethic extends to your family, and you take your role in it seriously. Despite spending a lot of time with your family, guilt burdens you because time with them never seems enough. You're afraid of not meeting your children's needs, letting your partner down and being a bad parent. You treasure pictures of your children when they were little, but seeing them gives you a tinge of sadness, pricked by the fear that they will never be little again, that the precious time has been lost and you're getting older. Once in a while, you remind yourself to just relax and enjoy your family. These moments, when you're able to master your fears, are rare for reasons you're yet to understand.

You feel bad that you haven't seen your elderly parents in a while (fear of failing your filial duty). When you visit them, you spend most of it resisting having an argument with them (fear that they might die and you don't want the last thing you say to them to be something negative). Their old-school politics gets under your skin (fear that people who should know better don't know better). You resent being treated like you're still twelve years-old (fear of being told what to do and how you should live your life, and fear of not getting the respect/credit you deserve).

You try to be careful about your weight. You are good 80% of the time, but it's the moments of weakness that let you down. The odd snack, the occasional second serving and the midnight pantry raids are hard habits to break.

We live in an overfed society where eating has little to do with nutrition, and more about our irrational fears. The fears are: going hungry, not getting enough nutrition, food going to waste, and fear of boredom.

To compensate, you over exercise. You take up running and set yourself a goal to run ten kilometres in under an hour. It's difficult to achieve this for two reasons: (1) you're busy, and (2) at any given time you are nursing an injury. Right now your knees are sore, and at other times it might be a bad back or a shoulder strain. The cause? Over-exercising. Over-exercising leads to injuries, which causes you to fall into a rut. This, in turn, causes you to overeat.

You don't weigh yourself, you probably have gained no weight, but you feel bad about your eating habits anyway. Not having the discipline to control what you put in your mouth, nor control of your body, is a real downer. So you overwork because pleasing others at work and keeping your inbox at zero gives you a sense of control.

You run from one thing to another, unconscious of your fears, unable to cast aside your compulsive worrying, being hard on yourself and others, and feeling incapable of relaxing to enjoy life's journey.

If only I could… I'd be….

Experts say we shouldn't over-train or be obsessed with get-fit-fast regimes. Instead, we should make exercise a sustainable routine to build fitness slowly. We over-train and risk injury because of our fears: a fear of getting fat, fear of looking bad, fear of being judged by our friends, fear of not being in control of our body, fear of being the kind of person who can't handle pain, and fear of the signs of ageing.

Ultra-marathon runners who endure distances of up to 160kms in desert or blizzard conditions are extraordinary people. Whilst they might be driven by ambition and the pleasure that comes from achieving something, for some of them somewhere deep in their psyche lies fear: of being ordinary, their life amounting to nothing, letting people down; fear of losing, etc. There is nothing wrong with that — I wish I could run 100kms myself — but doing it for the right reasons, as opposed to fear alone, ensures that we don't end up chasing validation that is unattainable no matter how many medals we win.

At the other extreme, many of us over-rest or avoid exercise unnecessarily because of fear. We have the irrational fear that our bodies are not up to it, even though moderate exercise is good for us. For example, some of us avoid running because of a weak achilles tendon, but running with a correct technique can, often, fix and prevent problems like this.[1] Some of us avoid swimming because we're afraid of catching a cold, but regular swimming may actually strengthen our overall immune system. Some of us spend too much time resting an injury because we have a fear that the pain could get worse (or become permanent). We let the fear talk us out of rehabilitation exercises.

The three excesses: overworking, overeating and overexercising are connected. Overworking leads to stress, stress leads to overeating (to make ourselves feel better), overeating leads to weight gain, gaining weight makes us feel bad about ourselves so we overwork and overexercise, over exercising leads to injury, injury undermines our sense of control, loss of a sense of control causes us to overwork (so that we can feel that we are in control), and so on and so on...

Chapter 3 shows how we can master our fears to break this cycle. We can live a full life without the pendulum swings of excesses driven by fear. Chapter 5 will specifically address how we can break out of ruts.

There may be good reasons for saying things like "If only I could lose five kilos, I'd be happy" or "If only I got that promotion... things would be ok". But it might serve us well to check: is there an underlying fear behind these motivations?

A SIMPLE FEAR MASTERY MODEL

How do we conquer our fears? How do we become aware of them, remain in control and live our lives to the fullest?

Senior executives hire management consultants to solve complex, high stakes problems such as how to compete, how to cut costs and how to affect organisation change. Good management consultants spend most of their careers trying to identify order amidst chaos, work out root causes, form concepts to de-muddle thinking and create ways to better understand the world. Having worked as a management consultant for over twenty years, I drew on old strategies and created a mental model of my own, along with a few templates, which I'll share with you here.

A Simple Fear Mastery Model

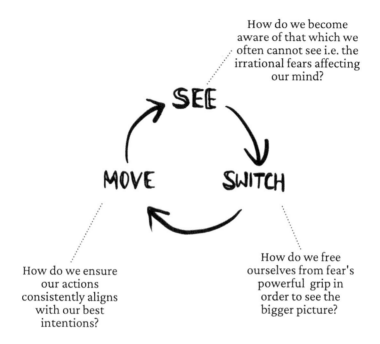

How do we become aware of that which we often cannot see i.e. the irrational fears affecting our mind?

How do we ensure our actions consistently aligns with our best intentions?

How do we free ourselves from fear's powerful grip in order to see the bigger picture?

I've asked myself often, "Does the world need yet another model?" My answer: a model makes it easier for everyone to grasp complexity, and most importantly, to put ideas into practice. Fear is a powerful force. In the grip of fear, we lose ourselves, our composure and our rationality. In these moments, what we need is a simple framework to get us out of trouble.

My peers in management consulting might regard the model as being too simplistic, and at first sight, you might agree with them. I believe its simplicity is its strength, not its flaw.

PART III

SEE

Fear is an invisible force, like the wind. To be blind to it is to flap about, veer off course, and become the people we said we would never become.

WHAT LURKS BEHIND EVERY BUYING DECISION

Be wary of sales and marketing tactics that manipulate us into buying things we don't need.

You're hosting an important dinner party tomorrow. The plan is to make a roast dinner with all the trimmings. It's easy and it's a crowd pleaser. This morning you discover the oven is broken. You need to get a replacement, fast.

You normally rely on your partner to make these types of purchases, however, your partner is unreachable on the phone. You decide to take matters into your own hands and go to the mall.

At a store, you decide which model you want, a $950 oven that looks similar to your current one, and get the attention of a store assistant who asks, "have you considered a double oven? They're very handy when you have a big crowd."

"I do have a big crowd tomorrow!" you say.

"There are two double ovens to choose from. A top Italian brand – which is on sale..."

The sticker price on the flash looking Italian oven says, "$3,500. Limited Stock."

Not wanting to appear cheap, you put on your poker face and try not to flinch at the price.

"Or we have a basic model," says the store assistant.

This one is $1,400.

"What do you recommend?" you ask.

"It depends on what you value. The basic oven does the job, but the Italian one gives you peace of mind, and it's what most people choose if they can afford it."

"Is the basic one no good?"

"It's a great machine. It will do the job for years, otherwise we wouldn't stock it. But in the end, you get what you pay for. We never see these Italian ovens come back because people love them."

"I see."

"Would you be interested in Premium Care?" asks the store assistant.

"What's that?"

"Premium Care gets you free replacement or repair if there is a fault with the oven within 3 years. It's $300. Which might sound like a lot, but it's a small investment for that extra peace of mind for your $3,500 oven."

You hesitate. The store assistant asks, "If you're interested, I can check if we have it in stock for you. Should I do that?"

"Yes, please."

The store assistant punches the keyboard on a computer. "I can see that there is one in stock, but let me go out back and double check it is still there. Give me a moment?"

"Sure."

Comparing the two ovens, the $3,500 oven is a beautiful,

eye-catching machine. *It would certainly impress my friends, and maybe even raise the value of the house!*

After a few moments, the store assistant returns wheeling a large box on a trolley.

"I found one – the last one! I grabbed it for you in case someone else gets it. They're very popular and can take weeks to order in!"

You're conscious that the store assistant has created a sense of scarcity. Although you're aware of this manipulation, you still can't help but desire the oven even more now because it's the "last" one. You feel compelled to grab it before someone else does.

"That's lucky! Thanks for grabbing it."

"Will you put this on your credit card or pay by instalments?"

You hesitate a little. The store assistant assumed that you have already decided to buy, but you haven't actually said out loud that you would. It's a sales tactic called "the assumptive sale".

"I'm not sure," you say, "it's a lot of money."

"It is. Would it help if I checked with the manager to see if I can get a better deal for you?"

"Yes, please."

"I'll ask, but don't expect too much. It's already heavily discounted, and they're very popular. I'll do my best. Give me a minute?"

"Sure."

After a while, he returns with a smile. "Good news, they have approved me to take another $350 off, which pretty much means you get Premium Care for free, plus an extra $50. This is an amazing deal – I've never sold one at this price. The manager must be keen to make her numbers this month. Would you like to take it with you now, or would you like it delivered?" The question is framed carefully to make you feel in control, but it limits your options to "take it home now" vs "delivered", as opposed to "buy" or "don't buy".

"How much is delivery and how long does it take?"

"$30. About a week."

"Oh, I need it today. I think I'll just take it then." The assistant has been hoping to hear these words, but the money is not in the bank yet.

"Will you pay by cash or credit card?" asks the store assistant. It's the assumptive sale tactic again.

You hesitate for a moment because it's a big decision. You'd like to take some time to think about it, gather more information, and consult your partner, but it feels awkward to back out now, and feel an overwhelming obligation to reward the store assistant's service.

"What the hell, let's do it. Credit card. Thank you for being so helpful."

As you motion to get your credit card out, the store assistant's phone rings. "I'm so sorry. I really have to take this call."

As you stand there waiting, you come to your senses a little. You feel you need more time. The break gives you the courage to back out of the verbal agreement. You point to your watch, feign shock, as if you're late for something. You mouth the words, "Sorry, I'm late, I have to go, I'll come back, thank you," and flee the store.

You find a cafe, sit down and reflect on what just happened. On impulse, you almost bought a double oven, spending three times more than you originally intended. *How did this happen?* You replay the situation in your head.

"For those special occasions when you have a big crowd..." That's what the store assistant said. It conjured up an image of a big crowd of people, aroused a fear of not being able to cater to everyone, failing to impress, and letting people down.

How often do I actually need to cater to a sizeable crowd? Maybe two to five times a year? Do I really need to spend so much more money to cover those few occasions? I suppose I could use the BBQ and the stove top rather than rely on the oven alone.

The store assistant said, "The basic oven does the job, but the Italian one gives you peace of mind, and it's what most people choose if they can afford it...you pay for what you get." These words aroused a different set of fears: fear of buying an unreliable machine, fear of making a mistake, fear of appearing cheap, fear of going against the crowd, and fear of going against conventional wisdom. We have a tendency to follow the choices other people make because it feels like a safer choice.

You do some research on your phone. There is no data to suggest that one brand is more reliable than the other. In fact, both products share common components – most of which are not made in Italy. The rubbers and seals are made in Malaysia, the electronics are from Taiwan, the convection fan from China, the baking elements are from Turkey, and so forth. The only thing "Italian" about the more expensive model is the brand name and the exterior look and feel.

The store assistant offered Premium Care, and you bought into it. The carefully scripted words were: "Premium Care gets you free replacement or repair if there is a fault with the oven within 3 years."

You wonder how much warranty comes as standard? You look this up on your phone. The consumer law in your country says: "Guarantees are not limited to a set period of time. Instead, it is based on general expectations of what is reasonable. Thus, for example, if high end ovens are generally expected to last over five years, then buyers have a right to replacement or repair within five years."

This makes the 3-year Premium Care completely superfluous. Why did I fall for it? You ask yourself. Fear of buying a lemon and losing money?

It's funny how fear causes us to latch blindly onto false assurances of safety.

At the store, you felt an obligation to make the purchase – backing out felt awkward. *Why is that?* The store assistant had said:

> "Let me go out back and double check it is still there.
>   Give me a moment?"
> "It's our last one... I grabbed it for you in case someone
>   else gets it."
> "Would it help if I checked with the manager to see if I
>   can get a better deal for you?"

These gestures come across as being favours, but they're also a set of sales tactics that makes you feel obliged to reciprocate goodwill. Owing to our tribal roots, we have an innate fear of causing disappointment, wasting people's time and creating disharmony. For example, once seated in a restaurant, given menus and served glasses of water, we're unlikely to walk out of the restaurant even if we don't like the look of anything on the menu. Many of us would rather risk stomaching an undesirable meal rather than cause offence. Each time you said "yes" to the sales assistant, you felt deeper in obligation, and by the end, it felt like you'd be letting down a friend if you backed out of making a purchase.

The more time spent in the store, the more committed you felt towards completing a purchase because of a fear of wasting time and walking out of the store empty-handed. You also didn't want to appear indecisive.

It's thanks to your fear of getting ripped off, fear of making a poor decision, and fear of having to explain to your partner your actions that gave you the courage to back out.

You search online to see if there are better deals. There are literally hundreds of models to choose from. You find a small oven on sale for only $900. It seems like a good deal, but you're unsure. You spend another twenty minutes looking for alternatives and come up with a shortlist of six models. You dig deeper into the features of each model, but it's difficult to make comparisons because they use jargon such as "3D" and "Cyclonic technology" – whatever they mean. After another twenty minutes, you're no closer to deciding. You wonder if you should look to purchase something second hand? Procrastination leads to more lost time. To add complexity to the problem, none of the online options will deliver an oven in time for your dinner party tomorrow.

You take a deep breath. With the luxury of time, and free from the pressure of the store assistant, you make a list of fears that you might harbour: fear that cheap ovens might break down (especially when you need it most); fear that your friends will think less of you for buying a cheap oven.

A part of you wants to give in and go back to the store to buy the Italian model, but you decide to embark on a thought exercise: *what if I had no choice but to purchase a cheaper one online?* You reason that if the cheaper oven breaks down prematurely, you can always return it under warranty. There is no evidence to suggest the store's Italian model is more reliable. Your friends aren't the kind of people that will judge you based on what oven you own. It's more likely that no one will notice. For tonight's dinner party, you could easily cook something else, using the BBQ and the stove instead of the oven.

The thought exercise helps you overcome your irrational fears. You purchase a $900 oven online, and in doing so, save your family over $2,000!

Feeling pleased with yourself, you can't help but wonder: *In what other ways are we paying too much money because of our irrational fears?*

On the way home, you reflect on the car you're driving. It's an SUV, a big car with off-road muscle. *Why do we need such a big car? What fears influenced this decision? Fear of your family's safety or that they'd be uncomfortable? Afraid of looking cheap? Or getting stuck somewhere without four-wheel-drive capability? Are these fears rational?*

You pull into a petrol station. At the bowser, you refuel your car with premium petrol. You wonder to yourself: *why do we pick premium over ordinary unleaded?*

Premium petrol makes a lot of claims: "the latest generation fuel", "Formula 1 power and innovation", "cleaner, smoother, further," etc. Claims such as "Dirt buster" imply that ordinary petrol is dirty. "Cleans your engine whilst you drive" conjures images of clogged arteries and sensitive engine components. Premium petrol only costs 20 cents more, which seems like a clever choice given your car costs $65,000. It's a simple decision really, so you feel good about filling up with premium petrol.

When you get home, you look into the value of premium petrol. A reputable motorist group says that filling up with premium petrol is a waste of money unless you're driving a performance vehicle that explicitly requires it. And experts say that the purported "extra mileage" is negligible[1] relative to the price hike.

You estimate that your family will save $500 per annum if you switch to ordinary, unleaded petrol.

You look around the house. There are so many consumer

products: an enormous $2,500 television, a $2,000 fridge, a $3,500 lounge, a $290 toaster, drawers chock full of kitchen utensils, an ice cream maker that was popular for only one summer, countless electronic devices: phones, laptops, tablets, eBook readers, smart watches, and a cupboard full of old devices and cables that were kept just in case they're needed one day. Outside is a neglected trampoline and a lonely basketball hoop.

You wonder to yourself: *what fears lurked in our minds when we bought these?*

~

Resist manipulation

In a sales situation, how could we counter the fear of not reciprocating? A polite way to do it is to apply brakes along the way, and switch mindsets to nullify the feeling that you're receiving a favour. For example:

When a store assistant says: "Let me go out back and double check it is still there. Give me a minute?". We can apply brakes by saying: "I am not making a commitment to buy yet, but yes, please check." And we can nullify the social debt in our heads by saying to ourselves: "A store can't sell something they don't have. It's their job to know what they have in stock." Another example, when a store assistant says, "Would you like me to see if I can get a better deal for you?" We can say to them: "I'm still undecided, but please check with your manager," and to ourselves: "This is just a sales tactic to deepen my commitment. It's their job to offer the best possible price."

Petrol companies appeal to a set of irrational fears to make more money: fear of damaging our vehicle, not getting value for money, and causing pollution. It works because in the absence of information, we go with our gut and pick the "safer" option.

We ought to be wary when sales and marketing people use words like, "safe", "quality assured", "government-backed", "warranty", and "peace of mind" because they're appealing to our fear of something going wrong; being confronted with unexpected problems; the hassle of asking for a refund or the need to organise repairs; being stranded in the middle of nowhere; getting ripped off; and fear of the unknown, generally. Often, the fear is unconscious and irrational. We choose premium and recognisable brands, with no evidence that they are better or more reliable other than the cheaper alternative. We associate familiarity (i.e. brand recognition) with reliability.

It's not just money that we waste. Fear can be a drain on our time and limited mental resources. All of us experience trepidation when making buying decisions, spending more time than we should shopping around, comparing options, and stewing over simple purchasing decisions. It stems from the fear of making a mistake; fear of being ripped off (or not getting the lowest price possible); fear of being stuck with a dud; and fear of looking stupid in the eyes of others.

BEHIND EVERY NEED IS AN EQUAL AND OPPOSITE FEAR

Fear impedes love and happiness.

Your employer offers you an opportunity to work in Dubai for six months. You tell your partner you really need to seize this opportunity. You're afraid that the opportunity might not come around again.

Your partner doesn't want to move to Dubai. "I want to stay here because I'm happy here." Your partner is afraid of leaving friends behind; afraid of living alone in a foreign country.

You say, "It's only for six months, maybe we could travel and meet each other every 4-6 weeks?"

Your partner says, "Long distance relationship? No thanks, I need you here." Your partner is afraid of losing you.

You say, "Now that you're not working, don't you think we need the extra money?" You're afraid of falling behind on bills and mortgage repayments, afraid of not building a nest egg, afraid of being vulnerable.

Your partner raises absurd questions: "Why do we need to have such a large mortgage? Do we really need to be living in the city? What if we moved to the suburbs?"

You say, "I love urban life." You're afraid of commuting, losing the conveniences of being in the city, of how suburban life might affect your identity, and being judged by friends and work colleagues for living in the suburbs.

Your partner completely overreacts. Now your lifestyle choices are being questioned. "What if we halved our expenses? We used to live happily on a fraction of our income. Why do we need all these things to make us happy? What if we gave up most of it and lived a simpler life? What are we afraid of?"

"I'm not afraid of anything," you say. "I like my job, I enjoy working hard, I enjoy moving up in the world and making more money. My sports convertible car wasn't given to me. I worked hard for it. I think I deserve to live in a spacious place in the city. Where is all this coming from?"

Your partner says, "I don't understand why you need a sports convertible! I know that you've earned it, but why do you need it? Is it a status symbol? Do you really need a sign to say that you are a success? Are you afraid that you're not? In fact, we have two cars – why do we need both cars? Why do we need a car at all if we live in the middle of the city? Shouldn't we cycle, use public transport or ride-share services more often? What are we afraid of?"

"You've gone mad!" you say with undisguised anger. You need to win this argument. There is too much at stake. Your anger stems from the fear that the things you've worked hard for, and therefore you feel entitled to, will be taken away from you; fear that your partner is behaving strangely, that things are getting out of control.

Your partner says, "I feel we need to return to a simple life." Your partner is afraid of being stuck on the corporate treadmill, becoming mindless consumers, and losing sight of what is important.

You fail to see this and say, "Look, I understand losing a job has hit your confidence hard. You need to bounce back from this. Don't be afraid of getting hurt again."

"It's not because of the job, I've been unhappy in this corporate world for a long time. I need more freedom. I'm afraid I have become just like my father – a slave to his job."

The two of you have been growing apart. Your partner is still the same person you met ten years ago, whereas your corporate career is flourishing, and you've grown as a person. It's a scary thought, but you wonder if you have outgrown your partner. Perhaps you need to move on, find someone more compatible with your current values. You're afraid that your partner has been holding you back. It's just a thought, though. You're too afraid to do anything about it. You're fearful that you might not find a better partner, afraid of messing up a good thing, afraid of upsetting your partner, afraid of losing the history between the two of you, afraid of being single again, and terrified of being alone in your old age. For now, you need your partner, so you choose your words carefully. "This is a great opportunity for me," you say. "I need your support. Isn't supporting each other's dreams what being in a relationship is all about?"

Your partner says, "Maybe we need to rethink this relationship."

These words strike fear and panic in your heart. You leave without saying a word. You need the conversation to end now because you're afraid you might say something that you will regret.

For the next couple of days, the two of you don't talk about the argument. It's as if it never took place. Conversation is kept to a functional minimum: "Could you drop this off at the post office? Have you seen my keys? What would you like for dinner?"

You're not prepared to admit fault. You need your partner to apologise to you because if not, you're afraid that you won't have the upper hand in the relationship.

At the same time, you feel the need to consider your partner's point of view. You're afraid you could be wrong, or come across as being cold and uncompromising. So you give in a little and reflect on the question posed by your partner: "Why do we need a car at all?". You make a list of your current car usage:

- Weekly grocery shop. Alternatives: use the bicycle, shop twice a week to lighten the load. Or have groceries delivered. *But what if it rains? What if we get hit by a car on the bicycle? What if we become ill?*
- Impromptu trip to the beach, visiting friends or going out at night. Alternatives: use taxi/ride-share, walk, cycle or use public transport. *But what if we get stranded because the taxi does not show up? What if we get mugged by the taxi driver? What if it rains and we get wet? Would taxis be a hassle and take up precious time? Seems like we would curtail our freedom.*
- Emergency trip to the hospital. Alternatives: use taxi/ride-share. *But what if a taxi/ride-share takes too long? It could be a matter of life and death.*
- Visiting family a 3-hour drive out of town. Alternatives: rent a car or take the train and have

someone pick us up at the station. *What if a rental car is not available during the holidays (the only time we need it)? What if the rental car breaks down? What if trains are overcrowded? It's better to own our car so that we can be in control.*

- Running odd errands like going to the nursery or hardware shop. Alternatives: use taxi/ride-share, cycle, borrow or hire a car/truck. *What if I have to cart large, bulky items? It would be so inconvenient.*
- Status symbol. Alternatives: Unclear. *I've worked hard. It's important for me to drive the car I want, to my identity and sense of self worth.*

You conclude it makes sense to own a car. Both cars, in fact, because the sports convertible is not suitable for running errands. You believe your concerns to be rational. Your unconscious fears stop you from seeing it any other way.

You show your partner the table you created. You assume your partner will appreciate your gesture and come to see your way.

"You haven't looked at the upside of not owning a car," says your partner.

"What upside?" you ask.

"Not having to look for parking, the money we'd save from avoiding traffic fines, the health benefits if we cycled or walked more often, the environmental impact, and the pleasure of train rides. And you give too much weight to the downsides. What is the likelihood that we'd get mugged? Who is to say that our car won't have a breakdown and cause us to be stuck in the middle of nowhere? We could lose our keys or have our car stolen – think of the hassle of that. If we were stranded somewhere, would it be so bad? It could be an adventure. You underestimate our tenacity, and overestimate the inconvenience because you're afraid of change. You're letting your fears rule your thinking."

The accusation hurts.

"It's you," you say. "You're the one letting fear rule your thinking. I've worked so hard to get us to where we are. Why do you need to hold me back? What are *you* afraid of? Are you afraid that we're growing apart? I've never felt so...so suffocated."

Your partner looks away and starts rearranging the cushions on the couch.

"Well? Are you going to answer those questions?" you ask.

"I'm thinking, I don't know what to say. That's the most hurtful thing anyone has ever said to me."

"Great, emotional blackmail, that's very...." You don't finish your sentence, grab your car keys, and leave the house.

Over the next week, a coldness descends over your household. You stay away under the guise of being busy, leave first thing in the morning, hit the gym, and find excuses to avoid getting home til late.

By the end of the week, your partner caves in and says, "I need you. I'm afraid of losing you. I'll support your career, I'll follow you to the ends of the earth. You're right, I need to get back on my feet, put myself out there again, and stop living in fear."

It's very big for your partner to say these things. You feel acknowledged. You hug each other.

As you hold each other, cheek to cheek, chins resting on shoulders, you feel a strong sense of relief, but there's something that is not quite right. It's as if the argument broke something between you. Perhaps it broke the illusion of safety your partner once represented?

At that moment, you decide you need to end the relationship because you're afraid that you won't be able to go back to how you once felt, afraid that you will be held back, despite your partner's promise.

The top three takeaways:

One. People have a tendency to be defensive during a quarrel and are less likely to admit to their fears. In the heat of the moment, it's more productive to acknowledge concerns, to be generous with assurances and role model fear mastery, rather than to point out the other person's fears. In fact, it's a great policy to:

Never point out someone's unconscious fears: they're more likely to raise their guard and take offence, rather than to wake up and thank you.

Two. We're all Olympic champions in terms of our ability to justify our fears. We find and give more weight to evidence that suits us. We overestimate the probability of downsides and dangers and dismiss or discount upsides and benefits.

And last, behind every need is a fear. Every time we feel a need for something, be it physical or emotional, it's an opportunity to investigate the underlying fear, and not just blindly make that purchase, pay a premium, upgrade or up-size. Doing so not only helps us save heaps of money over a lifetime, it frees our house from clutter, reduces our carbon footprint, and allows us to escape the trap of needing more money to buy things we don't need.

THE TRICK TO BEING A GOOD LISTENER

Paying attention to other people's fears is an act of love.

Your husband starts a new job tomorrow. He is nervous about it – to the point of being annoying.

You're trying to watch TV. He is fussing over the details of how he'll get to his new place of employment tomorrow. The details are trivial to you, and you'd like to think that he is more than capable of working it out for himself. However, you put this assumption aside; you want to appear supportive, to be a good listener, so you turn off the TV, and give him your full, undivided attention. "Let's start from the top. What's your plan for getting to work tomorrow?"

He runs through the details. There's some excessive padding, but it sounds alright overall. You say, "I'm pretty sure you could catch a later bus and still make it comfortably."

He isn't convinced. You try to prove your point by outlining different scenarios, tallying up the minutes.

Your brilliant logic does not win him over. This frustrates you a little. "Do the numbers not add up?" you ask.

"I don't think you understand," he says.

You sense that the next thing you say will catalyse an argument, so you pull back. He isn't appreciating your input, nor is he open to your expertise on the matter, so you decide to stay out of it. "Well, it looks like you've got it all figured out then. I'm sure you'll be OK."

You feel pretty good about yourself. *Good listener, tick. Supportive partner, tick. Presence of mind to avoid an argument about immaterial things, double tick and a gold star. Now, back to the show...will Mr Bates be found innocent?*

Later on, your husband pours himself a glass of wine without pouring one for you.

"That looks delicious."

"Yes," he says, without taking the hint.

You hit pause, get up and pour one for yourself.

"Are you OK?" you ask.

"Sure, I'm fine."

"Really? Are you sure?"

"I'm fine."

You hit the Play button and return to the show. As you're watching the show, the thought that he isn't fine distracts you. So once again you hit pause. You stare at him for a while. He says nothing. He stares at the TV screen blankly, sipping his wine.

You ask yourself: *what fears might he be dealing with at the moment? Getting stuck in traffic? Missing a bus? Catching the wrong bus? Getting lost?*

You dig deeper: *fear of being late? Making a bad first impression?*

You dig even deeper: *fear of not being able to perform in the new job? Not knowing what to do? Being humiliated? Bad things in the past happening again? That's it.*

They bullied your husband in his last job. He suffered from put-downs from his colleagues, and his boss treated him unfairly. *That's the source of anxiousness. That's why he's nervous. The fuss over the travel plan is a symptom of this deeper fear.*

Now that you think of it, it's as clear as day. Your husband is a proud man. He's not the type to admit to his fears. He is being distant now because he is afraid that you're failing to be more empathetic to what is going on in his head, afraid that you care more about what's on TV than you care about him.

The next challenge is: how can you allay his fears? You can't just confront his fears by saying something like: "You're afraid you're going to be bullied again, aren't you?" Even if it is the truth. No one likes to admit to weakness, and it would do nothing to build his confidence.

"What's your new boss like?"

"Err, well...she seems nice."

"Oh, how?"

"She called me last week to check that I have everything I need for the job."

"That is nice. Any different from your last boss?"

"Completely."

"Your last boss was a control freak and exploited people. How do you know she will be different?"

"It might be too early to tell, but the other people I met at the office had nice things to say about her."

He seems less distant now.

"Hey, I was thinking...I have to go in your direction for a client meeting. Maybe I could leave a little earlier to drop you off? It would be like a date."

"You'd do that for me?"

"Absolutely."

"Do you think Mr Bates did it?" he asks.

"Let's find out!"

You sit back with a content smile on your face. *Good listener? Tick. Mastery of your husband's irrational fears? Tick. Earned the right to go back to the TV show? Press play.*

To see the fear behind the words is to have empathy — the premise of trust in a relationship

WHY WE NAG, MICROMANAGE AND YELL FROM THE SIDE LINES

You pick your dad up from his home to go watch your daughter's soccer match. It was your idea. You thought it would be good to get him out of the house, but within five minutes, you're already regretting the decision. His constant nagging is driving you crazy.

"You're going too fast...don't forget to indicate...stay in your lane...keep both hands on the wheel...check your blind spot...green means go..."

Your father's behaviour is driven by fear: fear of getting into an accident, fear of putting your family in danger, fear of incurring a traffic offence, and fear of things not being done the right way.

You'd like to say, "Don't be a backseat driver, dad, I know what I am doing," but experience tells you that this will lead to an argument. And you're afraid to cause a scene, setting a poor example for your daughter sitting in the backseat. So you say, "Yes, Dad...OK, Dad..."

On your way to the soccer field, you stop at a restaurant for lunch. As usual, your father orders too many dishes. He's been told a million times by your mother: "Your eyes are bigger than your stomach!" He's afraid of not getting enough food, afraid of hunger pangs, afraid of being malnourished, and afraid your daughter is too skinny. You have the opposite fear: overeating, getting fat, wasting food, afraid that your daughter might have a tummy ache and ruin her game if she eats too much.

At the end of the meal, there is still so much food left. It's irritating, but you refrain from criticising your dad thanks to your fear of not wanting to sound like your mother. You'd like a doggy bag, because of the fear of food going to waste. The fear of adding more trash to landfill and destroying the planet over-weighs this fear. So you force you and your dad to finish what's left. Later on, you regret dumping all that food in your body. It's a shame your fear of overeating and getting fat didn't come into your thinking.

At your daughter's soccer match, you coach from the side-lines, more so than usual, because it's an important match. You don't think of yourself as one of those obnoxious, overbearing soccer parents, but on this day, you can't seem to stop yourself from getting worked-up. You hear yourself let out not-so-constructive cries such as "Shoot it!" and "For goodness' sake!".

Never shy about being blunt, your father says, "Why do you have to yell at them? It's not helping." He's afraid that you're embarrassing yourself and your daughter, and in doing so, spoiling the children's fun.

The words sting. Well practised at the discipline of not speaking your mind when you're angry, you pull your hat down and jut your chin out. The effort of restraint causes your breath to become measured and audible.

You try to compose yourself. *Why am I so amped up? I keep telling my daughter it doesn't matter if she wins or loses, or how many goals she scores, and yet I'm behaving as if the nation's future is at stake. Why is that?*

The three demons of fear

Fear is determined by three factors: stakes, uncertainty and control.

Backseat drivers nag because they don't have <u>control</u> of the car, they feel <u>uncertain</u>, and an accident at high speed can be lethal (i.e. the <u>stakes</u> are high).

Conversely, drivers will get easily frustrated with their navigator because the stakes are high (fear of getting in an accident or getting lost); there is uncertainty (e.g. the navigator gives unreliable or last-minute instructions); and because the driver doesn't feel in control (the driver can't see the map and doesn't know where they're heading or what is up ahead).

We yell from the sidelines because (1) the stakes are high (even though it's just a kid's game, we want our kids to be winners, to gain confidence, not be on the losing side, and not get hurt); (2) we have little control (we can't set foot on the field or influence the game, and we get especially irritated when we see injustice but we can't do anything about it); and (3) we experience uncertainty (the outcome of the game and our children's welfare is unknown). We resort to yelling because our vocal chords are the only instruments that give us a sense of control. Then we get amped up because the yelling doesn't actually do anything to ease our fears.

To deal with an anxious backseat driver, we might be better off addressing the fear rather than become defensive or take the criticism personally. For example, "You think I'm a bad driver?" is a sure-fire way to start an argument in the car. "Why can't you just relax and trust me?" might silence the less cantankerous backseat drivers, but it won't quell their fears. It's likely to make them even more anxious. Robbed of their voice, they'll sit in their seats and stew in silence, brewing up for a bigger fight later on. It's an unpleasant experience on both sides.

When people express their fear, the kindest thing we can do is to give them a sense of control and furnish them with plenty of information. Within the confines of safe boundaries, let them choose what will happen to them, let them order what they want to eat, inform them of the process at the start, update them along the way, make them feel understood, show them the range of options, demonstrate that you are listening and respond to their requests, show them the overall plan, praise their progress, point out their efficacy, let them decide what happens next, and so forth.

Back on the soccer field...

"I suppose you're right, dad," you say.

"Just let them play," he says.

"OK."

He persists, "Look at that parent yelling over there – do you think he's making a difference? Is it about the kids, or is it more about them?"

You reply, "They're spoiling the fun and making everyone tense. You were always so cool on the sidelines when I was a kid. I'm grateful for that." With this, you furnish him with a sense that he is being heard.

Your daughter's team wins the game. Everyone feels a lot more at ease, not because of the win, but because the uncertainty is over.

One parent still looks dissatisfied, pointing out the mistakes his child, the coach, and the referee made. It's as if he is trying to control that which has already happened, which is a futile act. Some people just can't let go of their fears even after the uncertainty passes.

On the drive home, you ask your father which is the best route to get to his home (giving him a sense of control). You play back your understanding of what he said so that he feels reassured you won't go the wrong way.

On the way home, you focus on making your father feel at ease. When he criticises your driving, you don't take offence because you're cognisant that it's not your driving skills that are in question, it's just him expressing his fears. When he asks you to slow down, you respond immediately, and ask, "Is this better?" to show that you're listening. It's irrelevant that you are driving below the speed limit. His experience and perception are what matters. He can relax because of the sense that he can get you to slow down simply by asking.

After a while, your dad stops backseat driving (he doesn't feel the need to), and relaxes to enjoy the ride.

You arrive at his house. He says thank you, "I have had the happiest time ever."

You muster the courage to ask, "Same time next week?"

He says, "Absolutely!"

It thrills your daughter that her grandfather will come watch her play again next week. Smiles all around.

The Three Demons of Fear

High Stakes

Uncertainty

Lack of control

JEALOUSY

Your girlfriend is beautiful. Maybe too beautiful.

Lying in bed, you ask her, "Here's a hypothetical question: if we break-up, and I'm not saying we're breaking up, but if we do break-up, who would you go out with?"

She says, "That's an awkward question."

"It's purely hypothetical. I promise you I won't get upset."

"I don't know...it's not something I think about."

"Well, think about it. Who would it be?"

She takes a moment. "Shaun at work, maybe, I don't know. Or John, your friend. That would cross the line, wouldn't it? I take that back. This is purely hypothetical, right?"

"Yes, a hundred percent," you say, but you wonder who Shaun is, and why John?

"The barista at the cafe up the road, maybe? Or Miles? Who knows? Maybe I'll mourn for eternity and never find a man like you again. How about you? Who would you go out with if we broke up?"

"Who's Miles?"

"My sister's friend. A firefighter."

It's like a dagger has been thrust into your chest. You picture a hot firefighter in uniform – it's hard to compete with that. You consider how much time Shaun and your girlfriend are together at work. You have no control over that. You didn't expect that she'd produce such a long list of men to replace you so easily. The thought of losing her feels palpable. Even though she has done nothing wrong, you feel awful, not just because you feel vulnerable, but the thought shatters the illusion that you are unique, the only man for her. You pretend nothing is wrong and end the hypothetical game abruptly.

Men hit on her all the time, at parties, at work and on the streets. She never encourages them, not that you've noticed anyway. She is friendly with John, your friend, but that's because he's your best friend. There is no reason to suspect that she might cheat on you, or even find another man attractive. She says she loves you, and as far as you know, she is completely dedicated to you. You'd like to check her phone to be sure, but resist the urge because you're afraid of getting caught invading her privacy and breaching her trust.

Days later, the unsettled feeling doesn't go away. You wonder who this Shaun character from her office is. You look him up on the web and find a photo of a handsome man. He looks fitter than you, with an excellent career track record: a good provider. You feel even less secure, and afraid of being cuckolded.

Knowing that insecurity can be unattractive, you try to hide it as much as possible. When you probe her for information about her dealings with Shaun, you feign nonchalance. You ask your sister about Miles, the firefighter, but do it discreetly. And when you're at the cafe up the road, you try to work out if the barista already has a girlfriend.

All three are single, good-looking men. The knowledge stokes your fears.

What began as an act of curiosity, a tiny ant, is now a monster in your mind. You spend too much mental energy fighting off jealous thoughts. When she is texting on her phone, you can't help but become anxious, wondering who is at the other end. You put her through love tests. For example, you'll suddenly go quiet or look sad and see if she notices. You don't like it when she goes out without telling you where she is going or who she is meeting. Fear changes the way you see things. For example, when she used to go out with her friends, you used to feel happy for her because her friends make her happy. Now you question why she has to go out without you so much. In the past, when she got dressed in her little black dress, you used to take in and enjoy her beauty, but these days you see it as a threat because it invites enemy eyes and seductive hands. It's all in your head, of course. Or is it?

One night, your girlfriend is unusually late getting home from work. She doesn't call or leave a message. The hour's anxious wait turns into two. You send her a message, but don't hear back. You resist sending her a second one. Time crawls slowly. Your emotions oscillate between anger and fear. When she finally gets home at midnight, you pretend to be fast asleep. You lie awake with the same terrible thoughts, the same unanswerable questions going around and around in your head. Jealousy throbs in your head and beats in your chest hard. It's the Thumping.

The next morning, you leave home early without leaving a message. You don't call or send a message and ignore her attempts to reach you.

You're punishing her for what she did to you, but in reality, she did nothing to you. She was at her friend's birthday party. She told you, you just forgot. If you'd bothered to look, it was in the calendar on the fridge. She didn't respond to your messages because her phone ran out of battery.

Poet John Milton said, "The mind is its own place, and in itself can make a heaven of hell, a hell of heaven." The pain and suffering that you're experiencing is entirely the making of your own mind.

You try to put her out of your mind and play it cool. You want to be free from fear, to show to yourself that you're fearless. The situation affects how you behave in other aspects of your life. You don't follow rules at work, drive recklessly, humiliate your girlfriend in front of her friends, and flirt with other women. The behaviour makes you think you're in control, but it's actually a compensation for feeling out of control. Deep in your psyche is the fear that another person, your girlfriend, can have so much control over you; fear of being cuckolded; fear of being alone.

One day, arriving home at 1am, your blood spiked with alcohol and a cocktail of vengeance, self-loathing and fear, your girlfriend asks, "Where have you been? I've been worried sick about you, have you been drinking?"

"Why? Can't I have a drink?"

"Babe, what is wrong?"

"Nothing."

"Where have you been? Why didn't you tell me?"

"Out with some girlfriends."

"Girlfriends? Why didn't you answer my messages?"

"You didn't answer my messages either."

"When?"

"Last week. You were out late. Look, it doesn't matter, you can do what you want."

"You mean at Jen's birthday party? I told you about it, remember? It has been on the calendar for weeks."

"Why didn't you answer the phone?"

"I ran out of battery."

"That's convenient. You couldn't borrow a phone to call?"

Your girlfriend can act in one of two ways. She can succumb to a set of fears: fear of being treated like a child, fear of not being trusted by someone she loves, fear of being suffocated by your possessiveness, fear that you are behaving like an overbearing, jealous boyfriend, and fear that your paranoia will cause you to become violent. These fears could cause her to lash out at you.

"Oh, babe, I've been so worried about you," she says. "I am so glad that you are back." She wraps her arms around you, and cries on your shoulder. You place your hands on her hips, not quite ready to be vulnerable. She says, "I'm so sorry, my phone ran out of battery, and I didn't realise until I was on my way home."

You still have your doubts.

She continues: "I love you, you know. You are the centre of my universe. You know that, right?"

You draw your arms around her shoulders and hold her tightly. All your fears are gone in an instant.

DISCERNING RATIONAL FROM IRRATIONAL FEAR

The key to mastering fear is to not be free of all fears, but from the irrational ones. This is much harder than we think. How often have we looked with hindsight at certain events and thought ourselves foolish to have wasted our nervous energy? If we were honest with ourselves, though, we'd probably behave in exactly the same way when put in the same circumstances.

Some of us go through our entire life living under a fear that everyone but us can see. We might dish out advice, laugh at or pity those that can't see or control their baseless fears, and yet, be unaware that we ourselves are guilty of being influenced by the same fears.

We are most vulnerable to irrational fear when we overestimate the certainty of occurrence, the stakes and our ability to control the situation (the Three Demons).

Overestimating the certainty of occurrence

This happens when we rely on our 'gut instinct', let our emotions get hold of us, or fall for biases, such as the availability heuristic. Remote or improbable outcomes become palpable.

> "She's so good looking, men check her out all the time, she's probably already cheating on me."
> "Our son is going to kill himself, we'd better not let him ride a bicycle, it's just not safe in the streets anymore."
> "I don't want to buy a secondhand mattress because I don't want to catch a disease, even if it is from someone we know who claims it to be new."

The best way to avoid overestimating the probability of occurrence is to gather data or look at the full picture, rather than to rely on our gut instinct.

> "She is honest to a fault, she is faithful, and she loves me. Sure, men check her out, but she chooses me."
> "A child is 3.6 times more likely to die in a motor vehicle accident compared to riding a bicycle. We live in a safe neighbourhood. He always wears a helmet. He'll be fine."[1]
> "At hotels, we sleep on mattresses hundreds have slept on, maybe thousands of people before us. What's wrong with buying a second hand mattress from someone we know who claims it to be new?"

Magnifying the stakes

This happens when we over-project, make things bigger than they are, and amplify the severity and impact of consequences.

*"If she leaves me, it will devastate me, my life will have no
        meaning, my life will be over, I can't live without her."*
*"If he is this lazy at eight years old, he'll end up being a
        bum. We'd better not be soft on him."*
"The ice arriving late will ruin the party."

*Again, the best way to avoid magnifying the stakes is to look at
the data and the big picture.*

*"He's eight years old. Just because he forgets to take the
        rubbish out, it doesn't mean he's lazy. He's diligent
        when it matters to him. Besides, a sense of responsibility
        takes time to develop. Let's not over-project. We just
        need to set clear expectations, and give him gentle
        reminders until it becomes a habit."*

*Alternatively, we can run a thought exercise: imagine the worst
happens, would things be as bad as we imagine them?*

*"If she leaves me, I guess I will be single again. It's hard to
        imagine life without her, but I was perfectly fine for
        decades before I met her."*
*"If the ice doesn't arrive on time, I guess people can drink
        whatever is in the fridge first. It's no big deal. What
        matters more is that I relax and enjoy the party."*

Illusion of control

*We have a tendency to overestimate our ability to control things in
our lives, particularly those of us who come from individualistic
cultures that subscribe to the view "if we put our mind to it, we can
accomplish anything". We:*

- *Seek in vain to have control over our environment when there are greater forces at play*
- *Try to make sense of chaos even when there are endless variables*
- *Spin our wheels trying to know the unknowable*
- *Take matters into our own hands in situations that are unlikely to change no matter how much we interfere*
- *Confuse competency with chance*
- *Expend effort and money to express our identity, when in actuality we are largely a product of our demographics and social circumstances.*
- *Believe we can bring about world peace by making a noise on social media when in reality, broader geopolitical issues have been at play for centuries.*

A jealous boyfriend is trying to control the uncontrollable when he says: "Why do you need to go out with your girlfriends so often? Were you flirting with that man? Where were you this afternoon? Who are you texting now?"

Ultimately, we don't own our partners and we can't tell them how to feel. The only thing that is within our control is our thoughts and our own behaviour.

Hosting big family meals during festive celebrations such as Christmas lunch or Chinese New Year can be an anxious time for many of us because we worry about things like, "Will the turkey be cooked? Is Bill going to get drunk and ruin everything? Will there be enough space? Are we going to run out of food? Will the kids like the presents? Am I going to overeat?" These are irrational fears. The stakes aren't as great as we think they are. A better framing: "If the turkey isn't cooked, we can stick it back in the oven again. It's not

the end of the world. Bill will do what Bill always does. We could never control him. If there isn't enough space, someone will find an extra chair. When was the last time we didn't have enough food at these festive meals?"

And even if everything goes wrong, and you forgot to make the gravy, as singer-songwriter, Paul Kelly, says:

"That's the great thing about Christmas, it comes around every year so we will always get another shot at it."

DON'T CALL IT LOVE

Love has the power to quell our greatest fears...but it can also amplify it.

You love your mother, but she can be overbearing.

She insists you take supplements. You say you eat a well-rounded diet so there isn't a need to take supplements. She says, "Nowadays, food is mass produced and lacks the nutrients we need." You say that supplements are an expensive way to make nutrient-rich urine. This annoys her a lot.

You tell her she should eat fresher food, and not keep things in the fridge/freezer for so long. She says everything in her fridge is fresh. You point at a container of old meat in the fridge and question how long it has been in there. She says she just got it out of the freezer that morning. You doubt this and the smell horrifies you. You say that the apples looked wrinkled. Rather than admit fault, she goes on the offensive: "Well, if you take me out shopping more often, then maybe I would have fresher apples."

The two of you have diametrically opposing beliefs, yet both carry the same fears: fear that the people you care and love most will be malnourished and fall into poor health; that those closest to you aren't listening to you; fear of not being trusted; afraid of becoming subservient once we admit to being wrong; and fear of loss of control.

You have the same argument with your mother on a weekly basis. Tired of this routine, you decide that things have to change. She is, after all, your mother.

On your next visit, on your way to her house, you mentally prepare yourself by chanting: *Love is kind, love is patient, love is not self-seeking, love is not easily angered, love keeps no record of wrongdoings...be kind, be respectful, don't argue – no matter what, no matter what.* You repeat this mantra in your head repeatedly until you arrive at her front door.

Within the first fifteen minutes, she brings up supplements into the conversation again. This time, thanks to the mental preparation, you don't get defensive or uptight. "Tell me more about these supplements," you ask her, "Which supplements are good for what?"

Seeing that you are finally listening to her thrills her. She runs through a list in her head. You listen attentively.

"OK, I will take a few supplements," you say, "but only if you promise to do one thing."

"What?"

"Eat fresher food. Don't keep so much in your fridge and freezer. Throw away old stuff."

"Everything in there is fresh."

"Mum, is it a deal? Will you try to eat fresher food?"

"OK, la."

It feels good to have struck an accord with your mother.

She's finally listening to you. "What's the best place to buy these supplements from?" you ask.

She says, "You don't need to buy, I can give it to you." Then she goes to her pantry, and returns with a pile of colourful plastic jars. She hands over one container at a time to you, along with the directions for each, "take two of these twice a day..."

You pull back, appalled by how much there is.

She goes back to the pantry to get some more. When she returns with another arm full, you complain it is too much. "You eat all this? This could cause more harm than good! I don't even know what half of these things are! What the hell is Coxanntinium XF12? Isn't that a heavy metal? Won't it poison you? No wonder you look a little blue sometimes. And how much is all this costing you?"

Fear is causing you to lose your cool, the mantra you practised earlier abandoned.

She is visibly upset. "Do you want them or not?"

"All this? No. And you shouldn't be eating all this. No wonder you get sick all the time."

"I'm not sick all the time."

"You really shouldn't be eating all this, Mum. There is no medical evidence to support that these supplements make a difference. It's a waste of money. It's a giant con."

She looks away.

"I'm only saying this because I love you, Mum. I don't want you to get sick."

She says nothing. It's the silent treatment. Her fears have turned into anger. It's her way of trying to gain control of the situation.

You're angry that she's not listening to you. You can't stand the silent treatment. "Please don't give me the silent treatment, mum."

She says nothing.

"Come on, mum, don't be so childish."

"Well, if you don't want to listen to me, then you can go to hell." She storms off to her bedroom, slams the door and locks it.

You may have made your mother happy for a moment with your "love is kind" mantra, but now the rift is greater than ever.

You leave the house, and in a state of fury, you decide that you need to take a stand. *How can she be so closed-minded?* You're sick of the silent treatment. This time you're not going to yield. It's a matter of principle. You're going to cut off all contact with her, and she won't be allowed to see her grandchildren until she listens to you on this matter. You're going to tell her friends that she is wasting money, putting toxins in her body, and being a fool for falling for the lies perpetuated by the supplement industry. You're only doing it because you love her. You're afraid that she is putting unknown substances into her body, afraid that she is poisoning herself, afraid that she is being manipulated by these companies, and afraid that she is wasting her precious retirement money. It terrifies you that your own mother would listen to someone else over you, that you have no control over her.

Love amplifies fears

There are two kinds of love. Love that is patient and kind or a love that is volatile and harsh. Love that does not dishonour others, is not easily angered, and keeps no record of wrongs, or love that causes humiliation, is wrathful and holds grudges. The difference between the two kinds of love is, of course, fear. Love amplifies our fears because the more we love someone, the higher the stakes are, the more anxious we feel when faced with uncertainty, and the more we feel the need to be in control.

Love drives us to extremes of human behaviour, from unnecessary worry, to betrayal, and violence. For example:

> *"I don't want to embarrass her in front of her friends. I'm only doing it because I love her."*
> *"I'm giving her the silent treatment because I love her."*
> *"I'm hitting her because I love her."*

It's not really love when it's fear-driven love. There ought to be a different word for it. The next time we do something for the sake of love, we should ask ourselves: "Is it love, or is it something else?"

BEHIND EVERY CONFLICT, EVERY ARGUMENT, AND EVERY GRUDGE LIES…GUESS WHAT?

Your daughter recently got married. Her husband, your new son-in-law, is a genial soul, easy to get along with, and quick with a joke or two. The two of you see eye to eye on most things bar one issue: free trade. He is dead-set against it, to the point of being an ignoramus.

"Buying local means you keep jobs in this country," he says.

To which you say, "Two hundred years ago, an economist named David Ricardo figured out that relative cost, not absolute cost, should determine the efficient allocation of resources."

"What does that mean?"

"We should buy foreign products if they can produce it more efficiently than we can." He still doesn't get it, so you elaborate: "Buying local might keep jobs in this country in the short term, but not over the long run."

"The long run? We've had decades of free trade, and look at what has happened to our manufacturing sector. There are abandoned factories and ghost towns all over this country.

Think of the millions of people out of work, think of their families and their shattered lives. Think of young people with no purpose, no skills, no self-esteem and no prospects. The future of our nation is in grave danger."

Surprised by his vivid descriptions and the emotion in his voice, you know it would be wise to change the topic, to keep the relationship amicable, but the stakes are too high, and it bothers you that a member of the ignorant class has penetrated your inner circle. You're afraid that it could infect others and you can't resist righting what is clearly wrong.

You say, "Human labour is a precious resource. We must put our people to work in areas where we can add the most value relative to other countries. That our manufacturing sector is in decline suggests we're better at other things – such as software design, health care and entertainment. It would be wasteful for our people to work in unskilled-labour-intensive industries, when other countries have a bigger reserve of lower cost unskilled labour than we do. They can produce some things at a lower price than we can – such as rice, fabrics and car components."

"Their prices might be lower, but these foreigners don't have the same standards as we do. They use slave labour and exploit children. They don't have the same safety regulations as we do. You might get a cheaper product, but they may fill them with cancer causing toxins. And consider the environment: they don't have environmental protection laws, they're poisoning rivers and oceans. And who knows where the money goes? To fund nuclear programs? To arm terrorist cells so that they can plant bombs in our backyards?"

Your pupils dilate, your synapses charge up. How dare he bring all this xenophobic scare mongering sewage into your house! You know you can't win against emotionally charged arguments, but this is a battle you can't afford to lose. You take a different tack – dumb down the message even further for him. It won't be easy.

"May I explain why free trade makes sense in a more relatable way?"

"Alright," he says. At least he's open minded – you give him credit for that.

"When your car breaks down, do you fix it yourself or take it to a mechanic?" you ask.

"I use a mechanic."

"You strike me as someone who is good with your hands, so why take it to a mechanic? Can't you figure out how to fix it yourself?"

"Sure, I can, but it would take me too long. They do it all the time. They have the equipment."

"This is what free trade is. Even though you can do it yourself, there is someone else who is relatively better at it than you are. You're happy to pay the mechanic because it saves you time and money."

"I'm not sure it's as simple as that."

"Stay with me. Imagine you decide you're going to fix your own car yourself. If you were a country, the advantage is that you'll keep a job from going overseas, and you'll stop money going into the pockets of foreigners. The money you save is the "salary" you pay yourself for fixing the car. However, is the money you save worth it?"

"Could be."

"But we've established that it would take you too long. You said it yourself. They do it all the time. They have special equipment."

"Maybe they're not as thorough, or maybe they're ripping me off. I don't enjoy doing business with crooks."

"That makes sense. So how do you decide which mechanic to use? How do you find a plumber, a tailor, and a lawyer?"

"I get recommendations, I check out their reputation, and stick to the ones I can trust. Local ones."

"In terms of free trade, that's the equivalent of buying from certified fair trade suppliers, or dealing with ethical companies that are trustworthy. So let's assume that you find a mechanic that you can trust, and the price they charge is sensible. Would you say that the money you pay them is worth it?"

"Yes, I suppose."

"The logic behind free trade is the same. You focus on the things that you're good at relative to other people, and this enables you to make the most money that you can. With this money, you pay for goods and services that other people can produce more efficiently than you can. Other people focus on what they're good at and rely on you to produce what you're good at. Everyone is better off."

He's looking unconvinced. You persist, "When a country decides to not trade, to manufacture things in their own country even though someone else is better at it, they're really harming themselves even though they've kept a job from going overseas. It would be like you deciding to fix your own car, do your own plumbing and sew your own clothes. You might keep all the jobs to yourself, but you're worse off. All these jobs might keep you fully employed, but it's stopping you from doing things you're better at, and you'd make less money. The salary you pay yourself, the money you save, is not worth it. It's a false economy."

You sit back and enjoy the simple analogy you invented. It's a masterpiece. The logic is so flawless, even a simpleton can't argue with it. But your son-in-law doesn't seem to appreciate it. He shuffles in his seat and looks at you sternly. People do this when they hear things that don't reconcile with their beliefs. Fear of being wrong troubles him. He says, "It might sound good in theory, but it's not how things work in reality. In the real world, evil exists, people don't play by the rules, greedy capitalists exploit workers, countries dump heavily subsidised imports that destroy our local industry, and they steal our intellectual property. Did you know that we're now entirely dependent on hostile governments for basic things like steel, telecommunications and vehicles? Imagine if we go to war, and we don't have enough steel to make bullets to defend ourselves, or they shut our communications down, or lose our skills to make cars. Free trade is a threat to our way of life."

The words have a powerful punch behind them because they're spiked with fear and emotion.

You become frustrated, afraid of not being able to persuade him of your arguments, that intelligent people can be so easily taken in by fear mongering, that your daughter has married an imbecile. You're afraid of the future of your yet-to-be-born grandchildren.

"You're wrong, Joe."

"No, I'm not. And most of the voters in this country agree with me."

"Will we win the next war with steel and bullets, or will we win it with bioweapons, drones, and cyber attacks? Do you want your children, my grandchildren, to be working in dirty steel manufacturing plants, or do you want them to be working in biofabrication, robotics and nanotech? Please, Joe, open your eyes. Don't buy into fear mongering designed to fool the uninformed. Don't succumb to it."

You regret these words as soon as they leave your lips. If only you were more in control of your fears.

He says, "This is a pointless conversation. I don't have to stand here and let you insult me," and leaves.

Thanks to your fear, or more precisely, your lack of awareness of it, you've put your daughter in a difficult position.

Fear, the gatekeeper

*Fear causes cognitive bias. We become more receptive to informa-
tion that triggers or confirms our fears, and tend not to apply the
same validity checks as we normally do. It's unkind to regard people
biased by fear as being stupid or ignorant. Intelligence has nothing
to do with it.*

Consider this exercise:

*Imagine you are skydiving for the first time. You are in a light
aircraft wearing a parachute. At 3.6 kms above the ground, the dive
should take 5-7 minutes, assuming everything goes well. If something goes wrong, you will hit the ground in roughly 27 seconds,
travelling at 956km/h. You're standing at the edge of the doorway,
waiting for the green light to come on.*

*Now consider this statistic: "We are more likely to die as a
passenger of a car (over a year) than taking a single skydive."*

*Do you believe this statistic? Will it convince you to take up
skydiving? If you are standing at the doorway of a light aeroplane,
3.6kms above ground level, would the statistic make you feel more
assured? Will it make you relax and step out of the plane gleefully?*

*If you are like most people, you'd be sceptical. You'd want to
check the source and validate the accuracy of the data before taking
up skydiving. Or you might dismiss the statistic altogether because
you're never going to believe anything that tells you skydiving is
safe.*

*Now imagine your 16-year-old son is going skydiving for the
first time. You don't want him to do it, but he isn't listening. You do
some research on the web and come across a statistic: "1 in 1,000
skydiving jumps result in death". How likely are you to pass this on
to your son to warn him of the dangers? How likely are you to check*

the source and validate the accuracy of the data before sending it to him?

For those interested, here are some statistics: 1 in 357,000 jumps result in death.[1] The chances of a car passenger dying over a period of a year is 1 in 48,439.[2] In other words, we are seven times more likely to die as a passenger in a car over a year than taking a single skydive.

This cognitive bias explains why we are seeing so much political conflict today. People who are against immigration (e.g. because they are afraid that it is the cause of domestic terrorism and higher crime rates) will downplay the benefit of immigration, disregarding evidence that suggests immigration creates wealth and reduces crime rates over the long run. The converse is true: people who welcome immigration (e.g. because of a fear of racism) will downplay evidence that suggests immigration is bad, disregarding evidence that suggests excessive immigration leads to economic and environmental decline.

People on both sides of the political debate aren't necessarily stupid. Fear causes them to be biased, they take in information selectively, and are deaf to anything that feels incongruent.

We are emotional creatures. Telling us not to worry, showing us statistics and other abstract arguments will not do much to change our minds.

The implication is that we ought to be wary when news is spiked with fear. The more emotive and visual the message, the more likely it will capture our attention, make an impression on us, deceive us and diminish our cognitive defences.

The implication for policymakers and business leaders is that we can't persuade people who are under the grip of fear to change their minds with facts, statistics, logical arguments and expert studies. The "dumbing down" of communications might not be effective either, because failing to comprehend isn't the problem. Opponents of free-trade use emotive words like "shattered lives", "exploit chil-

dren", "cancer causing toxins", "poisoning rivers and oceans" and "terrorist attack". These words conjure terrifying images and make the fear palpable. By comparison, experts and government officials use words like "absolute cost", "comparative advantage" and "unskilled labour-intensive industries". These words operate at the cerebral level, not the emotional level. To win over hearts and minds, we need to first address the most powerful gatekeeper: fear.

PROCRASTINATION

Fear isn't just bad for our health, it undermines creativity and productivity.

Your manager assigns you a work project in another part of the company. "It's a great opportunity to develop new skills and strengthen your resume." You wonder: *Was I not up to scratch? Did someone stab me in the back? Or was it something else?* You don't ask, of course, because you don't want to sound insecure. Instead, you show you are a go-anywhere, thrive-on-change kind of person by saying, "Sounds great! When do I start?"

You mutter to yourself: *must see the upside...new skills... strengthen resume...grow my network....*

At the first video conference meeting with your new team, you're put on the spot to introduce yourself. You fumble the start and recover with some well-worn anecdotes. You try to strike the balance between self-deprecation and humble bragging. *Am I banging on? Am I showing off?* Not sure if the little faces on the screen are even listening, you cut yourself short with, "And that's me." *Better to leave people wanting more.*

"Welcome to the team," says your new manager.

The attention shifts to another topic. The manager asks for a volunteer to produce a short video to announce policy changes, or something (you weren't listening because you were sussing out who's who on the screen). No one volunteers. After a moment's awkward silence, you put your hand up, keen to prove yourself.

"Are you sure?" she asks.

"Yes," you say, "I've done lots of these before". You want people to feel that you are a great addition to the team.

She offers, "Shall I walk you through the details after the call?"

"I think the brief is pretty clear," you say, "how about I create a first cut and run it by you so that we have a strawman to work off? It'll be more productive that way." You once heard someone say this and thought at the time that it sounded so cool and professional. You're glad that you could re-use it on this occasion.

"That sounds great," she says.

After the call, you replay how things went in your head: *How about I create a first cut and run it by you...it'll be more productive that way.* You like the way you sounded. *She said "that sounds great" in front of everyone.* This pleases you.

After the meeting, you read the brief more carefully. You have a lot of questions. *How long should the video be? What structure should I follow? What tone of voice?* You're afraid to ask your new manager. *I don't want to sound incompetent, not when I said I would create a first cut. Besides, I have done this sort of thing many times before. I can do this. I don't need hand-holding.*

You read the brief again. Make a few notes. Write a few sentences, which turn into paragraphs. Review what you read, and feel smug about how it reads. Take a break.

A thought pops up while you're in the bathroom: *What if it's not what they're looking for?*

Return to your desk. Read the brief again. *I should ask for help, but I'd look like I don't know what I'm doing.* You feel awkward about inconveniencing others. *I don't know anyone. What will they say about me? Must make a first good impression.*

Soldier on. Rework a few words. *Is this too long? Have I gone into too much detail? What if I'm missing the point? Who is the audience?* Re-read the brief again. Still don't know.

Stop work. Put it aside. Get a cup of tea. Tidy up the home office. Check emails.

Return to the task. Read what you have written so far. *It's alright, but is it what they want?* Worry that it is not. *What if I'm off the mark?* Procrastinate. Check notifications on the phone. Afraid to start because you don't want to waste time adding to something that is on the wrong footing. Don't feel you have enough to show your new manager. *I don't know what I'm doing. She'll be unimpressed, regret taking me in.* Want to show you are deserving of your senior status in the team. Want to be highly valued. Need to get it right.

You're not conscious of these fears in the same way you're not conscious of your heart beating, the biting of nails and the release of stress hormones.

Read the brief again. Go over notes again. Think. Come up with options in your head. Not sure which direction to take. Fold some laundry. Eat a sugary snack. Revisit options in your head. No obvious answers emerge. Return to desk. Browse social media. Check the clock and see you have wasted time. Think of what to do. Revisit options again. Use up a lot of mental energy. Take a break. Lunch.

Do some research after lunch, gather some ideas. Rework what you've written. Take a break. Check emails. Go back to what you've written. Your shoulders hunch over without you noticing. *What if I am completely misjudging this?* Lie on the couch for a while. Stare at the ceiling. No simple answers emerge. Return to the desk. Review notes. Put it aside. Check emails. Pay a bill. Do some research. Re-read the brief. Watch a few videos. Call it a day. *Clarity will emerge overnight.* Watch TV to distract your mind. Help yourself to another sugary snack.

Next day, same struggle. Procrastination, prevarication and much hoopla over what you're supposed to do. Read what you wrote yesterday. Don't like it. Start over. Write, delete, write, delete, write. What normally takes you two hours tops has taken you two days. It's like watching a tennis champion choke and forget how to serve. Fear can occupy our mind without our knowing, sapping our cognitive powers like a hidden parasite, and making our decisions for us without our say.

Day three, same struggle. Stress accumulates without you noticing it. By the end of the day, you are up to your gills. You find your son annoying, your partner insensitive and your usual barista chatting too much and taking too long. You don't realise that it's you, not them.

You suffer a poor night's sleep. Wake up with the Thumping. *What is going on?* Notice the signs of stress: anxiousness, tightness, constant snacking and generally not looking forward to the day.

Eat a healthy breakfast. Meditate for 10 minutes. Notice that your chest is tight and you are hunched over. Relax shoulders, push your chest out and straighten your back. Walk your son to school. Give him your full attention. Get your journal out and reflect. Make a sketch to depict what is going on in your mind:

Confidence Phase	Stress Building	Fear Detection	The Better Me
I can do this!	This is harder than I thought	Letting people down	I have done this before
How hard can it be?	I don't have all the answers	Getting it wrong	Just do: create an imperfect 1st cut, we'll iterate it as a team
Everybody will be so impressed!	My reputation is at stake	Doing a bad job	Ask for help - people like to help
		Loss of face	

Feel better. Crack on with the task. You are more decisive. The words come out easily. You find Flow, become more creative, and come up with a catchy pun that makes you chuckle.

You hit a snag. *How do I...? What is the right...?* These doubts turn into fear. *This feels amateurish. Will they like it? It's too pushy. I've taken too long to do this simple job. Someone else would have done a better job. They're going to find out I'm a fraud.* These thoughts pop into your head unknowingly in the same way thoughts come into our minds when we are meditating.

Walk to the kitchen. Stand at the pantry to look for a pick-me-up snack to get through the bump in the road. *What shall I eat? Wait...what am I doing here? I don't need a snack. I'm not even hungry.* Go for a walk around the block. Figure it out. *Fear of getting it wrong. It's OK to get it wrong. What matters is the tenth draft, not the first draft. Fear of loss of face. Just do, don't think.*

Back at your desk, you deal with uncertainties by taking your best guess. *Is this right? Doesn't matter, I can revise it later.* Plough on. Not sure if the example you're using is relevant. *Doesn't matter, it will work for now.* Plough on. Missing graphic design assets. Post a request on the team chat. *It doesn't matter if I should already know where to find these assets. People like to help.* Someone on the team responds with directions. Plough on.

You get into Flow. Free from the noise in your head, the burden of anxiety, the second guessing and the fear of failure, you produce more in three hours than the past three days. The experience is uplifting.

You create a first-cut mock-up video. It brings a big smile to your face every time you watch it. You send it to your manager, a little nervous, and request a meeting to get her feedback. You don't hear for hours. Finally, she responds with, "Let's show it to the team on Monday for feedback."

You didn't think it was ready to show everyone yet. *I meant it for her eyes only. Maybe she didn't even watch it. People will think I'm stupid.*

Monday. You show the video to the team. There are smiles. Four people chime in with praise and ideas. Your new manager is impressed and says so in front of everyone. You glow with a sense of pride and belonging.

That night, in bed, just before you fall asleep, the final thoughts in your head are: *if only I could have got my head together earlier.... How do people spot the signs of stress as soon as they appear so that they can deal with it?*

You come up with answers in your head, a list of ten practices. *I should get out of bed and write them down, but I'm so tired. It's okay, I'll remember them.*

That's the last thought in your head. You fall asleep, and sleep soundly.

In the morning, not only do you not remember the contents of the list of ten practices, you completely forget that you had made a list. As if blown away by an invisible wind in the night, they are lost forever.

Seeing the invisible

Fear Masters have a kind of detector, an automatic sensor that picks up signs of fear as they appear, within them and around them. The rest of us take days, sometimes years, to identify fears that underlie our behaviour (and sometimes we never do).

The good news is that fear mastery is a learnt skill. The more practiced we are at seeing fear, the more likely it will become second nature. Here are ten practices that help cultivate this ability:

1. ***Keep a journal.*** *Document worries, concerns and dilemmas to work out the underlying fear.*
2. ***Know your clan.*** *The immediate people around us heavily influence our well-being and our decisions. For this reason it makes sense to pick up the signs of fear experienced by those closest to us so that we can avoid getting caught up in their fear storm (i.e. overreact, get into an argument, do or say hurtful things, get upset and become fearful ourselves). Look out for excessive negativity, neediness, anger, absence or disengagement,*

excessive need to be in control, territorial and meddling behaviour. Another telltale sign is when people complain and bring up the same rants, e.g. "My father never understood me". Most people, even those closest to us, won't admit to their fears because they're either unaware of them, too busy coping with them or trying their darnedest to bury them. It's up to us, the fear masters, to recognise them, and in doing so, be able to help those closest to us.

3. **Meditate.** *With practice, meditation enables our mind to see what we are feeling, to catch our thoughts and emotions as they appear, to avoid acting on irrational fears, and to release us from unnecessary worry. It's a huge topic that I won't cover here because there are already a lot of excellent resources on meditation – books, apps and courses.*

4. **Walk.** *Some of the greatest minds in history, Aristotle, Churchill and Steve Jobs were habitual walkers. During these walks they allowed their minds to think freely, unencumbered by to-do lists, gripes, and modern distractions such as podcasts. They allowed their minds to wander, discover feelings, and gain perspective.*

5. **Analyse desires.** *Behind every need, ambition, desire and buying decision lurks fear. For example, if we're anxious about getting a promotion at work, often it isn't the extra income that is at stake but a fear of not getting what we deserve, fear of being taken advantage of, fear of inequity ("I'm better than them"), fear of failing in people's eyes, and fear of loss of status / loss of face. We should always ask ourselves what fears we're facing when making major purchasing decisions or when we hang on to objects that we utilise little. A*

worthy exercise is to write down our top 5-10 goals or ambitions now. This may include fitness goals, career goals or relationship goals. Then ask ourselves: "what are the fears driving these goals/ambitions?" To reiterate, fear is an important emotion that can bring out the best in us. The point of identifying the fears behind our goals/ambitions is to enable us to focus on what is genuinely important to us, and help us avoid irrational behaviour and unnecessary stress.

6. **Retrospection.** *Think back over the past day or week and search for moments when we've experienced fear or symptoms of fear. These might include tasks we've struggled with, arguments we've had, people we've tried to exert power over, moments when we felt out of control, times when we were obsessive, issues we were preoccupied with, etc..*

7. **Root causes analysis.** *Aim to discover root fears by asking "what is the root cause?" repeatedly. First, identify a fear, then ask ourselves, "what fear is driving this fear?" It's likely that you'll discover more fears. Repeat this until we uncover the fears at the very core of our being. The deeper we dig, the more we learn about ourselves. Knowledge of the fears core to our being is vital because they will be recurrent themes throughout our lives. (See an example of root cause analysis at the end of this chapter.)*

8. **Seek input.** *Ask a select few for their opinion. Use questions such: What do you think are some fears that are holding back my career (or what stops me from being an even better parent, spouse, leader, sports person etc.?) Which fears cause me to be overly anxious? What do you think I ought to worry less about? Why? What are my hot buttons? Why? It may be too*

confronting for some to point out your fears, so it may be necessary to offer a set of prompts. Often we don't seek the opinion of others because we already know what they're going to say. They may bring up old gripes, or be too mired in their own fears to have good insight about you. For example, a jealous partner might accuse us of being afraid of saying no to our friends, but this might come from a fear of losing control over you. Selecting someone close to us whose feedback we can trust is key.

9. **Identify symptoms of the Thumping that are particular to us.** *What are the things we do when we are burdened by fear? This might include overeating, having mental loops, becoming overly preoccupied, obsessing, being withdrawn, procrastinating, looking for distractions on our phones, consuming alcohol, smoking, bingeing on television, online shopping, watching internet videos, shouting or having tantrums. What emotions or physical sensations do we feel when fear first takes hold? This might include feeling lost, frustrated, uncertain, anxious, sleeplessness, impatient, angry, defensive or sad. Everybody is different, but throughout our lives, we respond to our fears in a consistent way. Fear Masters are familiar with the symptoms that are particular to them and are always on the lookout for them. It's a good idea to identify formally and write your top three symptoms. I have included mine at the end of this chapter. The picture is stuck on a wall next to my desk so that I can catch myself earlier than I otherwise would.*

10. **Partner up.** *It helps to have a running mate, at home and at work, to keep an eye on us, and give us a nudge when we need it. It would be even better if your running*

mate has read this book. Even if they haven't, a common framework and language will aid discussion. And if we trust them, we can share our list of common symptoms with them. The benefit of a good running mate is that they may pick up on the symptoms before we do, and alert us to them earlier than we would ourselves.

My top three symptoms and their root causes

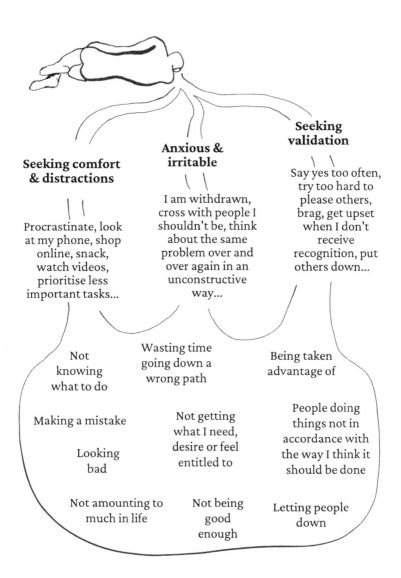

Seeking comfort & distractions

Procrastinate, look at my phone, shop online, snack, watch videos, prioritise less important tasks...

Anxious & irritable

I am withdrawn, cross with people I shouldn't be, think about the same problem over and over again in an unconstructive way...

Seeking validation

Say yes too often, try too hard to please others, brag, get upset when I don't receive recognition, put others down...

Not knowing what to do

Wasting time going down a wrong path

Being taken advantage of

Making a mistake

Not getting what I need, desire or feel entitled to

People doing things not in accordance with the way I think it should be done

Looking bad

Not amounting to much in life

Not being good enough

Letting people down

WE WEAR OUR FEARS ON THE OUTSIDE

You get along with parents at your child's school and look forward to a chat at the school gate pickup time. There is one parent that you try to avoid, because he often has a gripe about some school issue, and you'd rather not get involved. But today he's spotted you across the playground and walked over to you.

He seems to have a bee in his bonnet about a teacher. "I don't know what the kids are learning or doing in the classroom," he says, "there should be more transparency. You know what the problem is?"

"What?"

"The bad kids. They waste too much time and attention on them. My Rhonda isn't getting enough attention. I mean, I'm not asking for special attention. Rhonda has so much potential."

He bangs on. You don't agree with anything he says, so you withhold comment. After a while, perhaps because of your silence, he asks you a question to test that you're actually paying attention: "Did you hear about the incident?"

"What incident?" you finally ask, after an inaudible sigh.

"A group of kids got in trouble for bullying. My Rhonda was one of them. Rhonda says she wasn't involved, that she was just watching."

You have heard this story, and according to your sources, Rhonda isn't as innocent as her father believes.

He continues: "You know my Rhonda, you know she would not get involved in something like this. Can you believe that they put the blame on a group of kids rather than find out who actually did the bullying?"

You play it neutral. "Hmmm, yes, I heard about that."

"I'm going to do something about it. Speak to the Principal. Will you say something too?"

You weigh your options:

Option A: Say "Yes, but do nothing." This would be the path of least resistance, but dishonest.

Option B: Say, "I'm sure the teacher is doing his best." He'll conclude that I'm not on his side. Maybe this is a good thing. Maybe I should stand up for the teacher. What am I afraid of here? Fear of offending someone that I don't know very well? That he might gossip behind my back? The other parents might ostracise me? Am I afraid of not fitting in?

Option C: Be non-committal and say: "I'm not sure." This won't quell his anxiety. What if he follows up with, "Why not?" Then I'd be forced to say what I really think.

I don't want to cause offence, not because I'm afraid, but because I don't want to add to his consternation.

You stall for time: "What would you say to the Principal?"

He rambles. This gives you the time to think and listen for his fears: *he's afraid of looking bad in the eyes of the school community because of Rhonda's bad behaviour....he's seeking validation from me....the complaints are a front....*

"Rhonda is a great kid," you say. "She deserves the best,

and kids like her are a credit to this school. You're obviously doing a great job with her."

With this, you can visibly see the fear disappear from his face. You prepare yourself to talk him out of going to the Principal, but much to your surprise there isn't a need. He doesn't raise the topic because you've allayed his fears.

The way you handled the situation pays off handsomely, not just in the moment, but he now tells everyone on the school committee what a nice person you are. He seeks you out every afternoon during school pickup for a chat. You've become his buddy, his trusted advisor.

A few months later, your new friendship pays unexpected dividends. You're anxious because your employer says they won't be renewing their contract with you. You'll be out of work. Your new "best buddy" comes to the rescue and introduces you to someone he knows, who later offers you a contract that pays even better.

Luck seems to have played a big role in this, or did it? People say it's not "what you know", but "who you know", but in this case, it's "what you did", a moment of insight, an act of kindness, a fear mastered that led to this opportunity.

Even the most self-centred people have the capacity for generosity if we help them overcome their fears.

One day, standing alone in the schoolyard, waiting for your child, you come across an important realisation: **people wear their fears on the outside.** You can tell from what they wear, how they walk, how they look. It's on their faces and in their body language. A parent standing on his own away from everyone looking at his device and avoiding eye contact has a fear of small talk (which is a fear of wasting time and fear of not knowing what to say). A grandparent watching his step as he walks has a fear of falling. A young boy yelling to get the attention of his friends has a fear of being left-out and fear of not fitting in. A teacher yelling at a boy has a fear of losing control over the other students. A parent waiting with her arms crossed and looking anxious is afraid she will be late for something. The mother making her child eat the contents of his lunchbox, which he should have eaten at lunch, has a fear of food going to waste, fear the child will suffer hunger. The parent driving an enormous off-road vehicle (that has no place in the city) has a fear of getting hurt in an accident, fear of appearing weak. It's Tee-shirt weather, but there is a girl wearing a jumper. Either her parents have a fear of her getting sick, or she is trying to hide something.

It amazes you how obvious it is. All you have to do is pay attention.

You spot a parent whom you can't read at all. She walks with an air of confidence, like nothing is troubling her. Her mind is present, her posture upright. You are strangely attracted to her, not sexually, but a desire to be a friend. You imagine her to be one of those heroic characters on TV who can muster equanimity when faced with adversity. That's what makes heroes attractive: it's not their super strength, it's their confidence, their courage, their mastery of fear that makes us want to be like them.

And then you have a second realisation of the day: "If we wear our fears on the outside, what fears am I currently displaying for the world to see?"

THE EPIPHANY

After I got out of hospital, I spent a lot of time searching for and working out the set of fears that underpinned my stress. I started out with some hypotheses, searched for fears motivated by deeper fears, and organised them into a hierarchy of concentric shapes (see next page).

This was hard for me to do. Even now when I read it, I feel the pangs of fear in my gut. I showed it to my wife, who said, "Hang your balls out there, Jerry."[1]

I believe these fears to be close to the very core of my being. They are behind everything I do, what I say, what I wear, the career choices I make, how hard I push myself each day, who I choose to be friends with, who I avoid, all my desires, my purchasing decisions, the reason I experience anger, frustration, self-doubt and grief. It's difficult to shake them. In moments of happiness, I may forget them momentarily, but they are always there, pinning me down, blowing me in different directions, causing a flap.

After working this out, I lay on the couch in my office. The fears went in circles in my head, growing in magnitude. My heart rate increased, my blood pressure rose, and a sense of hopelessness gripped me. I was experiencing the Thumping.

Digging deep to discover my core fears

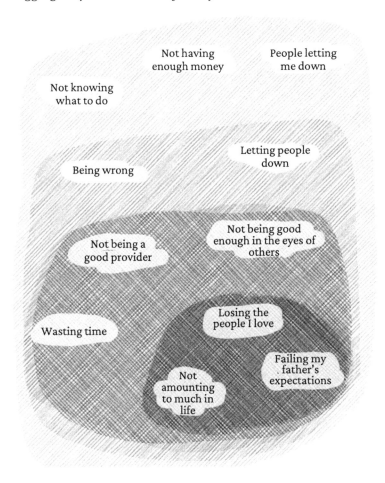

This is my point: seeing fear might be an important step, and some-times it's all we need to do. However, often it's insufficient. In fact, it can make matters worse. We can become consumed by it.

What do we do with the knowledge? What do we have to do to overcome it? How do we make the Thumping go away?

Bruce Lee said, "Courage is not the absence of fear, it is the ability to act in the presence of fear." At the time, I hadn't yet mastered this.

How do we be like Bruce Lee?

This comes next.

4.SWITCH

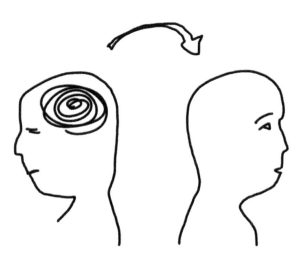

PART IV

SWITCH

Fear entering the mind is tension. Fear inhabiting the mind is stress. Fear released from the mind is relief, happiness, and peace. But what if it's stuck inside and can't get out?

If the first challenge in mastering fear is to "see it", then the second challenge is to "unsee" it.

THE FOUR LENSES

If we believe that we're at the brink of bankruptcy, would we be less fearful if we're told to "Relax, don't worry...everything will be alright"? Should our child be bullied at school, are we likely to be comforted if the school principal says "Don't worry about it, things will work out themselves"? And what if we suspect our husband is having an extra-marital affair? Would we find peace if he says "It's all in your head"?

Our fears may well be in our head, but it's not like there is a switch that enables us to turn it off. Once our brain senses a threat, rational or otherwise, it doesn't let go of it easily. The unease, state of alarm and emotion can linger on, or as is sometimes the case, never go away.

If the first challenge to master fear is to "see" it, to be aware of it, the second challenge is to "unsee" it: to release ourselves from its suffocating grip, make room for a deeper, more complete and balanced understanding of what we face.

Consider this analogy: Imagine that you live in a house with views of majestic mountains and rivers. One day, despite community protest, the government builds a manufacturing plant, a six-

storey concrete monstrosity with a chimney. The building is thirty kilometres away from you, a great distance, so it shouldn't materially affect you — the smoke that it emits doesn't travel anywhere near you, you cannot hear it, and you can barely see it, especially on foggy days. Despite this, you are upset because you know it's there. When you look out, your eyes are automatically drawn to the coal plant, so much so that it becomes all that you can see. Even when it is foggy, you know it's there. The intrusion irritates, infuriates and rules your mind. It's all that you can talk about. Even though the building makes up less than 1% of your view, you're no longer able to enjoy the majestic views of the mountains. "They've ruined my view," you think.

In this analogy, the manufacturing plant is fear. Fear can be so dominant in our minds, so prominent in our outlook, that it makes us lose perspective and become blind to the bigger picture.

The solution is theoretically simple: a Zen master would say that the majestic mountains and rivers are still there. We just need to acquire the skill to "unsee" the manufacturing plant.

How do we "unsee" something if the image is stuck in our heads? How do we unseat the fear that is sitting on our throne ruling over us?

There are four lenses we can look through to help us accomplish this. Here's an overview below. The stories that follow in this chapter will show how they can be applied.

The Four Lenses

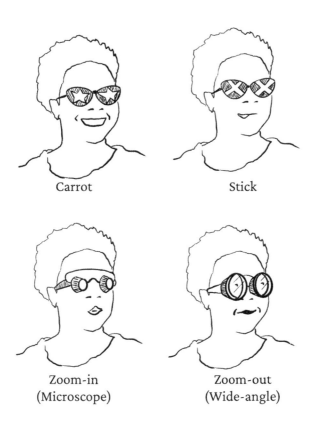

Carrot

Stick

Zoom-in
(Microscope)

Zoom-out
(Wide-angle)

The carrot lens

Look at the upside. Do this in one of two ways:

1. *Find gains in losses; or*
2. *Reframe constraints as advantages.*

Example: "They delayed my flight because of mechanical issues. I'm afraid I'll be stuck in this airport for hours. Grrr!"

Switch to: "I like an airline that is thorough and takes its time to ensure we get to our destination safely. The delay means I get extra time to think and have quiet time for myself. Great!"

Note that seeing the flip side isn't the same as wearing rose-coloured glasses. I'll elaborate in the next story.

The stick lens

Counter one fear with another fear.

Example: "Should we have a second child? What if the pregnancy doesn't go well, or I lose my wife in childbirth? Can we afford it financially?"

Counter with: "Can we afford not to have a second child? What would our first child be missing out on? Will we regret this decision when we reach old age?"

The microscopic lens (zoom-in)

Fear can be like a giant ball of fluff that blocks our thinking. If we can unravel it, we might find that it comprises smaller fears that aren't that scary after all. In other words, we can overcome our fears by breaking it into its component parts.

The wide-angle lens (zoom-out)

Looking at the bigger picture can help us think more rationally. Often, it can be difficult to gain perspective. A few thought exercises can help. Here are four examples:

1. *Time travel. This exercise works best for fears related to an uncertain future. Imagine time travelling forward and seeing that everything has worked out as we hoped they would. This is not about creating fantasies, it's about visualising plausible scenarios, and doing it in sufficient detail to help see all the possibilities, not just the negative ones. For example, if we're worried about not having enough money at retirement, create a spreadsheet with cash flow projections, and do this assuming that things will go to plan, and that there will be no major mishaps (e.g. we won't be unemployed if we choose not to, the stock market will continue to grow at 4% on average per year over the long term, our expenses will remain roughly the same etc.). Now assume this rosy picture to be the most likely outcome. All we have to do is to be our normal selves in order for this imagined future to take place. The aim of this exercise is to free us from obsessing over improbable, worst-case scenarios.*

2. *Let go. Imagine what it would be like to lose something we love or desperately want to hold on to. For example, if we're afraid that our partners might leave us for another lover, then try imagining that scenario happening. What would we do after we overcome the grief? What would our lives be like? Presumably, we'd be single again, and eventually we would find love again. We'd hopefully realise that we'd be OK, but more*

than that, we'd realise that we have the resilience to thrive. This exercise is about helping us appreciate what we have rather than fear what we have to lose. It's a gratitude exercise. For example, we might come to realise that every hour we get to spend with our partner is a gift, not an entitlement. They willingly choose us!

3. *Cheat death. This thought exercise is similar to the previous one. Imagine we are dead, we've lost everything. Now imagine that we've been given a second chance at life. What would we do differently now that we've been given this bonus time on earth? Is the fear we face still significant in the grand scheme of our lives?*

4. *Realise that we have less control than we think. We have little to no power over the nation's economy. If we're anxious about being promoted at work, whether certain managers will endorse us at tomorrow's meeting, realise that we have little control over it.[1] If we're experiencing the Thumping because our start-up is failing, realise that luck plays a bigger role than we think. The point of this exercise is to help us let go, to avoid trying to know the unknowable, or control things that are outside of our control, and to help us focus only on the things that are genuinely in our sphere of influence. Remember that the lack of control is one demon of fear. We can nullify a sense of lack of control if we let go of the need to control.*

The aim of looking through these four lenses is to enable us to put things in their correct perspective.

Returning to the manufacturing plant analogy, the lenses give us the capacity to enjoy the majestic mountain view again, to see the

99% and not narrowly focus on the 1%, to cherish what we have, and to return us to equanimity. Do it the right way and we may even learn to appreciate the manufacturing plant itself!

AGEING

Dealing with humankind's oldest dread.

It's your birthday today. You're turning 45. You get out of bed, look in the mirror and notice something miraculous: your grey hairs have disappeared!

How can this be? Is it because I've been feeling less stressed lately? Is it because I've been eating well? Have I discovered the fountain of youth? You smile at this thought. *Or perhaps it's genetic? Did this happen to mum and dad also?*

And then you come to your senses: *It's my eyes, my poor degrading eyes.* You turn the light on, lean in to take a closer look, and see, much to your dismay, that there are even more grey hairs than before. Great streaks of it.

You've been in denial about your declining eyesight for a long time. You haven't been able to read the small font on your phone. Rather than blame your eyes, you've been blaming the software engineers for their poor design. *Whoever designed this should be shot!*

One day, browsing in the shop of an art gallery, your partner suggests trying on some reading glasses. When you put them on, you're stunned by how clearly you can see. "My God! Look at all the lines on your face!" you say to your partner.

"Oh, thanks!" your partner says sarcastically.

"I didn't mean it that way. I mean, I can see with so much detail, I can see all your wrinkles."

"I don't think those glasses are right for you at all." Your partner leaves you wondering if you said something wrong.

You buy the glasses. They're great at first, but you can't get used to them. They don't make you look intellectual, as you assumed glasses would, they just make you look, well, middle-aged, which you are, but you don't see yourself that way. Deep down, you still think you're in your twenties. It's the benefit of having poor eyesight: looking at yourself in the mirror without your glasses on makes you look at least ten years younger.

The glasses give you headaches, which causes you to lose productivity. You try living without them, but it's no good, you can't see without them.

There is a bigger psychological problem. The glasses mark the end of your claim to youthfulness, and it catalyses a profound sense of sadness. You don't say this to anyone because it sounds vain. It's not just the eyes: your knees ache, which stops you from being active; your sexual energy isn't what it used to be. You still desire, still want to feel the excitement and pleasure of sex, but by nine at night, all you want to do is to go to sleep.

Sick of all this self-pity, you flip the switch and go full throttle with positive thinking. You don't want to be someone that whines about ageing. It's boring. Helplessness is unattractive. You dye your hair to hide the grey. *There's nothing wrong with my eyes. I don't need glasses. My knees are fine. I can run a marathon if I want to.* And you decide sex isn't a priority. *I'm just busy, and that's OK.*

One day, at a work conference away from home, you bump into an old colleague that you never liked much, a large man, famous for his bluntness. He greets you with, "Whaaaa! You look so old! What happened to you? I really could not recognise you!" The outburst causes heads to turn, you blush from the unwanted attention. "I remember when you...wa-wait, have you dyed your hair?" he asks, far too loudly.

"No, I haven't dyed my hair. It's totally natural!" You force a smile, step back to avoid his closer examination, then ask, "How come you are still so fat? Is that cheese on your shoes? I suppose you can't see it because your big belly blocks your view." It's not the most gracious thing you've said lately. Onlookers avert their eyes.

"Never mind la," he says, "we all get old, but you know what is the best thing about getting old? We get to eat as much as we want." He puts his pudgy arms around your shoulders, embracing you as a comrade in the war against time. "Shall we get something to eat?"

You play along, the amiability paper thin. *I am not old. He is just delusional and jealous.*

You catch a reflection of yourself in the windowpane. At first glance, you look middle-aged. You tilt your head to catch a more sympathetic angle, jut your chin out to hide the second one under it, suck your tummy in and successfully take off ten years. Much better.

At the end of the night, after the more sensible conference goers have retired to their hotel rooms, you go to the bar. You look at your phone and see that by now it is too late to call home. It's not clear why you are here, you should be in bed so that you're fresh for tomorrow's lectures. You sit at the counter, order yourself a drink, look around the room, and catch the eye of someone too young for you, who after holding eye contact for just the right amount of time, comes around to ask, "I haven't been able to take my eyes off you since you walked in the room, can I buy you a drink?" It's sleazy under any circumstances except now, coming from someone so young and good looking. Loving the validation, you play along, have momentary amnesia about the fact that you're not single, and say, "Sure, what's your name?"

Frame losses as gains

Fear of ageing can cause us grief, undermine our confidence and age us in a not-so-graceful way. One feature of being human is a tendency to over-project. The smallest signs of ageing can trigger panic, anxiety, and depression. The fear itself can precipitate the undesired outcome e.g. doubts about our sexual adequacy deflates our sexual virility.

With ageing, the trick is to avoid being saddened by what we're losing, over-project and worry about what is to come. Focus instead on what we still have and what we have gained. For example:

Don't think: "I'm losing my eyesight, I hate wearing glasses"

Think: "Thanks to these $29 bits of plastic (ie, reading glasses) I can continue to enjoy the miracle of sight"

Don't think: "My God, I'm going grey!"

Think: "Look at all that hair I've still got – I'm a silver fox!"

And instead of lamenting the loss of our sexual prowess, be thrilled that our brains are no longer preoccupied with getting laid every night.

Cautionary note: carrot lenses are not rose-coloured glasses.

A little over-optimism and self-deception may be beneficial but too much of it puts us at risk of being over-confident, apathetic to threats or in denial of reality, so that injury, humiliation, bankruptcy and other dangers are only a step away.

The "carrot lens" isn't the same as "rose-coloured glasses" because the aim of wearing the carrots lens isn't to paint everything in a positive, blinding light. The aim is to see the entire picture, unblemished by fear.

IMPOSTOR SYNDROME

Framing constraints as advantages to overcome fear.

You're the founder of a small software company. Business is good, you are profitable, customers like your product, but growth is achingly slow.

It takes guts and deep wells of self-belief to start a business. You are full of self-belief, but you're human, and therefore vulnerable to moments of insecurity. At the back of your mind, deep in your psyche, furtive as a termite nest, lives the fear of being a fraud.

I'm not a proper business.

We can't afford to have a CFO, or even an office for our business.

My company isn't solving big, sexy problems, such as building an electric car or solving world hunger.

I lack knowledge and expertise in so many areas, such as social media marketing.

I can't afford to hire the best people in the market to help me.

How can we compete with global software companies that can afford the best UX designers and engineers? Their products have so much sophistication, so many features.

We don't have big advertising budgets. We are too small to be noticed by newspapers and investors.

We don't have a sales force. How can we win when competitors have sales executives that wine and dine decision makers?

Why would big companies do business with us when we are so small and vulnerable?

You never express these, what you consider "lame-ass" doubts, out loud, not to your partner or even your dog because you don't want to appear weak. Nor do you formally address them in your head because you don't want your mind to dwell on negativity. You quash and bury these thoughts as quickly as you notice yourself dwelling on them. You choose to place faith in yourself. *I will bend reality.* You choose to send positive vibes into the universe. *If I work hard, I will be rewarded.* This blind optimism is the central problem. Whilst the fears remain unacknowledged and untreated, they sabotage your business without your knowing. You understate your value to potential clients. You're not as forthright in the marketplace as you need to be. At sales meetings, you're too pushy because you lack the confidence to let clients make up their own mind. We're all masters at justifying our fears. Your rationale for being pushy: *it's what other salespeople do…if I want something, I have to ask for it. Clients don't know what they want. It's my job to push them to help them make up their minds and close the sale.* You give up on sales leads earlier than you should because you don't want to "trouble" your contacts. *I hate to be pestered, so why should I pester others?* You charge too little because you doubt the value of your products. *It's better to underprice than charge too much.* You avoid raising money from investors because you can't guarantee they would get their money back (which is an unrealistic expectation). The lack of funds hinders your capability to grow. *Investors are likely to act in their own short-term interest. Besides, do I really need advisors to meddle in my business?* It's almost impossible for you to see fear covering its tracks because these justifications make sense. In other words, every decision you make is perfectly rational to you.

Too much self-doubt is bad for our health. Like termites to a house, fear quietly eats away at the foundations of our mind and the structure of our body. After four years of grinding in the business, it starts to take a toll on your health and well-being. You put on weight, have terrible sleep hygiene, and fall ill often. You give your friends and your family very little mind share. Every hertz of your brain's computing power needs to be dedicated to the business. There is too much at stake.

One day, you confess to your mentor, half-jokingly, "Maybe I should quit and find a proper job. I'd make more money and not have to worry so much."

Helen, your mentor, asks, "Why do you feel that way?"

In a rare moment of vulnerability, you open up and share all your fears and doubts. You feel ashamed to say these thoughts out loud. It makes you feel unworthy of calling yourself an entrepreneur, and you apologise for being so lame.

Helen says, "They're pretty good reasons to quit, but before you do, let's try a thought exercise. Let's look at the flip side of the constraints you face, to frame them as advantages instead of disadvantages."

"Why?"

"To walk a tightrope, we have to keep our eyes on the horizon. Too much focus on the ravine below, the negative, puts us off balance, and causes our decisions to be out of kilter. This exercise is about helping us gain a balanced view. Shall we try it?"

"Frame constraints as advantages?"

"Yes. How about I start you off? You said that you're too small, but small equals nimble. Nimble means you change tack much faster than your competitors. You don't have entire departments of people dealing with regulation and red tape."

"Hmmm."

"Your turn. What's another constraint?"

"I don't feel like a legitimate business because we have no investors, no board of directors, no CEO."

"The upside of that?"

"Well, I suppose the advantage is that I don't have to write board papers, sit in board meetings and answer to investors who might have a different agenda. I am told by another founder that this takes up half her time. We're free from all that."

"You can do what you want. My turn: you might not be tackling big, sexy problems, but you're solving problems that matter to a small group of customers. They choose you because you meet their needs exactly. Niche businesses are so hot right now."

"True. We might lack the expertise in some areas, but this gives us the opportunity to look at things differently. Novices create some of the best inventions because they bring fresh perspectives."

"Yep."

You continue. "Giant software companies might have the best designers and engineers, but they waste so much time in meetings and dealing with internal politics. We get things done in minutes, not months. We are free to make spot decisions and don't need relationship managers. Their products might be sophisticated, but they are sometimes bloated with too many features. Ours is simple, easy to change. Our customers prefer simplicity."

Helen adds, "Serial entrepreneur Jason Fried said: 'Less is a good thing. Constraints are advantages in disguise. Limited resources force you to make do with what you've got. There's no room for waste. And that forces you to be creative.'"

"That describes us exactly! We don't have advertising budgets, and this forces us to make better products."

"How so?"

"Because the only way we can grow is to make products that are so good that people will tell others about them."

"Word-of-mouth is the best form of advertising."

"We don't have a CFO, nor a place of business, but this is a conscious choice. It means we carry minimal fixed costs, and we can survive longer than anyone else."

Helen nods in agreement.

You continue: "We don't have a sales force – thank goodness because I hate dealing with salespeople."

"Ha ha. That's a tad negative. One day you will need a sales force in order to scale, but let's go with it for now. You're right in that right now you're not swamped with recruitment interviews, onboarding, arguing over forecasts and doing performance reviews. What else?"

"Growth has been slow. We don't have a lot of clients. I feel vulnerable. I don't know if there is an upside to this?"

"The advantage of not growing too quickly is that you get the benefit of time. Time to listen to customers more closely, time to experiment and refine your product, time to build a stronger foundation."

"Yeah, but investors will only look at startups that grow 5-10% per week. Otherwise it's not a startup, it's just a lifestyle business."

"I can see how a comparison with what they expect can make you feel you're not a legitimate business. It's difficult to put aside the impostor syndrome. Here's a different perspective: growth is an outcome. It's not something entirely within your control. What you can control is making good products, serving customers well and delivering great value. 5-10% growth per week is great, but it's also a big distraction. Right now, you have the advantage of time and customer focus."

Half-heartedly, you say, "I see what you mean."

"It's easy for me to say all this, but I'm not in the hot-seat. Being an entrepreneur is one of the hardest things one can do. There is so much risk and uncertainty. The majority don't make it. Some don't just lose all their money, they lose their mind."

There is a long pause. You say, "Uncertainty and risk are difficult to deal with but the flip side to that is that there is so much to learn and discover. I'm not going to the same old job, sitting at the same old workstation, doing exactly what I did yesterday, dealing with the same stiffs. I'm hungrier than anyone else out there."

"Nice flipping."

You sit taller, eyes towards the horizon.

Helen asks, "Are we guilty of telling lies to ourselves here? Are we being overly positive?"

"Maybe, but isn't that what good entrepreneurs do, put a positive spin on everything? Crush negativity? Bend reality?"

"No. There's a world of difference between positive spin and seeing the flip-side. Too much positivity is dangerous. It causes us to be out of touch with reality, make skewed decisions, ignore important signs and fail to change direction when we need to, which is how bankruptcy happens. A great entrepreneur is the opposite of this. A great entrepreneur sees with more clarity than anyone else."

"I see."

"Ultimately, only you can decide what is the truth."

There is another long pause.

Helen resists saying anything.

"On balance," you say breaking the silence, "I feel like I'm just at the beginning of a journey, and we have a lot going for us."

"It's natural to have doubts. You might feel a strong resolve now, but the uncertainty is likely to surface again. When this happens, I'd encourage you to surface them, write them down, and do what we did today: look at the flip side of constraints and disadvantages."

You finish your coffee, thank Helen, and say goodbye.

Although there is a great weight off your shoulders, fear remains. Fear of not being good enough, fear of not knowing what to do, not knowing if the business will succeed, afraid you're a fraud and terrified that you're already failing. It's all there, deep in your psyche, furtive as termites.

RACISM

If at the heart of racism is fear, then what can we do about it when politicians stoke it and modern media amplifies it?

Your father is a good man, but he's a closet racist (well, maybe not so closet lately). Your partner can't bear it, and wants you to do something about it.

"What <u>can</u> I do?" you say. "He's an old man. You think he's going to listen to me? You think we can change him?"

"Sometimes there's a need to fight fire with fire," says your partner.

You're proud of your father in many respects. A retired teacher, he now volunteers at a neighbourhood centre coaching kids, and has been a blood donor for the past five decades. Your kids love him. He always has time for them, playing board games or taking them on little excursions. And, like a Hobbit, he seems to have an endless supply of cake, chocolate and cheese in his larder.

Behind this generous persona is a racist. Once in a while, your father will say something that jars against your liberal values. "These damn moths are like the Wayans*. Once they get into your larder, they multiply and take over everything."

[*Wayan is a fictitious country, and Wayans are a fictitious race of people. Fabricated here to avoid causing offence and perpetuating stereotypes.]

Although horrified, you say nothing for fear of upsetting him. Whenever he says something racist, you take a big mouthful of cake, not caring if it has moths in it, swallow, and try to change the subject.

One day in your garden your child kills a cockroach with a shovel, yelling out, "Die, you Wayan bastard, die!"

"It's just an expression", you say, trying to make light of your partner's fears. "He probably doesn't even know who the Wayans are."

This disgusts your partner. He blames your father. "How can you let this racism into our house? You need to do something about it."

Having been a victim of racism, your partner has zero tolerance for it.

"It could have come from the school, or TV, we don't know," you say. "It's all over the news and social media. Everybody in this country seems to be against the Wayans lately."

"The problem is you're afraid to stand up to your father. Where will you draw the line? When our kids abuse Wayan people in the street? When offended Wayans hit back and our child loses an eye? Where's the line? Tell me, so that I'll know who to blame when our kids join militant forces and plant car bombs."

Your partner is pitting one fear against another fear: a fear of who your children might become versus fear of confronting your father.

Your partner continues: "If we want the world to be free of racism, our streets to be cleansed of it, we have to start in our homes. Your father's home, actually."

You ask: "What am I supposed to do? Tell my dad to stop being a racist? He thinks he's doing the right thing. I feel sorry for him."

"Sorry for him!? Why? For seeing Wayans as cockroaches?"

"Show me a racist and I will show you a scared and confused human being who is just wanting to make right what they think is wrong."

"What fear?"

"Fear that others will take what is ours, fear that our values and way of life are under threat, fear of social degradation and unemployment, fear that danger will come to us, fear that the world as we know it will change forever and no longer be the same...I could go on."

"So your father is a saint, then?"

"No, he is not a saint. He's scared, vulnerable and fallible. News and social media are the problem. They aim to inflame rather than inform."

Your partner says, "Well, if social media is the problem, then let's fix it."

"How?"

"The next time we visit your father, you distract him while I get into his computer. I'll unsubscribe and unfollow him from racist influencers and groups. I've been thinking about this for a while."

Your eyebrows hit the top of your forehead at hearing this suggestion.

Your partner presses on, "I'll go through his social media feed and report racist posts...I'll cancel his newspaper subscription."

"Isn't that an invasion of privacy?" you say with great alarm.

"Sometimes we have to fight fire with fire, darling. I'll subscribe him to more reliable sources of news and information."

"And what about his TV?" you ask sarcastically. "He has Cyclops News running in the background 24 hours a day. Are you going to cut his antenna?"

"That's not a bad idea, you know. He'd benefit from having a break from it."

"This all sounds extreme. I can't believe we're having this conversation. Please don't do any of that."

A week later, at your father's house, you notice something not quite right with your partner – flushed neck, sweaty palms, the smell of fear and adrenaline in the air, and then a long absence. You go searching, room to room, and catch your partner at your father's computer, covert as a secret agent.

"WHAT ARE YOU DOING!!" you whisper loudly. You already know the answer, of course.

What you don't know is that your father is in the next room. He hears you and appears in the corridor. "Is everything all right?"

"W-we, we're trying to settle a bet."

"A bet?" your father asks with scepticism. "What is it?"

You stare blankly at him. "Well," you say, "It-it's about a quote I heard recently. 'Once fear gets possession of the soul, it does not readily yield its place to another sentiment' – who was it that said that?"

"Dostoevsky, wasn't it?" your father asks.

"Close, Tolstoy," you say.

Your partner, frantically clicking away at the computer shutting down open windows, says, "Oh yeah, I thought it was Jon Bon Jovi. Yep, confirmed right here. Tolstoy. I wasn't even close. You were right, darling."

You turn to your father and say half-jokingly, "I've married an idiot, haven't I?" angry that your partner didn't listen to you. "Jon Bon Jovi! Ha ha ha. So what's for lunch, Dad? I'm starving!"

Two weeks later, your partner takes every opportunity to justify the misdeed. "Look at the difference it has made. He's a new man!" Although it wreaks of confirmation bias, your partner isn't wrong. Your father was irritable in the first week when something "strange" happened to his social media account, and when the TV mysteriously broke down, but now he seems to be his old generous self, less tetchy and grouchy.

"I didn't think it would make a difference, but..." you concede.

"It's OK, you don't need to thank me. I didn't do it for you alone. It was an act of mercy. Being pounded by threats of danger every day takes a toll. I'm glad he's better."

"I was going to say that it's still an awful breach of his privacy."

"You have to fight fire with fire, fear with fear. The means justify the end."

Social media algorithms have a way of finding our fears and insecurities, however small, and amplifying them. They learn about our desires and our fears by monitoring what content we look at and engage with, and feed us with more of the same. The most inflammatory content naturally gets the highest priority on our feed. It gets placed in front of more people because they are more likely to get a response. Social media platforms thrive on user engagement. Once we see it, it's hard to forget it. Exaggerated truths and misinformation stick to us, layer upon layer, accumulating to a point where it can become difficult to ascertain the truth. The sense of uncertainty is part of its effect. We can't fully blame social media algorithms, as they often amplify that which already exists.

It doesn't take long for your father's feed to return to the way it was. A river of political lies and sewage flows through his computer, causing him to be irritable and stirring up anti-Wayan feelings again. Also, your father gets his TV working again and pays far too much attention to it.

The two of you drop in to check on him one day. Out of context, he says, "The Wayans cannot be trusted, you know, they're the biggest threat to our way of life."

"I'm not sure any of that is true, Dad," you plead.

Your partner picks up on your soft stance. "What do you mean 'not sure'? It's total bullshit!"

"You people have had a blanket over your eyes," says your father. "Did you know the Wayans have invested more money in biochemical weapons in a year than we have spent on hospitals and schools over the past ten years? Why do you think they do that?"

"That's all fake news," says your partner. "Our nation's defence budget is ten times bigger than theirs. I've been to Wayan, and I have studied their government. Their leaders are rational people who love their children as much as we do, and not at all bent on destruction. The Wayans are good people. Some of my best friends and colleagues are Wayans."

You cut in, "Oh goodness, look at the time. We need to pick up the kids from sports!"

Your father ignores your effort. "Well, I'd keep a shovel close by if I were you. Never know when your so-called friendly Wayans will turn on you."

You sense blood sizzling on both sides.

"That's disgusting," your partner lets loose. "I can't believe you just said that. There are 240 million people in Wayan. Are you saying every single one of them is evil? Think about what you're saying here."

"Yes, that is what I am saying. The Wayans do not respect human decency. They are rapists and human traffickers. They'll come into your home at night, take everything you own, and slit your throat just for fun. I've sent you so many news articles – don't you read them?"

"No, we don't, because they're all lies. Stop spamming everyone with lies. You're embarrassing yourself."

Your father is bright red, "Alright, you people are so smart you don't even have to read anymore. Is that what you're saying?"

"You're accusing us of being closed-m....," your partner turns to you, "Aren't you going to say anything!!? Please don't be so spineless!"

"He's my father!"

"I think you should leave," says your father.

Your partner looks to you for the next move, eyes wide, full of rage. You say nothing, and in doing so, make both of them feel betrayed.

Your partner says to your father, "Please do us a favour. Stop watching news and cancel your social media accounts. It's corrupting your mind. You're so racist you don't even realise it."

"Is that why you pried into my computer and messed around with it?"

Embarrassed, your partner says, "C'mon, let's go! We can't save those who aren't willing to be saved." Your partner walks away, expecting you to follow, and adds (addressing your father), "You are to stay away from my children from now on. I don't want them infected by your bigotry."

Hurt, your father retreats in the opposite direction towards the backyard.

You're torn. *Who needs me the most? Which way should I go?*

You choose your father. You find him in his backyard, unsure of what to do or how things will play out. The noise of the honk of your car interrupts your thoughts.

What do I say to my father?

"Dad, I admire your sense of civic duty, your generosity and protective instinct. When you talk about the Wayans, I can see that you're trying to protect us, to defend our country, to ensure that we pass our values and way of life on to our children."

Must resist trying to change him. Not now.

The car honking escalates – it's now a long, continuous sound that says, "Get your ass over here now or else!"

You persist, "I need to go now, Dad, to pick up the kids. I just want you to know that I love you no matter what. And of course you can see your grandchildren anytime you want. You are a wonderful influence on them."

You rush to the street to find the car no longer where it was parked. Instead it is down the street, rounding a corner, tires screeching, and then it is gone.

How to fan the flames of racism

Certain journalists, politicians and influencers fan the flames of racism because it helps them gain attention, mindspace, followers, political might and revenue. It's only a minority thank goodness, but these inciters dominate public discourse because they're good at provoking fear, hatred and anger. They do this by stoking the three demons of fear:

    1. Inflate the stakes. *We're led to believe that the stakes are higher than they are. For example, with all the noise and hoopla about building a wall on the Mexican border, you'd think the number of unauthorised Mexican immigrants in the US is rising exponentially, but in reality it has been in steady decline since 2007. The number of illegal Mexican immigrants in the US fell by 29% from ~7 million in 2007 to ~5 million in 2017.[1] We regularly hear of misdeeds of certain countries such as the Wayans: they're always stealing our intellectual property, polluting the oceans with plastic and bullying other nations in terms of trade and territory. But do we always get the full picture? Do Wayans contribute intellectual property freely to the World? Do they steal more intellectual property than other nations (especially historically)? How significant is Wayan foreign aid? How does trade with Wayan benefit us? How does Wayan compare against other countries in terms of carbon pollution (in total and per capita)? Are other countries just as guilty of territorial bullying?*

    2. Create the illusion of lack of control. *They make us feel disempowered with sentiments such as: "things are getting worse, nothing can be done about it, and worse, no one seems to care". They downplay law and order with headlines such as: "Politicians bribed", "Police overwhelmed" and "Wayan hackers impossible to catch". The overall feeling of being out of control isn't entirely the fault of the inciters. It's a function of the digital age we live in. We receive so-called 'breaking news' on an hourly basis these days,* *which creates the illusion that problems are persisting (and that no one is doing anything about it). In reality, racial tension and international conflict evolves over decades (and centuries). The competition over limited resources and shifts in demography are global issues that no one individual or government can control alone. Unless we're tasked with running a country, for most of us learning about the misdeeds of the Wayans on an hourly or daily basis doesn't actually do anyone any good.*

3. Increase uncertainty. *Some of the tactics used by fear mongers to create uncertainty include:*

- *Make the enemy faceless or undetectable e.g. "They are everywhere and they are amongst us."*
- *Make the racial threat seem unpredictable e.g. "They might take your job, buy up the surrounding land, and turn us into slaves."*
- *Discredit reliable sources of information to create confusion and doubt, e.g., "The masses are being lied to, so don't be a sheep."*
- *Undermine the institutions we rely on for law and order, e.g. "The Wayans run our government" and "Authorities have no clue what to do".*

To reduce the uncertainty, we become obsessive about obtaining information, turn into heavy news watchers, scroll through pages and pages of our social media feed to look for answers, and this makes us prone to buying into "alternative facts" and unsubstantiated opinions (because they seemingly offer knowledge about the unknowable).

To regain a sense of control we behave in ways that we otherwise wouldn't: become easily agitated, justify discrimination, hurl abuse, spam people with racist content hoping to raise awareness, join rallies, stock up on weapons, gang-up on minorities, inflict psycho-

logical and physical abuse, and at the most extreme, commit murder, plant bombs and order military attacks. On the other hand, many of us switch-off altogether, and this is a problem because apathy, as we know, is toxic to the proper functioning of society.

Tackling racism

The racism that is widespread in our society, the kind described in this story, happens when good, ordinary folk like you and I are prompted to harbour irrational racist ideas and emotions that are inconsistent with their own cultural or personal values. These are good people, with sound moral values, motivated by the need to right a wrong and not sit idle while evil takes place. They harbour racist feelings because they perceive a threat that, in reality, isn't material, and only exists because of media bias and populist politics. Should we admire their good intent or admonish them completely? They're doing what they feel they must, based on the information available to them. Isn't that what we all do?[2]

What not to do and why

We put people offside when we try to correct them, tell them they are wrong, call them stupid or racist, ridicule their beliefs, and discredit their sources of information. Although ineffectual, we often do it anyway. Why? Why do we have these pointless arguments that divide rather than unite? It's because the stakes are too high. We can't help it. We feel compelled to attack the threat we see, not realising that we are stoking rather than subduing fears.

Unfortunately, our attacks have the effect of exacerbating the situation. We increase the stakes (e.g. we make it personal), create uncertainty (e.g. we challenge their worldview), and make people feel out of control (e.g. they feel distrusted, unsupported and unable to protect their reputation).

The fear that our view is wrong is a big deal. Our worldview is a set of beliefs that our brain uses to make sense of the chaos, without which we wouldn't feel safe. We use it every day to navigate through complexity and decision-making. Having our deeply held beliefs challenged makes us feel lost and uncertain.

Being ambiguous about where you stand or being duplicitous (saying one thing but believe another) can backfire because it spawns further distrust and uncertainty.

What to do and why

Racism can be subdued if we address the three demons of fear.

Reduce uncertainty

- Take a long-term view to see the broader picture (e.g. over the past 100 years, has discrimination improved or gotten worse?)
- Ask: "What are the likely outcomes given there will be counter-balancing forces when things go bad?"
- Increase awareness of our media consumption hygiene (e.g. are we trying to know the unknowable? Does this news channel aim to

inflame or inform? Is the injustice actually widespread or is it the exception?)

Boost sense of control

- Acknowledge and give praise for what people are trying to do e.g., "I admire your sense of civic duty and thanks for trying to protect us."
- Make people feel good about their higher moral standards — make them feel that they are not alone by talking about other people exhibiting these standards.
- Give examples of order and justice to dissipate the sense of chaos and lawlessness, e.g. "1 million illegal immigrants were evicted last year".
- Give people a sense of control generally. If people feel in control in one aspect of their lives, a spillover effect takes place where they are less likely to feel out of control overall.
- Role model critical thinking, and empower people to get better at discerning the accuracy of information (without making people feel judged).
- Refocus attention on what we are in control of (and not worry about the things we aren't in control of)

Ascertain the stakes

- Size the problem e.g. "What percentage of our population do these ethnic minorities represent? And of this, how many behave in an undesirable way? How do these statistics compare to the broader population?"

- Break down the risk into its smaller parts and rate each risk in terms of "probability of occurrence" and "severity of impact"

Lessons from history on dealing with racism

In the 1950s, prior to the American Civil Rights movements, equal rights were a threat to many white Americans because of the fear of loss of social, political and economic privileges.

Public opinion changed thanks to Civil Rights leaders who:

- *Countered one fear with another fear: by pitting the fear of not living to one's own moral standards against the fear of loss of privileges;*
- *Reframed losses as gains and reducing the stakes: by shifting the focus away from what Americans would lose (e.g. a seat on a bus or a place at a school), but what they have to gain i.e. a just society, peace and harmony for all Americans;*
- *Made white Americans feel in control: by not telling them what they should do, by avoiding zero-sum "I'm right, you're wrong" arguments, but by asking people to vote based on their conscience (i.e. giving them the choice).*

Why only "subdue" racism?

Why not eradicate it and be free of racism altogether? Racism is a fear, and fear is an innate human quality. As demonstrated by the swings of the pendulum in history, we never lose our fears, we only learn to live above them.

Interestingly, those of us who are aggressively intolerant of racism, to the point of being distressed, angry, offensive and ineffective, are driven by the same set of fears as people with racist attitudes. These are: fear of inequity, fear that we're being taken advantage of, fear of social degradation, fear that evil will compromise our social values, fear for our personal safety and that of our family, fear of economic loss, fear of loss of our way of life, fear that the world isn't the way it should be, and fear that people with deeply wrong beliefs are trying to manipulate us. Both the racist amongst us and those intolerant of racism are crying out the same thing: "How can you not believe me? How can you not see what I see? Did they brainwash you?"

JOB SECURITY

Take a microscope to fear.

The rumour is that the next round of job cuts will be the most severe in the company's history. You're afraid that you might lose your job.

For sixteen years, you've stuck to a job you don't love, but you do nothing about it because it's not clear that there is anything better out there. Unemployment is high. You loathe going through the job application process, feel uncomfortable promoting yourself, dread being judged by interviewers, and you don't fancy the prospect of having to start over in a new environment. *I am well paid, the benefits are good, I'm good at what I do, I have many contacts and people I like here, so I shouldn't complain.*

The timing is awful. You've just borrowed a whopping amount of money to buy a house, the family's dream home. You're up to your eyeballs in debt, there is no cash buffer, mortgage repayments eat up the bulk of the family's income, and your partner isn't working at the moment. *If anything happens, the bank would force us to sell the house, and we'd have to downgrade or find a place to rent.* You calculate the sums in your head, work out worst-case scenarios, recalculate the sums, reconsider the scenarios, read into what people are saying at work, come back to the scenario again, do the sums again, and so the mental loop goes. This drags on for weeks.

You cannot confide in your partner for fear of loss of confidence in you. Deep in your psyche is a fear that you're not good enough for your partner, that your partner deserves someone better. You're afraid of losing everything, not just the house. This keeps you up at night.

To avoid losing your job, you volunteer for extra work; you do extra unpaid hours, get into the office before anyone and make sure you're the last to leave. You don't challenge bad decisions by senior leaders, and you practice the art of the humble brag e.g. "I feel silly because last night I didn't know how to switch the lights off when I was the last to leave", and "My greatest challenge at the moment is balancing my productivity versus taking time out to teach junior staff." OK, so maybe the bragging isn't so humble at all, but you feel it is justified because everyone else is doing it. This behaviour makes you look desperate.

The stress felt by everyone in the office surfaces in strange and awful ways. There is incessant gossiping and slandering behind people's backs. The huddle of smokers standing outside behind the building is bigger than ever before. People are stealing cutlery and stationery, presumably because they feel entitled to. It's hard to get a word in at meetings because people cut each other off, leaving no room for the introverts to say anything. Everyone is trying so hard to prove their value that no one recognises anyone's value.

Some fears are difficult to block out of our mind. Telling yourself that "everything is going to be OK" feels like a hollow promise. You've heard that it helps to imagine the worst-case scenario, but this is unthinkable to you and only exacerbates the anxiety. *Lose my job...fall behind on bills and mortgage repayments...lose the house...what will everyone think of me?*

You don't like how you sound. *I've never been materialistic. Why am I afraid of losing the house?* You attempt a thought experiment. *Do we need such a big house? Wouldn't we be just as happy in a small house?* You draw a table listing physical and psychological needs associated with your dream house, and analyse them:

Zooming-in: why a big house?

Needs	Fears	Analysis
Spare rooms for guests	Not being able to host friends/family; not seeing enough of my adult kids (i.e., they don't visit because there is no room). Fear of loneliness.	Guests can sleep on the couch, share a room or stay at a rental home nearby. The money saved from downsizing would pay for holidays with my adult kids. It's silly to have spare rooms for the 10-20 nights that we need for guests. There'd be less cleaning and maintenance if we had less space.
Third toilet	Having to "hold it in".	The situation in which 3 people need a toilet at once urgently is very rare. Fellas can take a pee in the garden. We'd have one less toilet to clean.
Double garage	Having our car stolen if we park on the street. Needing to walk to/from the car in the rain. Loss of convenience.	We could sell one car and save even more money. Car theft is unlikely these days. Getting caught in the rain isn't the end of the world.
Second living room	Losing a lovely room to impress and entertain guests. Having to fight the kids over what to watch on TV.	We can use the existing living room to entertain guests. We'll have to "impress" our guests in other ways. It would be good to watch TV as a family more often.

...continued

Needs	Fears	Analysis
Pool	Loss of living standard (pleasure from taking a quick dip on a hot day, and hosting the kid's friends)	Pool maintenance is time-consuming, boring and expensive. I hate being a slave to it. It's not great for the environment. The pool only gets used 30-40 times a year, and less as the kids get older.
Outdoor dining	Loss of standard of living.	We were able to get by fine without it before.
Happy partner	Letting my partner down. Afraid my partner might leave me.	Is this true? Don't know.
Status	Not gaining the respect from people we care about.	We don't need a fancy car or a big house to prove ourselves. It's not how I judge others, so why should I care about being judged this way? People like us because of our values (such as generosity and kindness), not because of what we own.
Security	Not having a nest egg for the future.	We are better off with a balanced portfolio rather than having all our eggs tied up in one asset. Not having an overbearing mortgage gives us financial breathing room and freedom.

Having broken down your fears into its parts, you deduce your fears are almost entirely unwarranted. There is one exception: you're afraid of disappointing your partner, afraid to appear weak, and ashamed of the risk of losing your job. You decide it's best to say nothing rather than worry your partner unnecessarily. *Maybe I won't lose my job after all.* The trouble with this approach is that you play out the same conversation in your head repeatedly, revisiting the same fear. You do this alone.

One night, you blow up and yell at your teenage daughter for wasting money and behaving like an over-entitled child. Afterwards your partner asks if everything is OK. That's when it comes out, you bare your soul, the fears about the job, the house, and how you could lose it all. Your partner is equally concerned. You feel relieved that it has all come out, but desperate to reassure your partner that everything will be OK.

"What do you mean everything will be OK?" your partner cries. "We could lose everything."

"Look at this," you say, showing your partner the table of needs and fears you drew up.

After studying it, your partner says, "When you break it down like that, it makes things really clear. We don't need a big house to be happy. At this stage of our lives, we ought to do what we want to do. I don't want you to stick to a miserable job you don't love or feel suffocated by a mortgage we don't need."

"I feel like I'm letting you down."

"Darling," your partner places a hand on your shoulder, "that fear is just in your head. You could buy me a mansion by the beach and still feel like this, you know what I mean? Home for me is wherever you are. All I need is this tiny little space right next to you to be happy."

Just like that, the power of love melts away all your fears, the heavy burden off your shoulders, and the hundred thoughts knocking around in your head are silenced.

Back at the office, you're no longer affected by the threat of job cuts. You stroll like a man in a park without a care or a worry in the world, as if you have an invisible coat shielding you from the fear and insecurity everyone else is feeling. You are generous with praise; give credit where it is due; unafraid to challenge poor decisions; behave in a way that is true to your purpose and values, and leave work on time to be with your family.

Envious colleagues wonder why people like you exhibit no fear. "Maybe they're clueless about the looming job cuts? Are they mortgage-free? Do they know something we don't? Are they in cahoots with the executives? Maybe they're performing sexual favours?"

The air of confidence inspires others to want to work with you. Which is why people are devastated when they learn that you're leaving for another job. You put in your resignation because the culture of the company is too toxic, and find work in a smaller outfit with an ethic that aligns with yours.

Those left behind say things like, "It's always the good people that leave." They whine and complain about the company, "it's so political, this company is doomed." For fear of sticking their neck out, being out of work, not being able to make ends meet, mortgage foreclosure, letting their partners down...year after year, they do nothing about it, they stick to the jobs they loathe, put up with people behaving badly, and worry about the next round of job cuts.

CHEATING DEATH AND TIME TRAVELLING

This story contains a couple of examples of how we can use thought exercises to help us switch mindsets.

You are the product manager of a chemical company, but the patent of the product you manage will expire in a few years. The implication is that competitors can enter the market with generic substitutes and erode margins. Corporate headquarters will downsize your department unless you can figure out a way to grow sales or defend margins. Having your team downsized is a tremendous loss in status. There'd be a cut to your budget, your team size, and possibly your salary. Or worse, another department could absorb your product, making you and your entire team redundant. You've known your team for years, and they look up to you. It would be a significant loss to disband them.[1]

Your only hope is to be assigned a blockbuster product, but

the managers responsible for these products look well entrenched in their positions.

It's common to bring forward the problems of tomorrow. We can't help ourselves. As if diagnosed with cancer, everyone in your team has lost the ability to smile, and morale is down even though the expiration date is several years away. Previously agreed budgets are revised frequently by senior management. They force you to make budget cuts on a monthly basis, and scrutinise every expense claim.

Here is a case in point: you had approval to bring your team leaders together for an offsite workshop, but now a lowly finance person is blocking the purchase order. You once wielded the power to swat these bureaucratic gnats out of the way, but now you seem to have to answer to them.[2]

"We have the budget. Why are you holding it up?"

"It doesn't matter if you have the budget, it's no longer inside your delegated authority."

"How do you expect me to keep my people motivated? How do we solve problems if we can't get together to collaborate?"

"I'm just following policy."

You give up reasoning with the irritating finance officer and go above his head, but the finance manager isn't helpful either. "I understand your position. I can't do anything about it either. Perhaps we should ask Ron?"

You take it to Ron, the group executive, hoping he can pull a few strings. Ron is likely to be sympathetic because he is business-minded, but you're conscious you shouldn't call on him too often,[3] so you practice and hone your pitch before the meeting.

"The workshop would enable us to do a month's work in a single day," you say. "Twelve people for twenty days is roughly $150k. We're talking about an investment of $20k in expenses.

It's worth it, isn't it? Plus, think of team morale – you can't put a value on that."

It's a hard sell, but you get your way. Ron approves the budget. You stick it in the face of the lowly finance officer. It surprises your team leaders to learn that the workshop is still going ahead, and they admire you for standing up for the team.

The workshop is a tremendous success. Everyone works together to agree on a set of strategies, and everyone feels energised about the future – which is a big deal given the bleak and challenging prospect. Your team is full of admiration for you, and you leave the workshop on a high.

Almost immediately after the workshop, you are told by the finance manager, "We need to cut 20% of your team before the end of the month."

Outraged, you ask, "Why!?"

"We need to redeploy resources to where the greatest return will be. I know you're upset, but you and I know that it's going to have to happen eventually."

"But we've just spent twenty thousand of my budget to get the team together. I brought everyone in and energised them towards a common plan. I can't let them down now by letting one in five go!"

"Again, I appreciate this is upsetting. The question we ought to ask is, 'What is the right thing to do for the company?'"

"I'm taking this up with Ron."

"Ron asked me to tell you."

"This is coming from Ron?"

You decide to go to Ron, anyway. This is the last straw, and you're prepared to burn your bridges. In truth it is the fear of loss of face and loss of control that is driving you. You put off telling anyone in your team, or take any action until you see Ron.

Ron doesn't respond to emails, and you cannot get a meeting with him. You're frustrated. The anxiety builds. You know you need to cool off, but it is hard to stay cool when so much is at stake: your team, your reputation, your ego. You try meditation. It calms your mind for a while, but it doesn't take long for the peace to vaporise because in reality the difficulty and uncertainty remain.[4]

The fear causes you to procrastinate further. You take a week's vacation and book a beach escape to take your mind off things.

Sitting on the beach, your mind returns to the losing battle you're fighting. You replay conversations in your head repeatedly. It's difficult to delight in what the kids are doing, and you have no appetite for adventure. You've turned into a grouch. Your partner tries to cheer you up and include you in the fun, but you can't get into the spirit.

You send your family off on a boat cruise so that you can sit on a beach alone with a book. It's a book about fear that a colleague gave you just before you left the office. At the time you thought to yourself, "I don't have a problem with fear," but you were gracious and accepted it.

The book suggests that there is one of two exercises that can help you put things into perspective (to master fear).

Exercise one: imagine cheating death.

Imagine you die of a heart attack suddenly and unexpectedly. You don't get a chance to say goodbye to your children, your partner, your parents, or your friends. Never will you walk up the driveway of your house again, or set foot through your front door, or sleep in your bed. All your possessions are not yours anymore: not your mobile phone, your computer, not even the shirt you are wearing. You won't complete anything you started: the portrait you are painting will remain half-finished, and you won't see your children graduate. You won't enjoy the benefits of the money you have been saving for later life. There will be no opportunity to fulfil any of your ambitions, write that book you always thought you would, won't become fluent in French, travel to New York with your best friend, comfort your partner or hold your children. You are dead.

Now imagine having a second chance at life. You come back alive and return to exactly where you are now. What would you do differently? Would you remain preoccupied with the problems you currently face? Be too busy to play with your children? Stay upset with your mother? Carry a grudge against that colleague at work? Choose to be buried in fear and worry about deadlines, finances and politics? Or would you consider these matters trivial now that you've had a second chance in life? How would you like to spend this day now that you have a second chance? Would you focus on your children? Start that book that you always wanted to write? Would you be more cheerful, more grateful for what you already have, and what you've accomplished?

Almost instantaneously, the thought exercise lifts the dark clouds over you. You look around, take in the beach scenery, feel the breeze on your skin, become amazed by how blue the ocean is, how bright the sand is, and you notice for the first time since you got here tiny colourful shells in the sand. You wiggle your toes, the sand satisfyingly scratchy between them.

When your family returns from the boat trip, you shower them with attention. *I get to see them. How lucky am I? Look at my beautiful partner!* You reach into your bag of tricks that always make them laugh, such as your suite of superhero impressions. You've never been so present in your life, and this seems to double the joy in your family.

After the kids go to bed, you consider the second exercise in the book:

Exercise two: look at your life over a longer time span

Step one: travel into the future, say ten or twenty years, and imagine that everything has worked out "fine". This isn't about indulging in unrealistic fantasies such as winning the lottery or becoming a rock star. It's about imagining a plausible future. A couple of examples may help: if you are worried about your teenage son, then travel forward twenty years and imagine your teenage son has become a kind, competent and responsible adult. Visualise what your son will look like as an adult, for example, how he speaks, what he is like as a father, etc.. If you are worried about work, perhaps because you are in over our head, then travel forward ten years and imagine reaching your career goals, whatever that may be. It helps to do this in some detail. For example, you might visualise yourself addressing a vast audience at an industry conference.

Step two: take a leap of faith by assuming that what you have imagined in your mind's eye will happen, in fact it has already happened, that there is nothing to worry about because all you have to do is to be yourself and you will fulfil this destiny. It doesn't mean that you can sit back, do nothing and assume you can leave every-thing to fate. You can't abandon your parental duties or stop trying to make progress at work. The exercise is about relieving short-term anxiety by taking a leap of faith into an imagined, plausible future.

Step three: return to the present moment, and acknowledge the progress you've already accomplished. For example, you might look at your teenage son and congratulate yourself for the great job you've done so far, and what a great kid he already is. The point is, there is no need to panic and over-project at the first sign of disap-pointment. You should keep doing the right things, make small adjustments if you need to, but recognise that you're well on your way towards the bright, imagined future. You have after all been working towards it all your life. Give yourself a pat on the back.

This exercise makes you cringe. You're too cool for this self-help, "power of the mind" malarkey. This said, you decide to give it a go because you're still not yet out of the frying pan. *What have I got to lose?*

You close your eyes. You travel forward ten years and see yourself as an executive in charge of a portfolio of blockbuster products. *I am already a success, a group executive with a lot of clout, recognised widely, celebrated for my contribution to the industry.* You picture yourself in a corner office with a magnificent view. *I have a brilliant personal assistant, and a team of top gun product managers.*

You open your eyes. *Step 3: I have already made progress towards this vision. I have the skills and experience. There is nothing to worry about. The current problems are just hiccups. I will bounce back.*

As cheesy as the exercise is, it works in that you feel less panicked about your current circumstances.

The book suggests that one way to overcome fear is to "embrace constraints". You try it.

The upside of cutting my team is that we get to be leaner, there'd be less noise, and we'd be able to move faster. It's not all bad. I get to prune the weaker members of my team.

It's unlucky that I got handed a dud portfolio, but this gives me the opportunity to stand out from the crowd. I will make a success story out of this. Every success story needs obstacles, every superhero needs evil villains, like Thor needs Loki. This bit of luck is a blessing in disguise.

When you get back to work, you no longer act entitled to past privileges. You decide to cut one in four members of your team, rather than one in five. This will give you the discretionary budget to run your business your way. You decide which individuals to let go, meet them individually to inform them of the bad news, and get the entire team together, including those that are leaving.

"It's been a tough day," you say in front of everyone. "I hate doing this. It's a lousy consolation, but it's true that we must do what is right for the company as opposed to what is right for us. As sad as I am, I know in my heart that this is the right thing to do. We've been fighting with one arm tied behind our back and dragging around like victims. It's time to embrace the constraints put upon us, and take the future into our own hands. Those of us remaining will build a turnaround story. Every hero needs a challenge, a villain. Without Loki, there is no Thor."

Everyone in the room was with you up to that point. You regret making the Thor reference. You press on, "It won't be easy, but that is the point. If there is no difficulty, there would be no triumph. We will adapt. No longer will we look like the weakest member of the pack, sickly and limping, ready to be picked off by wolves. We will, instead, be the strongest, fastest and healthiest in the pack." This seems to resonate with some in the room. People lift their heads up, literally.

"Those of you leaving, we are grateful to have shared this part of your journey with you." You name each individual and say something gracious about them. "Our lives are better off because of your friendship, hard work and creativity. You are all professionals, highly talented and qualified, and you will be a tremendous success in another role. I am sure of that. I know this is disappointing, but the silver lining is that you are embarking on a new journey now, rather than in a year's time. And in a year's time, you will be stronger and happier than if we had held you here for another year fighting fights with one arm behind our backs. We're not on this planet for a long time, we ought to make the most of it. Let's thank each other for the journey so far and wish each other the best for the challenges ahead."

You don't win everyone over. Some are angry but

restraining themselves from saying anything out of respect. Some are too fearful about their future to know how to act. A few are teary. Those remaining behind feel sad that they're losing their colleagues, and at the same time worry about their own future.

You make a mental note to buy everyone a copy of the fear book, the one that was generously shared with you.

Later, a departing team member says, "We know you've tried your best to protect us. It's time for us to emerge from under your wing. Thank you for being the best leader I've ever worked under."

"Thanks for saying that. None of you ever worked under me, you were always ahead of me," you say, hoping to sound magnanimous. *Perhaps I was too hasty in letting this one go.*

One day, back at your desk, you flick through the fear book and find an interesting line:

Sometimes we need to fight fire with fire, fear with fear.

It gives you an idea: to tap into your customer's fears in order to defend your product's market share. Nobody wants to pay higher prices for fear of wasting money, but with the right marketing campaign, this fear could subordinate to a whole slew of bigger fears, such as the fear of failing to keep our family safe.

You sell your idea to the leadership team. You don't call it fear-mongering, of course, this sounds too manipulative. Instead, you call it the "Premium Positioning Strategy".

"As you know, the generic suppliers will swamp the market in a few years when the patent expires. The expectation is that suppliers will enter the market with generic products, start a price war, and destroy our margins. We can take inspiration from pharmaceutical companies: marketers of branded painkillers claim 'faster relief', 'greater efficacy', and 'higher standards', planting the idea that generic brands are potentially less effective with substandard quality." You omit the fact that such claims of faster relief and greater efficacy aren't statistically significant according to experts, and that branded and generic pharmaceutical products basically have the same active ingredient composition.

You press on, "Pharmaceutical companies aren't alone: industry lobbyists, such as those working for car manufacturers, gain tariff protection from foreign competition by stoking public fear. Motorists don't want to pay higher prices, but they're persuaded by a fear of economic decline and job losses."

Ron chimes in, "In the U.S., insurance companies don't want governments to provide affordable health care because they'd lose customers, so they run campaigns to stoke fear of deterioration in quality of health services, fear of government intervention and rising taxes."

"So you want us to run a scare campaign?" asks another group executive.

"No, that is bound to backfire. We don't have to. We can rise above it simply by occupying the premium position. Imagine this: at the point of purchase customers choose us because we're the familiar and trusted option. They'd happily pay us three times the price if we can achieve this.[5]"

"What would it take to achieve this?" asks an executive.

You reply: "A big marketing budget, and by big, I mean astronomical."

"Sounds risky," says an executive.

You reply: "It would be a gutsy move, but we did a market study and Finance has looked at my numbers. The returns would be in the order of five hundred percent."

"Five hundred percent?!"

"That's the conservative estimate," says the Finance Manager, handing out a detailed report.

You secure the funding and lead an aggressive marketing campaign. Advertising increases your brand's awareness. As you had hoped, market surveys confirm customers are conflating awareness with trustworthiness. You've successfully shifted the customer's buying criteria from "saving money" to "getting good value".[6] From "What is the cheapest?" to "Which is the safest?"

"The magic of this strategy is that customers aren't even conscious of it," you brag to Ron. "The generics have been in the market now for six months and have taken almost no market share of us. They've now priced their generics at a price point similar to ours, seeing that they can capture a large margin, just like us. We've avoided a price war."

The success story spreads throughout the company, making you a superhero.

Success breeds success. They put you in charge of a blockbuster product. And soon after, a competitor poaches you with an attractive salary package to look after a set of blockbuster products.

Sitting in your corner office, one with a wonderful view, you get a phone call from a journalist that has been pestering you. You decline the interview and hang up. The journalist runs a report that says your company has been making exaggerated product claims to inflate margins. It becomes a media scandal. The industry watchdog launches a formal investigation. You're worried that it could tarnish your reputation. Having climbed so high, you have so much to lose. You could face a lawsuit, maybe even jail time.

In your office, you have a framed copy of a book on your wall. It's the book on fear that you first read on the beach many years ago. It is now yellowed and tarnished. Sitting in your corner office, you look at the book and it prompts you to see the set of fears you're experiencing. Rather than yield to these fears, you think to yourself, "It looks like another opportunity has presented itself!"

It's a reality: people use fear to serve their agenda, often, at the expense of others. This story isn't a lesson on manipulation, it's an insight into the machinations of political animals, con artists, and bullies. We'll find them at workplaces, corporate and government alike. They are effective only to the extent that we are oblivious to their methods.

PART V

MOVE

"You live if you dance to the voice that ails you."

Lorrie Moore[1]

ACTS OF FEAR

Some fears are too powerful, too deeply ingrained, for our minds to control. We know what we ought to do, but fear clouds our judgement; we forget earlier resolution, don't do the maths or look at the data; instead we become puppets to our fears: we overeat, nag, micromanage, waste money, bully, procrastinate and act in ways that let us down.

The point is, seeing the problem and knowing what the right thing to do isn't enough. If it were, then losing weight and getting fit would be a cinch. Ultimately, what matters is our actions.

How do we stay in control, master our actions and not be a puppet to our fears?

I've discovered that the simplest and best solution is to formally make a list of my fears, the mindset I ought to have, the set of fear-driven acts I should avoid, and actions I'd be proud of (fear mastery). What started as a list in my journal evolved into a matrix consisting of bullet points. I call it the Fear Matrix.

The Fear Matrix

Example: "I've put on weight, and I can't button my jeans."

1. Fears	2. The Better me
What are the set of fears affecting me?	**Looking through the four lenses, how can I better frame the situation?**
Example: fear of what others will say, fear I won't get back to normal, and fear of loss of freedom to eat what I want	Example: I've had a great time eating what I want, now I get to switch to a healthier routine (carrot lens). My friends won't judge me (zoom-in). I know what to do, I've done it before, I'll be back to normal in time (wide lens, time travel).
3. Acts of Fear	**4. Fear mastery**
What actions should I avoid?	**What actions enable me to be the best version of myself?**
Example: be anxious about my weight, obsess over it, develop an eating disorder, avoid social situations to avoid the shame, and lose confidence because of my weight gain. Do nothing: go into denial, continue to live an unsustainable lifestyle.	Example: set realistic goals, find an exercise buddy, commit to eating salads at lunch four times a week, and be proud of who I am.

This practice may sound overly simplistic, but it works in the same way taking notes in a lecture works. Writing things down increases understanding, memory retention and the likelihood of behaviour change. Plus, the permanent record becomes a useful resource to refer to later on or in the heat of a moment.

Acts of fear *are often reflexive, our brain's automatic response to regain control and make everything right again. Although fear-driven acts can be a good thing (e.g., we practice safe sex thanks to the fear of sexually transmitted diseases), for the sake of this exercise, let's define fear-driven acts as being <u>un</u>desirable. They include over-projection, over-reaction, looking for distractions, disengagement, chasing shadows, and expending too much time and mental energy on unconstructive things. Desperate to seize control, these actions often have no effect on the fear that we are seeking to nullify.*

Be mindful that action can also mean no action (i.e., do nothing). Fear can cause us to freeze, procrastinate, disengage, and avoid what needs to be done. For example, fear of failure prevents us from trying new things; fear of losing money stops us from liquidating stocks in a bear market.

Fear-mastery actions *are those that enable us to live the best versions of ourselves. They are the ones that heroes choose in the face of fear. We list them down because it gives us the best chance of taking these actions, instead of behaving like a deer in headlights. They are different to new year's resolutions in that it's less about goals and more about practices. To reiterate, action can also mean non-action – by this I mean deliberately choosing to do nothing.*

I'll elaborate further in this chapter through stories.

INFIDELITY

Why do we cheat on our partners? Why do we lie, break our vows, put our family and our reputation at risk and allow our lives to be disrupted with emotional pain and anguish that can scar many for life? Films and literature portray acts of infidelity as being driven by passion, lack of love (or neglect), lapses in judgement, or a lack of morality altogether. In Tolstoy's Anna Karenina, for example, the protagonist, Anna, commits adultery, which triggers her fall from grace. She loses access to her son, is banished by high society and becomes delusional, paranoid, and depressed. Sure, lust and morality have something to do with it, but there is another driver that can affect us all.

You love your wife, but you're experiencing the twenty-year itch.

The two of you met at university. You only dated one other person prior to going out with her. Like many others who married early, there is an iota of curiosity in you, a discontent.

What's it like to "play the field", to have casual sex with attractive women? What have I missed out on?

After twenty years of marriage, the sex hasn't dried up, but there is less of it. You miss the original passion, the inability to keep your hands off each other. Your wife seems content to do the same routine. Your fear is that the good times are behind you, a reminder of your limited mortality.

After twenty years, sex happens with less regularity, i.e. you can't be certain when she will be in the mood. The lack of certainty causes you anxiety: *Will I get it tonight? If not tonight, then tomorrow? Can I wait that long? She seems tired. Maybe it will not happen tonight. Maybe I should "take care of myself"? But if I do and it is on tonight, will it ruin my pleasure?* It's an exhausting thought process that congests your mind. You're afraid of getting stuck with unfulfilled urges.

You could ask for sex, but you're afraid of being rejected, afraid of being a burden, afraid of coming across as a dirty old man, the kind that pressures a woman into sex, and ashamed that you can't control your sexual urges. The greater fear, in most part unconscious, is that you're not an attractive, desirable man. This creates a Catch-22 situation: if you ask for sex, you won't be as aroused because you'd feel that your wife isn't into you, that she is doing it out of obligation rather than lust. On the other hand, if you don't approach the topic, no sex is almost a certainty because she rarely initiates sex. This is because your wife is driven by the same need: to be desired.

When you ask, "Wanna make love tonight?", it comes across as uncertainty to her — you seem unsure you want her. Plus it puts the onus on her to decide what happens next, which taxes the cognitive mind (not particularly conducive to helping anyone get in the mood). Her romantic ideal, what she needs to feel desired, is where a man, brimming with desire for his wife and only his wife, creates a setting, in the way bower birds do to attract a mate, and seduces her with creativity, passion, empathy and confidence, without a hint of fear, uncertainty, obligation or pressure.

At other times you are more direct and say things like: "I'm feeling horny" and "Your ass is beautiful" (accompanied by ogling or groping). To you, this is effective signalling. To your wife, they come across as you needing to satisfy your sexual urges, and it falls short of making her feel desired. You're oblivious to how your comments make her feel.

Is she really oblivious to my needs or is she's intentionally ignoring them? Does she not have any libido or is she just not into me? You are totally in the dark. The uncertainty messes with your mind. Bound up in a knot of fears and frustration, you blame your wife for not desiring you, not taking an interest in or responsibility for your sexual needs, and not paying enough attention to you. You feel emasculated.

To regain control, you embark on a mission to make yourself more attractive. You go on a diet, join a gym, hire a fitness instructor, take protein supplements, join a triathlon group, buy a new racing bicycle and a cupboard full of sports gear. The endeavour is expensive and takes you away from your family. The hope is that you will be more attractive to your wife, that she'll have uncontrollable, animalistic lust for you, as crazy as this sounds. You say to yourself that your motivation is to get healthy, but it's fear that is making you punish your body to great extremes.

After six months, you get what you want: a leaner, more muscular body. The effort pays off to some extent, but unfortunately, not enough. Whilst your wife compliments you on your progress, and she seems to enjoy sex a little more, you're still not getting enough sex, neither in terms of frequency, regularity or predictability. This is because a lack of attraction isn't the problem.

You feel cheated. You feel powerless. All this effort has been for no gain. You still have the same exhausting chatter in your head: *"Will I get sex tonight? Am I going to have to ask for it? Will she reject me?"* The fear of rejection makes you frustrated and angry.

Meanwhile, thanks to your improved physique, you're getting attention from other women, at work and in social settings. You update your wardrobe with slim fitting shirts, cufflinks, tailored suits and Italian leather shoes. Altogether, you've become an eye-catching package. What women find attractive isn't necessarily the clothes you wear, but the self-confidence.

Although adultery crosses your mind, you do nothing for fear of betraying your wife, destroying your marriage and ending up sad and alone in your old age. Yet you allow yourself to flirt, to hold eye contact longer than you should, to shower certain women with attention. These actions seem on the surface to be driven by our natural attraction to beautiful people, our need to feel desired, but what really drives it is a deep-seated fear of not being desirable. The tight business shirts, the new suit, the cufflinks, the flirting – they're a cry for validation.

Before long, you develop "friendly" relationships with several women. You hide all this from your wife. You rationalise you have done nothing wrong, since you haven't gone on a date or made physical contact.

The moment in which you cross the line takes you by surprise, but it shouldn't have, because the road to adultery comprises a series of actions (e.g. presenting the better side of yourself) and non-actions (e.g. not playing out consequences in your head). You allow yourself to walk through the multitude of gates that lead to adultery. A moment alone in the office, a kiss, a rendezvous for a drink and a walk home afterwards. As you walk through her front door, lust takes over, you let her remove your tie, then she turns around and asks you to unzip her dress. You know you should stop, but new fears emerge that cloud your judgement: fear of not seizing this opportunity (you may never get the chance again), fear of letting this woman down, and fear of not being man enough. You want to prove to her you're a great lover, and feel the need to please her to the best of your ability. You feel entitled to this act because you're a man, and your wife has been neglecting you. The combination of fear and lust is a powerful cocktail that thrusts you over the line into adultery.

The sex is awkward, partly because guilt weighs on your conscience. You're unable to fully lose yourself in the moment. It might not be the best sex you ever had, but the validation feels phenomenal. She's so much younger than you, you feel like a player, thus a lifelong itch is finally fulfilled. But the itch isn't physical at all.

You decide your wife must never find out the truth. You tell yourself that it is a one-time indiscretion. But then, you cheat a second time. Once we cross a line, it becomes easier to cross it again. You send a text message to your wife, "Drinks after work. I'll be home late xxx". Technically, it isn't a lie: you *are* having drinks after work.

The sex is fantastic the second time around. Lying in bed next to this woman, you feel gratitude and affection. She is giving you what your wife isn't giving you: the feeling of being desired. It wouldn't be such a massive ego trip if you didn't have a fear of not being man enough and fear of not being an attractive man.

To combat the guilt, you build resentment towards your wife: *It's her fault. She's the one who drove me to this, the one who neglected me, rejected me. My wife puts in no effort, no imagination, same old routines in bed. She never dresses up in lingerie unless*

I ask her to...frowns when I want the lights to be left on...brushes me off when I suggest sneaky or impulsive daytime sex...like as if I'm perverted. She performs oral sex like it's a chore. Is it too much to ask of a wife to devour her husband with lust and passion? Is it too much to ask of a woman to look after her man's most basic needs?

In reality, your wife loves you and would do anything for you. Your wife is dealing with her own fears, which can be encapsulated in the question: "Aren't you attracted to me just the way I am?" Your actions and demands effectively say: "No I'm not, I need more." You are blaming her so that you can feel good about yourself. You are afraid to admit to any wrongdoing. It enables you to continue the affair and still regard yourself as being a moral man.

Meanwhile, your wife is busy with her career and the kids. She is oblivious to your infidelity. There is even less sex than before, and this seems to suit her. You use this to justify the ongoing lies and betrayal. *Life is short. I owe it to myself to experience life to its fullest.* This is your fear of your mortality speaking. *She doesn't seem interested in me, anyway.* This is your fear of missing out speaking.

You disguise the dirty weekend away as a "business" trip. It's awfully cliched, which makes it even more exciting. It's like you're in a movie, just the two of you in a cocoon, set in the city of love, Paris, along the Seine.

Captured by the romance of the city, you make a promise to your mistress: "I will love you, always." It sounds like love, but it's an act of fear – fear that this good feeling, this love cocoon, this magic won't last forever, fear of letting your mistress down. The addition of "always" is a promise no one can keep. You add it as if buying insurance, hoping that it will protect you from losing this moment.

This goes on for a few months. You maintain your exercise routines. You continue to flirt with other women because the validation buoys you. All the love and attention you're getting doesn't sate your needs because your fear of not being an attractive man is a deep-seated, irrational fear. It can never be sated if you're blind to it, so you're always looking for more.

One night, at a bar, you catch the attention of a very attractive woman, and she appears responsive to your advances. Her name is Katarina. You talk about music, get a little drunk, dance with her. There is a hint of a nightcap back at her place. You rationalise: *Who is to know?*

Inside her apartment, you tell her you're a married man. She says in a mock tone, "I guess you better leave, then."

You kiss her on the neck, unzip her dress to reveal black stockings and matching garter belts. She kisses and makes love to you lustfully. It's as if she knows what you want. You feel special. You drive her to sexual heights like you have never done for any other women. The sex is outrageously good, the validation even more extraordinary.

You ask for her phone number, but in the weeks that follow, she rarely returns your call. When she does, you hookup for great sex. You have no control over her. There is no certainty of when you'll see her. This makes you think about her incessantly, to try and control the uncontrollable. You try to play it cool, but her unattainability drives you insane. This is a ploy of manipulative people. They arouse fears by withholding information, creating uncertainty, artificially creating a sense of scarcity and depriving us of a sense of control. Katarina is a master at this. To curtail your fear of not being able to attain her, you buy her an outrageously expensive sapphire necklace. You take her to top restaurants and pay for everything. You purchase a sports car that you don't need, because you catch her eyeballing another man in a sports car, but rationalise that you've always wanted one, and that you deserve a sports car. The purchase seems like a desire-driven action, but it's a fear-driven act. Fear that you're not in her league, fear of not being able to possess her, and fear that she might leave you for someone else.

By now, it's obvious to your wife that she is playing second fiddle to something or someone (unaware that she is actually third fiddle). It's difficult to explain the absences, physical and mental, and yet you maintain your lies. You accuse her of being distrustful, which causes unknowable damage to her mental wellbeing. You're too self-absorbed to realise what you're doing to her, and instead blame her for her failure to keep things together.

Meanwhile, your relationship with your mistress is taking a back seat. She suspects something isn't right, but she's unsure of what to do. She fails to analyse her fears, nor identify actions that are driven by fear versus those that are not, and as a result, she defaults to what a lot of us do in this situation: go into denial, do nothing, trust blindly. Had she produced a fear matrix (see example), she might have taken more practical steps to deal with the issue.

Fear Matrix

"I think he's cheating on me. What should I do?"

Fears	The Better me
Losing him (everything I've put into the relationship will go to waste). Being sad and lonely. Being lied to, made a fool of. To be judged by my friends. My mother telling me, "I told you so". Contracting sexually transmitted diseases. Facing confrontation and heartbreak.	• Zoom out: time travel 5 years forward: "I am fabulous, I am surrounded by people who love me" • Frame losses as gains: If the relationship ends, I regain my freedom and self-respect; I give myself the chance to meet the right person • Carrot lens: he's driven by fear, he deserves a chance to reform himself

Acts of Fear	Fear mastery
In a fit of rage, accuse him of cheating. Threaten to tell his wife. Intrude on his privacy. Douse his sports car with petrol and light it. Threaten to sleep with someone else. Sleep with someone else. Do nothing: pretend nothing is wrong, stay in denial, live in fear and doubt.	• Gather evidence in order to make an informed decision • Have a conversation in a way that makes him feel supported and not judged • Options: (a) end the relationship (overcome fear of loss and loneliness); or (b) learn to live with an open relationship and accept him for who he is; be the love and support that he needs; enjoy every moment you have with him (even if it doesn't last)

Your mistress lets the situation drag out for weeks. Pummelled by fear, uncertainty and self-doubt, she experiences the Thumping, and becomes a nervous wreck.

Two months after her first suspicions were raised, she loses it and confronts you with evidence that you've been lying, alibis that are false, text messages she saw on your phone, a conversation she overheard, what a friend saw, and airline boarding passes in the trash can. She threatens to sleep with someone else. The evidence is overwhelming, you have no choice but to come clean. In a panic, you promise her that the other woman means nothing to you. You beg for forgiveness. You say you still love her, that she is your one true love. You tell her anything to stem the pain and flow of tears. You want everything to be good again. It's fear that is causing you to over-promise: fear of losing her, fear of having to deal with the hurt you're causing, fear of what she might do (e.g. harm herself, damage your reputation at work, or upset your family life).

Much to your surprise, your mistress forgives you. You're grateful for the leap of faith, and make a promise that you will never see Katarina again. For the moment, you genuinely hope to return to the way things were, like those days in Paris when you uttered the words "I love you, always", and meant it.

Things don't get back to the way it was. Your mistress keeps you on a tighter leash, asks for an account of all your movements, and needs assurances all the time. Her pestering and anxiousness are driven by fear of being lied to again, and who can blame her? It strikes you that the relationship feels more like work rather than fun, dependency, not freedom, and burden, not excitement.

At the bistro where the two of you had your first date, you poke your salad absentmindedly. She's wondering if you're thinking of someone else. You're wondering if she will ever trust you again. Fear of loss taints every moment. It crosses your mind to end it here, but you're afraid to pull the trigger. You're afraid of upsetting her, losing her, and returning to a sex-less life. She isn't just a source of sex, she is a key pillar keeping your self-confidence from collapsing.

By this point, your life is a mess. Distant husband, absent father, compulsive liar. This is the context in which you call Katarina, the other woman, on impulse, and hook up with her again. It's an act that is supposed to quell your fear of loss of freedom, fear that your life isn't worth living, fear that you have ruined your life, fear that you're not a good person. But unfortunately, it doesn't.

You wish things could be better, but don't know what to do. You still love your wife, and have to think of your children, but you resent your wife, and don't want to return to a marriage that makes you feel undesired and unvalued. There is still love for your mistress, but her distrust is suffocating you, and you just don't feel the same about her anymore, no matter how much you want to. Katarina is exciting, but you can't see a future with her because you're afraid she is unattainable. There is no returning to the way it was. You could lose everything, including the last scraps of your ego. You wonder, *How did this all happen? Why am I like this?* It never dawns on you that it all has to do with fear, and nothing to do with luck, lust or a lack of self-control. The three women can't give you what you need because you're the only one that can deal with your insatiable, irrational fears.

You blame your wife: her selfishness and apathy towards you drove you to this. Your mistress is to blame: her insecurity is a drag on your happiness. You blame Katarina: there is something wrong with her that she won't allow herself to be pinned down. These are, of course, rationalisations. You blame your libido and lack of self-control, and this leads to deep, deep self-loathing. One that causes you to lose your moral compass, your happiness and everything important in life.

In the wee hours, Katarina watches you in your sleep, wondering where she stands. She knows that to yield to you is to destroy the reason you call her, and she is not prepared to risk that yet.

This story is <u>not</u> meant to be a moral lesson on sexual fidelity. Each of us faces a unique marital context, has different values, and lives within different social norms. What is aspirational to one person in one culture might be intolerable to another. The point of the story, is not to judge, but to help us recognise actions that are driven by fear versus those that are not.

An appetite for validation is insatiable if the fear is irrational

Our fears cause us to seek validation. We want proof that we're good enough, beautiful enough, manly enough, womanly enough, wealthy enough, still youthful, popular, useful, intelligent, and in charge. This can be a good thing, it can motivate us to achieve great things for humanity. Validation is essential to relationships. It's how we communicate, how we let people know how we feel, what we need, and what we think of them. However, the need for validation can drain us, causing us unnecessary stress and damaging our relationships if we don't keep our fears in check. It can cause billionaires to chase more wealth at the expense of their well-being; cause us to waste thousands of dollars on non-essential cosmetic surgery, putting us at risk of disfigurement; make us put our partners through suffocating love tests, and in doing so, we become burdensome and needy. It can undermine our resilience because we are more easily discouraged when we don't see signs we're on the right track. It can cause us to compromise our moral values and commit horrific atrocities.

Dictators like Joseph Stalin and Mao Zedong had millions of people executed, including officers closest to them, for fear of disloyalty. For them, no amount of validation was enough to quell their fears. Thankfully, our fears aren't as maddening as those of tyrants, but all the same, all of us seek validation all the time. As social creatures, it's in our nature to seek approval, acceptance and admiration from others. This said, resisting our need for validation can be one of the most graceful things we do.

GAMING ADDICTION

It is not the intention of this story to make parents feel judged about how much screen time they allow their children. Every child is unique, and each of us faces unique circumstances and has different aspirations. A child that has unlimited access to digital devices may flourish and become a philanthropic tech entrepreneur (if that is a good thing), whilst another child, perhaps even from the same family, may suffer depression and become a gambling addict if he has unbridled access to the digital world. The point of the story is to help parents recognise actions that are driven by fear versus those that are not, so that they can develop a policy that best suits their own circumstances.

Your eleven-year-old son is obsessed with an online game called *Chainsaws & Flamethrowers*. When he's not playing, he's watching videos about it, and when he's not watching videos, he's chatting about it online. When he's not on his devices, he's thinking about it: plotting, scheming, revisiting strategies, working out what inventory he has, what weapons he needs to acquire. He thinks about it at the dinner table, in the car, in the classroom, when you're talking to him, and in his sleep.

You cut him a lot of slack because you were exactly the same at his age. You were free to play for hours, often to the wee hours, and you turned out OK, so why should you worry? The problem is that your partner doesn't agree with you.

"We're supposed to limit screen time to an hour a day," says your partner.

"That's absurd," you say, "it's just one of those media lies that gets bandied around to make parents feel guilty. I can guarantee that no one is keeping their children to an hour of screen time a day, not even in Congo. I mean, do these experts include watching a two-hour movie as a family? What if the game helps build social skills? What if our son is learning a language, cutting code or sequencing DNA to solve cancer? Do you include that in the hour's limit? Ridiculous."

"The Finnegan's across the road ban their children from games altogether."

"Oh really? We're doing that now? We're keeping up with those control freaks? They ban their kids from television, anything with sugar in it, and I have it on authority that the kids aren't allowed to breathe without adult supervision."

Your partner's eyes roll.

You press on: "Before we take action, let's pause and consider what fears we are dealing with here. Are we afraid that our son will get fat, wear a moo-moo all day, have to be lifted by a crane because they can't fit out the front door, develop violent tendencies, and end up committing mass shootings? Is this what we're afraid of? Might I remind you that these so-called experts were making the same warnings about television in the 80s as they are about digital games today? TV was supposed to rot our brains and cause us to become serial killers, remember?"

"Chainsaws & Flamethrowers is not like anything we've seen before. Have you seen what happens when he gets rewarded with a special flamethrower? How high he becomes when he completes a stage? The extent to which his online image defines his status amongst his friends?"

"He's just a kid. He'll grow out of it. You underestimate his capacity for change. I was the same, and I worked out fine."

"I don't think your childhood is a credible reference. It's a sample of one. Extensive research data says that kids who are addicted to gaming are more likely to suffer depression, gain weight, perform poorly academically and be less social."

"Is that a fact or media exaggeration?" You suspect your partner is right. Game designers today have hacked the brain's reward and self-regulation system. Kids get a higher high than doing anything else, to the point at which kids can find the real world boring and not worthy of their attention. Your son is more deeply immersed, more anxious, more plugged in than you ever were. You just don't want to admit to being wrong, given how heavily you've invested in the laissez-faire approach you've adopted so far.[1]

Your partner can always tell when you're being stubborn, takes a deep breath, gives you a nod, and walks away.

Later that night, your partner takes your son aside to explain a new, more restrictive regime, and the rationale for it. Your son isn't happy about it, turns to you, hoping you might come to the rescue, but all you offer him is a shrug of the shoulders.

"You're being mean, and I hate you," says your son to your partner, and leaves. Your partner turns to face you, hurt and hoping for moral support, but all you offer is a shrug of your shoulders. Your partner takes a deep breath, gives you a nod, and leaves the room.

Here's what the new regime looks like: one hour a day of gaming, plus 30 minutes chatting on-line or watching videos. This entitlement only applies after your son has completed a set of chores. No screens after 7pm. No devices in bedrooms. And use of devices for coding, drawing and study is permitted under adult supervision. TV time with family excluded.

To you, the regime seems draconian, flawed, and impossible to police. Rather than question it, you decide to best let things play their own course.

Results from the new regime: a lot of friction in the beginning, but your partner doesn't budge, and much to your surprise, your son complies, albeit begrudgingly.

Over time, like a penned rabbit, your son finds weaknesses in the walls, sneaks in extra game time when no one is paying attention, and pretends to be doing constructive things on the laptop, but isn't. You don't intervene. In fact, you quietly root for him in admiration for his tenacity. You suspect your partner is aware of the infringements too, but does nothing about it, because it's emotionally draining to play "bad cop" all the time. Here's how a typical conversation goes:

"Are you still on it? I told you to get off hours ago."

"No you didn't."

"Yes, I did."

"OK, sorry then."

"Saying sorry isn't good enough...you're still playing, you're not even looking at me when I talk to you."

Your son slams the laptop screen down hard. "OK, fine, happy now?" And for the next two to three hours he's amped up, agitated, and hostile towards everyone, especially his younger sister.

These fights happen daily. You stay out of it, except, occasionally, unbeknownst to your partner, you grant your son extra game time. The intent is to release the pressure within the household; the effect is that you become the favoured parent; the outcome is a mockery of the regime.

The regime further unravels when you use game time as a bribe: "Unpack the dishwasher and you get an extra half hour of Chainsaws – how about it?" It's a problem because you've turned game time into a currency, and he expects payment every time you want something from him.

"Could you go answer the door?"

"How much extra gaming time do I get?"

"None. Go answer the door."

"Sorry, I'm busy."

An unforeseen side-effect of the regime is a deterioration in your son's sense of self-worth. There now exists an unhealthy parent-child dynamic in which your child takes little responsibility for his actions, seeks to exploit weaknesses in the regime, and feels like a failure every time he is caught cheating.

One day, your partner snatches the tablet from your son in the middle of a game.

"What the f...?!"

"I'm sick of being ignored. I'm banning you from all your devices for a week. You need to learn to respect the rules."

"This is so unfair! You're on your phone all the time, too. Should I be banning you from your phone for a week, too?"

"You're out of line. How about we make it a two-week ban?"

Unphased by the escalation, your son says, "Fine, I don't care."

"Alright then, how about a month?"

"Fine, I don't care."

"Oh yeah? Then how about I sell all your electronics and ban playdates for a year?"

"Fine, I don't care."

As a bystander, it's plain to see that your partner has lost control. When our fear-driven actions cannot achieve its desired effect, that is, to help us regain a sense of control, we're likely to escalate the severity of our actions, and if we aren't careful, keep escalating to the point of insanity. It's easy to see this as a bystander, much harder to refrain from escalating when we're in the hot-seat. You feel your partner is expecting too much of your son. He hasn't yet reached the age in which he has the maturity to de-escalate and back out of a confrontation. Being a proud person, afraid to show weakness, your son feigns nonchalance, which unfortunately aggravates your partner. Your instinct is to intervene, but you're afraid of going against your partner in front of your son.

It's not exactly what you were hoping for, but you got what you wanted: to be in a position to say, "I told you so." You don't get to say it out loud, unfortunately, because your partner looks too hopeless and defeated to handle a stomping. You muster the grace to ask, "What do we do now? How can I support you?"

"Don't ask me. I don't know what to do anymore, I'm a terrible parent, and I've failed."

"Things are not as bad as you think. Just relax, everything will work out, you'll see."

"He's put on weight, he has a lack of interest in anything else, he's not doing his homework, and he barely talks to us – you don't think this is a problem?"

"In my opinion, since you're asking, and no offence intended here, is that you're letting fear rule your mind. You underestimate his capacity for change, to grow. We ought to have more faith in him. Let's give him enough rope to decide for himself what is good for him. The price we pay for intervention is this nasty parent-child dynamic, where we give him reason to cheat, lie, become secretive and distrust us. Worst of all, we make him feel like a failure every time he isn't able to stick to the rules." It would be graceful if you stopped here, but you can't help but bang on because you want to fully secure your victory, "I warned you of this. This is so typical of what happens when parents act on their fears. The biggest thing at stake isn't your parental pride, it's our son's sense of self-worth. Your disappointment in him is toxic to his self-belief."

"Alright. How do I back out of the one-year ban?"

"It's OK, let me talk to him. I'll explain that you only want what is best for him. Let's give him his devices, and let's pretend the argument never happened. That way, no one has to lose face. How about that?"

Once again, you get to be the hero. As you hand over the devices to your son, you give him a wink, and he gives you a triumphant but grateful wink back. "We just want what is best for you. Remember that, OK?"

The both of you now take a hands-off approach. Your son's gaming time creeps up, from one hour a day to two, from two hours to four. He's given up on Chainsaws & Flamethrowers and moved on to an even more addictive first-person shooter game called Bao Palace. Five or six hours becomes the norm, and all day long on weekends. The behaviour is eating up your partner, but your partner lacks the confidence to take action.

"It's like we've lost our son," you confess to your partner. Your partner doesn't know what to do, or what to say, so it's up to you to talk to him, to give him a gentle nudge.

Your nudges have no effect. He is uninterested in anything you offer, not a bush walk or a trip to the beach. "I don't even like the beach," he says. Whilst this upsets you, you refrain from showing it, because you're mindful of the need to stay in control of your fears. You let out more rope. He gets his way and disappears further and deeper into his gaming world.

One day, you find a series of $20 and $50 purchases on your credit card, totalling $840 over a period of a month. The bank informs you they are legitimate transactions with a gaming company called Bao Palace. "Oh, God!" you cry out.

Your son says he didn't do it knowingly. It feels like a lie to you, but you give him the benefit of the doubt. You are, after all, the cool parent. After hours of negotiation online and over the phone, you convince Bao Palace to refund 85% of the charge, but that's still a $126 expense. It's important to you that your son takes responsibility for his actions, so you propose he pay half of it out of his savings. He says he's fine with that.

A month later, you discover another $480 in charges from Bao Palace on your credit card. Again, your son denies it. He says it must be from before. Your attempts to get a refund this time are not met with any sympathy, and the charges stand in full. You explain this to your son, who offers to pay half of it out of his savings.

"I think you're missing the point here. It's not your money to waste, you didn't earn it, your grandmother left it to you for when you will really need it."

"Well, I really need it now."

"When I say 'need', I mean important things like buying a house."

Your son can feel your disappointment, and changes tack. "I'm sorry. I'm bad, I don't know what I was doing. I feel so stupid."

"Well, if you've learnt your lesson, then there is no need to beat yourself up, but all the same, I will be removing the credit card from the game centre, got it?"

"If that is what you want me to do."

Game designers are good at extracting money from their players. For example, they will subtly raise difficulty levels, frustrating players, then dangle cheats or shortcuts that can be purchased with money. These cheats, such as a more powerful weapon or a better armour, make players who fork out money to look good in the eyes of their peers. They feel powerful, and are relieved of built-up frustration. Although your son was content to play with the free version for a while, over time the game's algorithm stalls his progress, lowly enemies kill his avatar, he isn't able to keep up with his teammates, and his best friend, malice unintended, calls him a loser.

Your son stops playing Bao Palace, and goes back to Chainsaws and Flamethrowers, but the game has lost its original buzz and attraction because his friends have abandoned it.

Soon after, you discover a $160 charge on your credit card from Bao Palace, plus a $160 deposit. It appears your son has worked out how to reconnect your credit card to the game centre, and made a cash deposit, thinking that you wouldn't miss the money.

At the risk of hearing 'I told you so', you turn to your partner, "What do we do now? Not only have we lost a son, we've got a credit card stealing addict in the house."

"This is the greatest challenge of our time, you know," says your partner.

It sounds a tad dramatic to you, but you say nothing and listen.

"I've been doing some reading on this. You were right from the beginning: it's all about fear. I've been projecting my fears, and this created a lot of problems. But leaving him to his own devices, literally, and doing nothing, is also an act of fear, fear of engagement, fear of making a mistake when faced with unknowns, and fear of confrontation. He is a child, we're adults, so he needs our guidance. We've let him down. Look at this..."

Your partner shows scribblings on a couple of pages of paper[2].

The Fear Matrix: What to do about our son's gaming?

1. Our fears

- He is wasting his life
- Too much gameplay deprives him of developmental needs such as reading, exercise and social skills
- The addictive behaviour and bad temperament becomes a part of his personality
- He'll become an adult who can't hold a job and become a burden on us and on society
- How his conduct reflects on us
- He might suffer depression
- Not being in control of him
- Upsetting him if we confront him (and ruining the family harmony)

2. The better us

- Countering one fear with another: the biggest thing at stake is his sense of self-worth
- Flip side: experts say some games can be good for child development (e.g. problem solving, creativity and social skills). We should admire his tenacity in getting what he wants. This is an opportunity for him to develop self-knowledge, self-discipline and good habits (it will be a lifelong benefit in other

areas, not just gaming). It's our job to prepare him to take on the real world in our absence.

- Time travel: our son will be a well-adjusted, loving son with healthy gaming habits

3. Acts of fear

- Get upset and blame him when he fails to stick to the rules
- Harass him to stop playing
- Rise to his emotional outbursts
- Place arbitrary bans
- Relax the rules to avoid emotional outbursts
- Shame him
- Make him feel that gaming is a waste of time
- Do nothing: assume it will be OK (or assume that nothing can be done); disengage and leave it to the other parent to deal with the issue; and be frustrated and give up.

4. Fear Mastery

- Help him feel he is in control e.g. let him define what a good week looks like; establish processes and habits (such as setting a timer); get him to reflect on whether he is sticking to the plan (i.e., ask "What went well?" and "In what ways can we improve?")
- Set boundaries (e.g. no devices in bedrooms)
- Focus on the positives of gameplay, e.g. praise teamwork, tenacity, creative problem solving, etc.

- Be interested in and knowledgeable about the games he plays so that he trusts us as adults within the gaming world (and not just in real life)
- Don't get upset by failures (he is not a failure, he just needs more practice at seeing the signs); blame the game's addictiveness rather than him
- Empower him with knowledge about the psychological tricks game designers use to get us hooked on their games and to extract money from us

Following this discussion, you agree on a new set of protocols with your son.

Instead of unlimited gameplay, you agree with your son that an hour and a half each day is reasonable, on a one-week on, one-week off basis. The week's break aims to remove the addictive hooks created by game designers, break habits, and create space for other interests to flourish. Your partner offers him a choice of sports camps, of which your son chooses football. You organise play dates involving outdoor activities, such as meeting his friends at the beach.

The two of you are engaged in his gameplay, ask questions, listen, make him feel like an expert, ride the highs and lows with him, warn him of dangers when you spot them and explain why. He never gets to the point where he has to lie, cheat and steal credit card details because you're there as a credible and trusted guide to teach him about the techniques used by the game designers (such as the illusion of scarcity, addictive rewards strategies, etc).

When he breaches his daily allowance and fails to stop playing, your partner doesn't get upset or shout. You offer a five-minute advanced warning, followed by an appealing transition activity, such as a snack, a game of ping-pong or a swim. You have a conversation later, when everyone is in a calmer state, "I know it's hard to stop in the middle of a game, but what can we do to get better at sticking to the plan?" You and your partner work really hard to be a united front. After some trial and error, the strategy that works is proposed by your son, where he sets up two alarms for himself, the first one being an early notification that he needs to wrap up, and a second for when time is up. With these practices, your son feels in control of the situation, and you avoid a negative parent-child dynamic.

When things don't go according to plan, your partner directs your son's frustration at the game's addictiveness rather than laying blame on your son.

The two of you have an accord to apply the rules consistently where no one is to use game time as reward or bribe. The stability gives your son a sense of control because it makes game time predictable, not something that can vary depending on the whim of a parent, which parent is in charge, how hard he negotiates or which emotional lever he pulls.

The transition journey is full of failures and difficult moments. You adults have a tendency to fall back on your old fears. For you, it's being complacent, avoiding conflict, and failing to enforce the rules when you lack the conviction to know what is the right thing to do. For your partner, it's panic at the first sign of failure. With practice, your partner gets better at remaining stoic. When faced with indiscretions and emotional barrage, your partner, more often than not, enforces the rules in a calm, matter-of-factly manner. It helps to remember that it's normal and healthy for children to test their boundaries.

Three years on, your son still needs reminders sometimes,

but that's OK. For screen time, don't we all need constant reminders, both grown-ups and children? On the whole, he consumes games responsibly, and feels no guilt or shame about his gameplay. He has other interests outside of gaming, and most importantly, a healthy sense of self-esteem.

OPPRESSION

The courage to stand up and sing when you want to.

As you approach middle age, you decide that the second half of your life needs to differ from the first half. Not that there's anything wrong with your life so far – you've travelled, fallen in love, had children, you're financially independent, and you have a sought-after job. What needs to be different? Well, you'd like to treat yourself with more respect, to worry less about what other people think, to not be so reliant on the affirmation of others, and to do what you want, more often, free from guilt. You want your voice to carry more weight, to not be taken for granted, at home and at work. You're determined to stop doing things that undermine your status, such as feigning ignorance or putting yourself down to give others a sense of superiority, pandering to egos for the sake of keeping the peace, or yielding to emotional blackmail.

This is easier said than done. In karaoke, everyone gets a

turn on the microphone, to pick the song of their liking, be the centre of attention, carry on like a diva, and live out their dreams. This is the way things should be in real life, where everyone gets a go at being the star of their own show, but it isn't always so. In real life, people wrestle for the microphone, make noise out of turn, and take more than their fair share of the limelight. Often what holds us back isn't a lack of self-respect, motivation or skill, it's the people closest and dearest to us, who, on a whole, might have our best interests at heart, but consciously and subconsciously hold us back, keeping us under their thumb. You recognise that change will be difficult because so much of it is outside of your control. It requires others to change, for example, to be less self-absorbed and more considerate.

Being the strategic thinker that you are, you know that a war isn't won in a single battle, rather, it's earned by gaining the upper hand, however slight, over a long series of confrontations. You steel yourself to wage a long war, and to win one confrontation at a time.

Confrontation #1: Sing when I want to

You love karaoke, but you never do it because your partner hates it. He doesn't forbid you from doing karaoke, the words "thou shalt not enjoy karaoke" has never been uttered, but you willingly choose not to because that's what unselfish people do: they anticipate what others want, and prioritise the desires of others over their own. A less charitable view is that it's an act of fear, fear of disapproval, of growing apart, and of marital disharmony.

The new you decides: "If he doesn't like it, that's his problem." You book a karaoke booth for Saturday night, invite three girlfriends, and ask him if he wants to come along. His response is as you expected, a frown across his face. "Great, we don't have to find a babysitter then," you say. You continue to ignore the frown, say thanks and leave without waiting around for his approval.

You score your first win, albeit with a tiny sense of guilt.

Confrontation #2: No one is beneath me, I am beneath no one

Your boss at work has an inferiority complex. He bosses you around, micromanages, puts you down and does spot tests to undermine your confidence, boasts about his political prowess, and gives you menial work, often in front of his peers, to give himself a sense of self-importance.

The new you decides you will not pander to his ego anymore. He is still your boss, so you'll need to tread carefully, to strike a fine balance between respecting yourself and respecting his status as your boss.

Today, at the morning check-in, he goes into a condescending rant: "You have to listen to people when they speak. Don't be thinking about the next thing you're going to say. Listen to every word, every syllable..." Normally you let him bang on, let him feel superior, pretend that you're actually learning something new. It's an act of fear: fear of coming across as being a "know-it-all", which isn't a reputation you want as a woman.

The new you cuts him off, "That's a good tip. Everyone should put that into practice. Is there anything else we need to cover today?"

Your interruption miffs him, but he composes himself, searches his memory, and asks about the status of the report you are writing. He's micromanaging, as he often does, because the report isn't due for weeks. You play along and give him a run down of where you are at. He interrupts: "Walk me through the government's AFKM scheme. How will it affect the funding model?" You fumble with the answer because nobody actually knows the answer, not even industry experts. The aim of the question is to put you on your back foot. A power play. Even if you knew the answer, he'd still achieve the desired effect, to remind you of your subordinate position to him. This power play is transparent to the new you, and you refuse to give him the upper hand. You blabber on about the AFKM scheme, without answering his question, in such great technical detail, you know most of it will go above his head. To save face, he pretends to understand what you're talking about. At the end of a long explanation, you ask, "Shall I go deeper?"

"No, that's fine," he says, "I've got things to do. When will you get the first draft to me?"

"You'll have it by its due date."

Confrontation #3: Here I stand

Later in the week, your boss asks you to take on additional work. The work, data verification, is beneath your pay grade, and saying yes means you will have to work nights and weekends for the next six weeks. He ought to hire temporary staff to deal with it, but he doesn't because he wants to save money, thereby looking good in the eyes of his superiors.

In the past, you've found it difficult to say no because he's your boss. He decides your pay rises and promotions; you need his support if you are to look for another job; he can deny you from getting training; can cancel previously approved vacations — make life miserable for you at work.

The new you knows that the inability to say "no" is an act of fear: of confrontation and of negative repercussions. Experience tells you that saying "yes" won't curry any favours because you'll be taken for granted.

You've been reading a book on assertiveness. The advice includes: practice saying "No"; use "I" statements; and use assertive words like "will" instead of "might" and "want" instead of "need"

In response to his unreasonable request, you put it to the test and say: "No, I will not do it. I will be on a vacation next week. I want you to find someone else to do it."

It's on the nose and overly confrontational. You know it, your boss knows it. Given the relationship history, the lopsided power balance, you expect the assertiveness to go down badly, but it's not like you haven't thought about this. You've played the conversation in your head many times. Anything less assertive like, "I'd love to help, but I'm on vacation next week, could we maybe find someone else to help?", and you'd be steam rolled like the hundreds of times before with emotional blackmail such as: "Oh, so you want us to cover for you while you go on holiday?"; "You can do what you want, but is this the right time to neglect your responsibilities and abandon us?"; or "I'm surprised and disappointed."

You reason that if you're going to come out on top over the long run, you're going to have to take a few bruises in the short run.

Your boss stares at you blankly, blinking. You stare back at him, doing your best steely cowboy impersonation. *My body language needs to back up my words.*

The two of you say nothing for what feels like an eternity before he says, "Alright, I'll find someone".

You're surprised that he conceded so easily. You leave the office with a mix of elation and trepidation. *Is this how bank robbers feel after pulling off a heist?*

You chalk up another win. Force your mind to not think of the repercussions.

Confrontation #4: Not a dogsbody

Your older brother left his seven-year-old son with you to mind for what was supposed to be 'a couple' of hours, but he's been gone nearly three hours. He doesn't call or text you – this is so typical of him, behaving like your time doesn't matter.

His son, your nephew, is not exactly pleasant company. He is antagonistic, whines all the time, bosses everyone around, gets on the nerves of your children, throws tantrums and makes a mess.

"Where's daddy?" he asks.

"I don't know."

It's now 1 p.m., and he is *"hangry"*. You offer him lunch: "Pasta? Can I make you pasta?"

"No! I want ice cream."

"Eggs? You like eggs, don't you?"

"No! I want ice cream."

"You can't have ice cream for lunch."

"Daddy always gives me ice cream for lunch."

You'd like to say: *And that's why you're a spoiled brat.* You bite your tongue and instead say, "You should eat something healthy. How about this: we eat something decent for lunch, and then we can have some ice cream."

"No! I want ice cream."

You refuse to cave in because you don't want to reward whining, and set an awful example for your children. In the calmest voice that you can muster, you say, "In this house. We always eat something good first, and if we behave well, then we get ice cream."

"No!"

"How about a sandwich?"

"No!"

"How about some cake? At least have some cake. I can see you're hungry."

"No. I hate cake. Where's daddy?"

"I'm sorry, but he is running late. He should be back soon."

He throws a terrible tantrum, topples over a dollhouse, and kicks a teddy bear in the face. It causes you to dig your heels in deeper, determined not to reward this kind of behaviour. Your eldest child screams, "Just give him what he wants!"

A switch flicks in your head. *What am I afraid of here? Fear that my nephew isn't eating well? It's not my problem, I'm not the parent, I'm the cool aunt. Fear of setting a poor example for my children? I wouldn't let my children behave like this. Fear that my brother will judge me? Well, he's late, he's in no position to judge.* You're sick of being taken for granted by your brother, sick of him not respecting your time. You take charge of the situation and give your nephew ice cream.

After three scoops, he asks for more. "Sure, here you go! Go nuts, my little man! How about some chocolate sauce? Here, have the entire bottle – pour as much as you want!"

Not caring what others think feels great. Another win![1]

Confrontation #5: I'm a role model

After eating half a tub of ice cream, your nephew throws up all over the toys, on the carpet, and on the couch. Just at the moment, your older brother steps into the room, in time to see his son wretch the final contents of his stomach over your shoes. It amazes you how much ice cream is coming out of the kid.

"Oh my God! What's wrong with him?" your brother asks.

Your eldest child dobs you in, "He ate too much ice cream."

"Why did you give him so much ice cream?" asks your brother.

"He had five scoops and the entire bottle of chocolate sauce for lunch," adds your daughter. "Eww, it's so gross!"

You shrug your shoulders.

Outraged, your brother asks, "You gave him five scoops of ice cream for lunch? What kind of parent are you?"

The old you would have taken the insult on the chin and apologised. You would have acted submissive and put yourself down before he can, in order to avoid a confrontation, e.g. "I'm so stupid, what was I thinking!"

The new you won't tolerate the insult and says defiantly, "I'm not his parent. I'm the cool aunt." You go on the offensive, and turn the tables on him: "Why are you late?"

"Excuse me?" he says. This is typical of him, acting like he doesn't answer to you. "No wonder your kids have no respect for you," he says.

It's a low blow. "Look," you say, "I don't want to have an argument in front of our kids. Isn't there somewhere you need to go? Because I have a lot of work to do here."

"So you can't spare a bit of time for your brother, huh?"

"Oh really? Straight to emotional blackmail, huh?" you say, annoyed. "What do you mean by 'I can't spare a bit of time'? I've just spent half my day looking after your son!"

"You are so ungrateful. Have you forgotten everything that I have done for you?" He turns to your children: "When your mother was little, she didn't brush her teeth or change her clothes for days. She got bullied badly at school, and always came last in class. I used to protect her from bullies, I tutored her in maths and chemistry, I made breakfast for her for years, I practically raised her."

Back to you, he says, "If not for me, you wouldn't be where you are today. Is this the gratitude I get?"

This is the point where you normally back down. To stand and fight now leads to a well-established pattern: silent treatment, and after weeks of emotional torment, you'd grovel for forgiveness. In the past, you rationalised that backing down is the gracious thing to do: he's your big brother, it's kind to let him win. You used to put yourself down by saying, "I should think before I speak, I'm so careless, I'm sorry." The new you knows this is an important battleground, if you are to change the power balance in your relationship, to change him, to get him to be more respectful of your time, to break the cycle of bullying, then you need to do something different from what you have done in the past.

"You must have very sore shoulders," you say.

"What does that mean?" he asks.

"You've been carrying that chip around on your shoulder for years. Actually, decades. How many favours do I owe you? How much humble pie do I have to eat before the debt is paid?"

"You've become an arrogant cow, you know that." He grabs his son's hand, vomit dripping off his son's chin, and marches out, leaving a trail of vomit flavoured footprints.

"Do you want to clean him first?" you shout after him, but he ignores you.

You're left standing there with your two children. They're just as surprised as you are by your act of defiance. You're not proud that you made your nephew sick, and in the heat of the argument, you forgot about your poor nephew's feelings, but you are proud that you stood up for yourself. What's at stake isn't just your dignity, it's standing up for yourself and being a role model for your children.

Confrontation #6: Rely on no one but me

Besides singing karaoke more often, there is another, bigger, more important ambition: to study a master's degree in international law. In the past, there has been little support from your inner circle. At work, your boss says: "I'm all for lifelong learning but it will take a lot of guts, years and years of study and a lot of stress...less than half get through to the end to qualify" (an attack on your fear of not being good enough, and fear of not being able to cope). At home, your husband says: "It's up to you, but is this the right time given the children are so young?" (an attack on your fear of not being a good parent). Even your father is unenthusiastic: "You already have a great job, you already work so hard, how will you squeeze study in?" (an attack on your fear of being too greedy, fear of being overwhelmed, and fear of losing your nice, secure job). They're not overtly trying to hold you back. In part, they're expressing their fear of losing you, and fear of being inferior to you, but mostly, they're afraid for you, afraid that you'd fail, or suffer unnecessary hardship.

It's hard to overcome your fears when those around you aren't supportive. We're tribal creatures. To go against them is to risk relationship disharmony, contempt, shame and retaliation, at home and at work. So far, you've put the ambition aside. In order to live with this decision, you reason that it's an act of generosity, not fear. *My marriage, my children and my employer deserve my full devotion.*

The new you asks: *What if it were the other way around? Would I support my husband if he wanted to pursue a Masters? Of course I would. If I were a manager, would I be supportive if my subordinates expressed the desire to better themselves? Of course, I would. In ten years' time, will I regret not doing anything? Absolutely.* The new you decides that you will no longer rely on others for moral support on matters as important as this. As writer and philosopher, Ayn Rand, said, "The question isn't who's going to let me; it's who's going to stop me." You apply to a prestigious university. The plan is to say nothing for now, because there's a real possibility that your application won't be successful. *I'll worry about what to do later, on the remote chance that they accept me.*

Confrontation #7: The Thumping

You complete the report on the government's AFKM scheme and send it to your boss. He returns it heavily marked with not-so-constructive criticisms, and entire paragraphs crossed out without accompanying justification. You're conscious that it's a move to undermine your confidence and keep you under his thumb. Despite this, you give him the benefit of the doubt and rework the report, making changes for the sake of appeasing him. The reworked version is great, better than anything he could have written. You prepare yourself to expect more criticism, but this time you don't hear at all.

Later on, you discover he presented the report to the senior leadership team without you. Although it's the manager's prerogative to do this, no one does it in practice because it's unfair to the subordinates who did the work. It's his way of showing everyone, especially you, that he doesn't need you. The old you can live with this because: "he's the boss, he's meant to take credit for my work, it's my job to make him look good." The new you knows that this is too magnanimous a position to take if there is no quid pro quo, if you know for certain he will not return the generosity in kind. When someone takes credit for your work, they are robbing you of the nutrients you need to grow your reputation in the company. The new you doesn't step away from a fight. You confront him.

"Could we maybe present my work to the senior leadership team together in the future?" you ask. The words that came out aren't as assertive as you had hoped because having the resolve is one thing, and having the courage to execute your resolve is another.

He feigns ignorance. "Oh, I didn't think you were interested in being in these long, boring meetings."

"I love long, boring meetings."

"OK, noted. Anything else I can do for you, madam?"

You later discover that he presented a subsequent report that you wrote to the senior leadership team, again without you.

At the next team meeting, your boss asks you to make a photocopy of a report for everyone. It's another power play. He should ask the more junior person in the room. Instead of saying "no", you say, "sure," and use the phone in the meeting room to call your boss's assistant, and ask him to do the photocopying.

He is passive aggressive towards you throughout the meeting, making sarcastic remarks at your expense, avoiding eye contact, and obstructing your ideas. At the end of the meeting he assigns "glamour" tasks, those that are interesting and sets people up for promotion, to others, and assigns menial tasks, the jobs that no one wants to do, with no opportunity for personal growth, the business equivalent of vacuuming under the couch and scrubbing the shower, to you. It's so blatant that everyone notices. A less senior colleague offers to trade tasks with you to save you the humiliation.

The old you would have accepted that you are getting what you deserve. The new you is furious. Furious because there is so much at stake, yet you're powerless to do anything about it.

There are no grounds for complaints to higher authority or to the Human Resources department. You don't want to quit your job, it's a sought after role, it'll be hard to find another like it, and working gives you a sense of purpose outside of raising a family. The old you would have sucked it up and tried to make amends, to work yourself back into his favour through subservience. The new you has no answers and is frustrated at the lack of options. You replay the entire episode in your head; mull over a set of futile options, repeatedly; the inequity of the situation causes you to become angry and anxious. You struggle to fall asleep at night, with thoughts racing around in your head and the blood boiling in your veins.

Meanwhile, your brother isn't speaking to you. The emotional stress is enormous. You'd like to call him, to be rid of the guilt, but you don't want to give in or grovel when you have done nothing wrong. Confiding in your husband about the row with your brother, hoping for moral support, he says unsympathetically, "What did you do?" You picture trying to explain the ice cream incident, and decide that it's going to make you look like the bad guy, so you say, "Never mind, I'll work it out."

It's too hard to explain to him what is going on at work without risking judgement, so you bottle it all up.

Confrontation #8: The Backdown

Your husband is in a bad mood. He always talks down to you when he is in a bad mood. At lunch, he says, "I told you never to put sugar in salad dressing. I hate it. How many times have I told you not to do it?"

"I forgot. I shouldn't have followed the recipe blindly, sorry."

After lunch, he throws another tantrum. "Why can't I ever

find anything around this house? Just for once, I'd like to live in a house that isn't a pigsty!" It bothers you that he undermines you in front of the children. This isn't the first time. No wonder your children use the same tone against you, and with each other when they're cross.

By a thousand cuts, your husband subconsciously undermines your confidence by saying things like:

- "Why are you so clumsy?"
- "What's wrong with your grammar? Didn't you go to school?"
- "I can't believe you did it again. Some people just never learn."
- "Are you blind? Can't you see what's going on?"

Experience tells you that if you stand up to him, you'll make him even more cross, but if you don't, then what stops your children from emulating how he treats you? You say nothing for now because you've run out of fight. You are already fighting too many battles on too many fronts.

"Why do you have to work so many hours?" your husband demands. "Can't you see that they're just taking advantage of you?"

You say nothing. You reason to yourself that he won't always be like this. *Once we pay off the mortgage...once things settle down at work for him...once his back pain gets better...once the kids grow up a little...things will be better.*

Meanwhile, you haven't heard from the university about your application. You worry they will reject you, afraid that you're not good enough. Your mind stews over the guilt that you should have consulted your husband beforehand. You worry he will be offended. *Isn't an omission a lie? Aren't lies toxic in a marriage?*

The old you loses confidence in the new you, regrets at having too much ambition, wishes that you had been content with what you already have, wishes that the emotional turmoil you're feeling will go away. The old you despises the new you just a little.

At dinner, you get a text message from your boss. It's about a report written by someone else, the glamour task. It's not to his standard. He wants you to take over, work on it tonight so that he can have a copy to read in the morning. It's Saturday, the night you're supposed to go to karaoke. An exchange of text messages ensues:

"I can't tonight. Can I send a good draft to you by Monday morning?"

"Monday will be too late."

"Too late for what?"

"Senior leadership meeting, 9am Monday."

"I'm sorry, I didn't know about that. How about you leave it to me – I'll work on it tomorrow and present it on Monday? WDYT?"

"No, I want a draft by tomorrow morning, so that I have all day tomorrow to prepare. Also, I want you to keep Sunday open in case you have to make more changes. This is non-negotiable."

"I can't do it. I'm sorry. You'll get it Monday morning, Sunday night at the latest."

"If you can't do it, then don't bother coming in on Monday."

"You're firing me via text message?"

"It's up to you. You know that there are plenty of other people willing to jump at the chance to work on this, right? Don't hold me for ransom."

"Alright, fine."

That night, you go to karaoke, get drunk and don't get

home till the wee hours. When you wake up, it's nearly midday, and you discover a half a dozen missed calls and several text messages from your boss. You don't bother opening the messages. Instead, you enjoy your Sunday with your family. You meditate on all that you have: the wonderful time you had last night with your girlfriends; the poppies swaying gently in the cool summer breeze in your garden; a pair of blue and grey finches searching for grubs on your lawn, the soft little lips of your youngest child when he kisses you on your cheek. It fills your heart with gratitude. It's the magic of karaoke that is liberating you from your worries. Get up on stage, sing like a fool, make everyone laugh, overcome inhibitions, and, in doing so, forget all your troubles. In the joyous moment of behaving like you're a teenager, you experience a moment of clarity, which looks like this:

Fear Matrix
"How can I rise above the oppression?"

Fears	The Better me
• Be taken advantage of or mistreated • Not being a good role model for my children (harming their future) • Losing my job • Loss of dignity • Fear that I don't matter	Time travel: I am already a success; a strong and independent woman, surrounded by people who love me.
Acts of Fear	**Fear mastery**
• Limit my options to fight or flight; think of myself as hero or coward • Be submissive, self-deprecate, sell myself short • Frame confrontations as win-lose battles, cause people to feel out of control (and further exacerbate their fears) • Get upset when I feel I'm being bullied	• Identify the fears others are driven by when they try to dominate me • Address their fears rather than focus on mine • Give assurances and help people feel in control

Confrontation #9: The Showdown

Two psychological drivers can explain your boss's behaviour. One, we have a tendency to treat others the way people treat us in our formative years (as a child or a junior in a work environment) because it subconsciously gives us a sense of order. It's why bullying and horrible, abusive acts between humans persist. Your boss experienced bullying early in his career, thus the power play and the put downs are behaviours consistent with a model of leadership that lives in his subconscious. He expects subordinates to endure hardship as he did, to be submissive as he was. Two, bullies act tough because of deep-rooted insecurity. The micromanaging, the criticisms, the tests of loyalty, the boastfulness, the hoarding of credit are all acts of fear. Fear that you are better than him, fear of appearing weak and incompetent, of not being consistent with his idea of what a leader is meant to be. He fears disloyalty and loss of respect and authority. Put simply, you threaten him. He's afraid of not being in control of you, and this annoys him. It disrupts his well-being and sense of order, and causes him anxiety.

Your instinct is to flee. To find another job with a better boss because you can't repair him. The new you says you have unfinished business in this job, and you'd like to stay. The old you would like to grovel, beg for forgiveness, and hope for mercy. You now know this would get you nowhere.

Monday morning, you get to work and head straight to his office. He doesn't appear surprised to see you, folds his arms, sits back in his imposing, black executive chair, and asks you to close the door behind you. "Take a seat. We need to talk." You sit. "It's time for us to part company. It has been a pleasure to work with you. You can trust me to be a good referee."

"That's very generous of you," you reply. "You can trust me

to reciprocate, to speak of your better qualities wherever I go, especially at the exit interview." He nods, glad that you won't besmirch his reputation.

"I'll go pack up my things," you say.

You get up, walk to the door, pause there and turn to face him. "Regarding the government's AFKM scheme, there's a lot more to be done. Your options are to give it to someone else to complete, or insist that I finish it. If you give it to someone else, they'll face a massive learning curve. I'm sure they'll work it out under your guidance, but it's likely they'll drag you into the nitty gritty. I know it well and can have it done in six months flat, well ahead of the deadline."

"You're holding me for ransom?"

"Not at all. I'm offering to help, to avoid losing all the work we've done so far, and to put you in a dominant position for the rest of the year." He looks sceptical. You press on, "I'll do the work, you'll have full control, and you will present to the senior leadership team. I'll stay out of the way."

"What's in it for you?"

"We've worked together for a long time, and I owe it to you to get this job done. There is too much at stake given how closely the senior leadership team is monitoring this."

He accepts your proposal. The both of you save face. He gets to feel superior, and you buy time to remain in the game. You're not afraid of the tenuous position you're in, that you might do the work, not get credit for it, get kicked out after six months, and in the meantime continue to suffer humiliation and bullying. This is because you have a plan based on the premise that when we allay people's fears, they'll come out of their negative, dog-eat-dog mindset, and exhibit better qualities – compassion, generosity and comradery. And even if it doesn't work out, you are buying yourself time to find another job. It's much easier to land a new job when you're coming from gainful employment.

Over the next few weeks, you work hard and execute your new mindset. You become adept at reading his fears, which allows you to make the right moves, staving off his need to be domineering. You furnish him with assurances when he feels uncertain; give him regular updates so that he knows what is going on; break big tasks into smaller tasks when he feels overwhelmed; involve him in key decisions to feed his sense of self importance; frame options so that he feels in control; show progress along the way when he feels out of touch; and praise him where it is warranted to keep his ego at bay.

Sure, he still falls back on old habits, pushes you around and uses you to flex his power. One evening, he gives you a task knowing that you will have to stay back and miss dinner with your children. The old you would have accepted the task begrudgingly, deepening the disrespect. The new you would have said "no", making him feel frustrated and not in control. The even newer you doesn't see it as oppression. The even newer you frames it as an opportunity to work on your leadership skills, and to continue to improve your relationship with him. You do the work, feed his ego on this occasion, but afterwards put in place a new arrangement whereby you gain visibility of what is on his plate. You help him get better organised, which makes him feel a sense of order, and in doing so, cut out the surprises that can cause you to miss dinner with your children.

To be clear, you haven't changed his personality, not an iota. The insecure male chauvinist continues to live large. Lion tamers who believe they can change the nature of their beasts are dead tamers. All that you are doing is making the creature feel safe, avoiding its territory and keeping it well-fed. In pacifying the beast, you might make room for the civility that is there to begin with, but the mood can change with the crack of a whip.

Over time, he is less controlling because he feels in control. He doesn't throw his weight around as much, nor constantly put you through tests of loyalty as much, because he feels assured of your respect for him. The two of you collaborate as peers, free from the friction on both sides, and together you produce great work.

Five months later, he offers you a glamour task, the kind that will give you good visibility across the business. It's his way of asking you to stay beyond the six months that were agreed upon. And having earned his trust, he surprises you by asking you to lead the presentation at the next senior leadership team meeting, to which you say, "I'm happy to present, but it's important for our success that you are seen as the one steering the ship. How about I walk through the presentation, you draw out the implications and facilitate the conversation?"

"Okay, but only if you insist," he smiles with gratitude.

It's a victory for both of you.

Meanwhile, you apply the same strategy with your older brother. Your insight is that his domineering behaviour is driven by fear of not getting the respect he deserves, and fear of being unworthy of love.

Fear Matrix: I want my brother to treat me as an equal

1. My fears

- Offending my brother if I take a stand (and causing him to be sad)
- Being punished with the silent treatment (needing to deal with the loneliness and emptiness)

- The humiliation and loss of upper hand from having to grovel for forgiveness

2. The better me

- Carrot lens: my brother has been a great ally in life. He has a tremendous sense of responsibility, and will do just about anything for me if I get into trouble
- Countering one fear with another: if I continue to be submissive, I'd be a bad role model for my children
- Microscope lens: I shouldn't get upset by the threat of the silent treatment. I can't control him. I am not responsible for his hang-ups, nor his emotional condition

3. Acts of fear

- Continue to be submissive and avoid confrontation
- Put myself down so that he can feel superior (he won't respect me if I don't respect myself)
- Frame the relationship as a competition i.e. *who has the upper hand?*
- Get upset emotionally, shout, take revenge and treat my brother the way he treats me
- Give him the silent treatment, cut off the relationship and endure years of loneliness

4. Fear mastery

- Practice seeing the fears he is expressing rather than get upset by his prickly words and criticisms. The prickly words are an expression of fear: fear of being inferior, and not being respected as the 'man' in the family. I can use his fears in my favour by hinting at the values of a great leader and praising him when he lives up to them.
- Accept that he is going to boss me around and tell me how to live my life. It's just him trying to gain a sense of control in this scary world. I don't have to argue, resist or comply with it – for I am a grown woman, not a teenager. All I have to do is furnish him with a sense of control, do this by acknowledging what he is saying and praising his generosity with advice.
- Realise that it's not my job to change him, and I may be the worst person to do it given our sibling dynamic. The stakes aren't that high because we no longer live under the same roof.
- Be generous with assurance and love. Make contact regularly. Show gratitude for all the things he did for me when we were little. If I mention it before he does, he won't feel the need to brag or belittle me.
- I am human – it's OK to make a mistake and lose my temper. Treat myself with kindness.

To really know someone is to know their fears. Seeing his fears allows you, for the first time, to admit that his behaviour is totally warranted. You haven't been treating him with the respect he deserves. At best, you tolerate him, do things out of obligation, not admiration or love. You hardly initiate contact or check in on him, perhaps because you feel oppressed by his domineering ways. With the benefit of this insight, the way to improve your relationship with your brother becomes obvious. If you praise him regularly, he won't need to fish for compliments, demand it, or belittle you to gain a sense of superiority. He won't feel lonely or unloved if you communicate with him daily, even if it's just a text message. Actions speak louder than words. You drop in on him more regularly, with a gift of fresh produce or sweets that the two of you ate as children. These incredibly simple gestures do amazing things to turnaround your relationship with your brother. He's become pleasant to be with, and the two of you are closer than ever.

One evening, your husband returns home and hands you a letter from the university. With feigned nonchalance, he asks, "What's that about?"

"Please sit. I have something to tell you."

"What?"

"I've been afraid that my life will amount to nothing."

"So don't let it amount to nothing: go and fix me one of your famous martinis."

"I've applied to study for a master's degree. I didn't tell you about it in case I didn't get in. No point worrying you unnecessarily, right? Or embarrassing myself."

With his voice a little strained, he asks, "A master's degree? How are you going to find time to do that? You already work on weekends. What about your responsibility as a mother?"

He becomes conscious of how he sounds and adjusts his angle a little. "I'm all for lifelong learning, and I will support you if this is what you want, but...shouldn't we ask ourselves if this is the right timing?"

You respond with, "Can I paint you a picture of what my schedule will look like and how it affects you?"

His fears continue to govern his mind, and this causes him to withhold a spirit of generosity.

"I plan to step my hours back, working only 3.5 days a week," you explain. "This is how I will fit in the fifteen hours of study per week." Pointing to your spreadsheet, "Here's the time for you and the children, and this is where we will need you. Exam time will be tough, but I am entitled to five days of study leave per year, more if it's without pay."

He appears less doubtful.

You continue, "I will always prioritise you and the kids, always. I'll quit the course at the drop of a hat if we feel things aren't working. I've been wanting to do this for a long time. It's really important to me. You are the most important person in my life. I can't do it without you."

"Well, if it's that important to you," he says, "then you have my support, one hundred percent. I'll quit my job to look after the kids if I have to."

You've never loved him so much as you do now. The affection in your eyes radiates like sunlight warming his face.

"Well, are you going to open the letter?" he asks.

You hesitate, afraid you might humiliate yourself in front of him.

He says, "It doesn't matter if you don't get in this time, you'll get in the next time."

You try to open the letter, but with him watching, you can't seem to get a purchase on the seal. Finally, you rip it and unfold the piece of paper inside.

You're in.

THE END

In the twentieth iteration of this book, this is where I felt I had run out of things to say. I stuck the words "The End" right here.

I had created what I thought was my best work, which helped me become a better father, a better husband, and a better person. I experienced life-changing epiphanies, gained insight into my deepest fears, and I broke out of mindsets that had me pinned down my entire life. Which is to say, I became less of a douchebag, and nudged closer to being a functional human being.

Filmmaker, Taika Waitiki, has the practice of putting written drafts away and coming back to them a year or two later to gain distance and perspective. I thought I'd do the same: let the concepts ferment, and see if they will stand the test of time. [1]

In the two years that followed, my father passed away, Covid hit, I shut down my business, and I fell into a confidence rut. All my demons came at me all at once, along with the behavioural and physical manifestations: the micromanaging, the nagging, the sleeplessness, the mystery rashes, the injuries, the feeling of panic all the time, the Thumping.

What I learnt (and I should have known this, being that I had just spent the previous decade working in behavioural science) is that knowledge alone is insufficient. If it were, then getting a six-pack and learning a language would be easy. So many self-help books don't bring about change because reading is a cerebral exercise, and resolutions are made when we feel rational. We suck at change and suck at doing what we say we should, because we're not robots. Humans buckle under fear and stress, and as I discovered, when life sends a tsunami at us, drowning us in a sea of fear and emotion, it's hard to keep our heads above water, let alone see what is going on.

The See-Switch-Move model remains useful in my kitbag, but it lets me down in times of crisis. And I knew it wouldn't work for those who needed it most.

There was more work to be done.

PART VI

INJURE

There is a point at which the Thumping breaks us, and nothing, not rest, nor money, can get us back to an even keel.

THE FEAR-INJURED MIND

Our mental fortitude, the ability to think straight in the face of pressure, stress and uncertainty, is a finite resource. In the same way our muscles fatigue with repetitive strain, our resilience to fear diminishes each time we expose ourselves to a fear, hold a fearful thought, or revisit the same fear. Fears that are more vivid, intense or relatable impart more damage.

Prolonged exposure to fear leads to injury. As a non-medical person I do not refer to physical injury, as in brain damage; psychological injury, such as childhood trauma; or mental illness like schizophrenia. In this book, when I refer to "injury", I'm speaking of the behavioural effects seen in a person resulting from prolonged exposure to fear. To avoid confusion, from here on, I'll use the term "fear-injured" mind or "fear-injury".

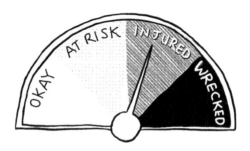

Possible symptoms

Repeating things ad nauseam, chronic
procrastination and avoidance, hyper
cautiousness, bursts of temper/tears, inability
to relax and enjoy, high levels of anxiousness
as a baseline, heavy confirmation bias,
addiction to news, etc..

We pay a heavy toll for being in a fear-injured state.

We feel less safe, less secure and opt for safer options e.g. we refrain from going out and being sociable, we triple check and lock doors and windows, we bark at others for taking what we perceive to be dangerous risks; stick with what we 'know' even if it no longer serves us well; are less open to trying new and potentially better things; hoard objects and spares "just in case".

We pay a "Fear Tax": that is, we pay a premium for things that represent poor value such as paying for five years' warranty on a technology product that will become obsolete in three years. We are vulnerable to marketers who use phrases such as "peace of mind" and "added security".

We are more susceptible to scams, e.g. a fixed-income pensioner might hand over her life savings not because of greed but because she is afraid that if she doesn't, she might miss out on a "sure thing".

It doesn't take much to cause us to fly off the handle, e.g. shout at our children, hurl abuse and death threats at other drivers on the road, yell at nursing staff for delays in the Emergency Department, etc..

We lose confidence in ourselves and fall into ruts.

We lose sleep, experience more stress, and this affects our health and well-being.

We become self-centred, lose our powers of empathy, and become blind to the needs of others.

We become fixated on trivial matters, procrastinate and become indecisive, e.g. "Should I make the chicken or the fish today? Should I catch a train or drive in?" We become reliant on others to decide for us.

We revisit past decisions and regurgitate grievances repeatedly, e.g. "I should have taken up painting when I was younger"; "the lawyer tricked us into signing the contract"; and "I never had the opportunity because my parents never gave me the chance". It's not that we don't want to forgive and forget, we're just unable to because they seem hard-wired into our thought patterns.

We become fixated on political issues that strike fear in our hearts (such as climate change, animal cruelty, immigration, over-population, corruption, corporate greed and terrorism). It causes us to consume too much news, to talk about nothing else, and to become repetitive (because we see it as our civic duty to stay informed, to know what is going on, and to speak up). We complain about the state of the world in every conversation, online and offline (fuelled by the fear that something needs to be done, but no one seems to do anything).

We are more likely to condone or commit extreme actions that we otherwise wouldn't, such as physical and verbal abuse, harsh punishment, discrimination, and even torture, murder and genocide.

The worst thing about a fear-injured mind is that it isn't always aware of its condition. We are all of the things listed above without *realising it, we get defensive when people try to tell us, and believe we are the ones behaving appropriately.*

If our fear-injured minds continue to be battered by fear or carry thoughts of fear, then over time we risk becoming "wrecked". In a wrecked state, the Thumping starts to pervade everyday life. It's as if fear and negativity are hard-wired into our brain.

Whenever we encounter extreme, hysterically emotional behaviour, we can almost be certain that we're dealing with people in a wrecked state, such as online trolls, people who own enough guns to start a minor war, and people who condone violence against defenceless people. This can all be the result of chronic fear.

It is very difficult to gauge our status. We're at constant risk of not realising that there is a problem until it is too late. It pays to check-in regularly and ask:

- *What is my fear load at the moment?*
- *How much fear have I exposed myself to today or over the past week?*
- *How much fear do I feel in my gut right now?*
- *Am I regurgitating the same fearful thoughts again and again?*
- *Am I speaking louder than normal to assert my point?"*

The best way to avoid an "injured" mental state is to avoid taking psychological hits to the head in the first place. In real life, this is easier said than done.

Some of us don't get a choice. Soldiers, ambulance workers, doctors and nurses, police officers and social workers – they're exposed to tragedy, death and the worst of humanity in the course of their work. When they appear cold-hearted or unsympathetic, we ought to be less judgemental: perhaps what we're seeing is their attempt to protect themselves from fear-injury.

News grabs our attention through shock, outrage, and fear.

Given this, how do we stay informed without taking hits to the head? How can we be the "better us", if we're afraid all the time? How do we avoid becoming apathetic to important issues?

In this chapter, I will go deep into the perils of the fear-injured mind, how it happens, the danger signs to be wary of, and how we are all vulnerable to it. Some of the stories may come across as a little negative and humourless, but I believe the importance of the topic warrants it. I don't offer simple answers because when we're talking about fear-injury, it wouldn't do anyone any good to pretend that there are simple answers.

CHRONIC LOW SELF-ESTEEM

Your son has reached adulthood, but he still lacks confidence.

He's a reasonably good-looking lad, but he doesn't have a girlfriend because he's too shy. He's an intelligent man, but doesn't apply himself. In your view, he should be the captain of his basketball team, but he's too self-conscious and lacks assertiveness. He should be out there expanding his network, but he wastes his free time with his one and only buddy from primary school.

Right now he is preparing a resume so that he can apply for jobs after he graduates from university. You say, "If you had done more networking like I told you to, employers would knock on your door instead of the other way around." As usual, he says nothing, neither acknowledges what you said nor protests, which makes your blood boil because it feels like he is not listening.

His resume looks weak, and his choice of words shows he doesn't believe in himself. Heck, you wouldn't hire him.

You: What do you want to do with your life?

Him: I don't know.
You: What interests you?
Him: I don't know.

He's always been like this. Here's a sample conversation with him from when he was 7 years old.

You: You can do it.
Him: No, I can't.
You: Yes, you can, you just have to try.
Him: I can't, I don't know how to.
You: It's OK if you fail, you just have to try.
Him: I don't like it.
You: You don't know that yet. Give it a go, and you'll
    see, you might like it.
Him: I'm not good at it.
You: How will you get better if you don't try? This is the
    one of the most important things I can teach you in
    life: to be prepared to take risks and try new things.
    If not, how can you learn anything?
Him: But I don't want to do it.
You: Why not?
Him: I don't know, I just don't want to.

He's been like this even though you've spent your whole life lavishing him with praise, and holding back criticism.

Him: I was terrible.
You: You were great out there.
Him: I was terrible. The other players are much better
    than me.
You: From where I stand, you looked amazing! I'm
    really, truly impressed! The ball didn't come your

way as often, but when it did, you made the most of
it. That's all the coach can possibly ask for.

Him: I missed so many shots.

You: You're focusing too much on your mistakes, which
is natural to do because you want to improve, but
you should also look at the positives, like the steals,
rebounds and assists. You were great!

Him: No, I'm not.

It frustrates you to have to have these arguments with
him. *Why can't he just accept the compliment and feel good about
himself like every other normal person? Why can't he see the
importance of self-belief? If he will not believe in himself, then who
will?*

In your lowest moments, you venture to think: *There must
be something innately wrong with him.*

His fear of failure undermines his confidence, but the
insight doesn't seem to help him:

You: You're letting the fear of failure hold you back.

Him: I just don't want to do it.

You: Why not?

Him: I don't like it.

You: You don't like it because you're afraid that you will
fail.

Him: [Exasperated] OK, I'm afraid. I'm scared. I have no
courage. Is that what you want me to say? Are you
happy now?

You've tried to switch his mindset: to frame losses as gains,
to zoom in on his fears to help him see the irrationality of his
fears – but none of these strategies seem to work.

You: Don't focus on what people will think of you. See
   it as a learning opportunity.

Him: I don't want to do it.

You: What are you afraid of?

Him: I'm not afraid of anything.

You: Aren't you interested in getting better at this?

Him: No, I'm not. I didn't want to do it in the first place,
   remember? You're the one who forced me to do it.

You: For goodness' sake, just back yourself! Be more
   confident! I don't really care whether you do it.
   What I care about is that you practice mastering
   your fear, practice being the person you want to be,
   because if you master your fears, then no one can
   master you. Don't you want to be great at this?
   Don't you want people to look at you with admiration? Isn't that what you want?

Him: It's what you want.

You: [Exasperated] OK, let's start over. Forget about
   what I want. What do you want?

Him: I want to go home.

This narrative is overly negative because that's how you
see it. There is another side of the story that you don't focus on.
Your son was well regarded at school, by his teachers and his
friends. He exhibits moments of being confident. He is, for
example, good at history and physics. And when he is amongst
the safety of old friends, he's good at making people laugh.

However, at certain moments of truth, when you think it
really matters, when you believe your son needs to dig deep
and find courage, he'll climb into a shell and opt for the easy
option. You try to be positive, but deep in your psyche, you're
afraid that it is already too late, that his low self-esteem is
already a part of his immutable personality.

To allay your unconscious fears, you've put him through tests, exposed him to challenging situations, hoping he would rise to the occasion.

When he was twelve years-old, you sent him to elite basketball training camp. Unfortunately, everyone was better than him. Although he gained some skills, he found the experience traumatic, and this further eroded his confidence.

In high school, you got him into the state's top academic school. You had hoped that the attitudes of other students would rub off on him. Surrounded by children who have been tutored since birth, your son felt inferior. Had you sent him to an ordinary school where he might have been the brightest kid in class, he might have become more confident, but you believe this would give him a false sense of confidence, and put him at risk of not making the grades he would need to get into a top university. Perhaps there is a Goldilocks zone, the right school for the right kid, but you lack the confidence to consider anything but the top schools.

You staunchly believe in the notion that "it is all in the mind", and you've said this often to him: "If you set your mind to it, you can accomplish anything." That he has fallen short of your expectations causes him to feel that he must be weak of mind.

Your son is now twenty years-old. When you say things such as "be confident", "this is not a criticism", and "you're doing well" it triggers a hard-wired response from him, he seizes up, backs into a bunker, gets ready for more of your tests and criticisms, and takes a negative view of whatever you want him to hear.

Even though you know that by now you should say nothing — not just because he is a grown man, but because anything you say has for a long time been counterproductive — you can't help but intervene anyway. You criticise and show disappointment. *Why can't he be like everyone else? If only he would listen. If only he tried harder. If only he believed in himself. If only he would take the opportunity. If only he could see his own fears.* The problem is you. You are blind to your fears which over the years have come to dominate your mind. He *has* been listening. He *has* worked hard and made the most of opportunities that come his way. He has moments of being confident and heroic. You just can't see it.

For years, the two of you repeat the same counter-productive argument. It exacerbates the pain and anguish on both sides, and cements the scars in your fear-injured minds.

Hard-wired fear

When learning a foreign language, we study the same words and phrases repeatedly, so that over time, the foreign material will become embedded in our brain, and as if by second nature, we can recall it without effort.

It follows that if our minds regurgitate the same fears and worries repeatedly, then over time being fearful, worrying and over-thinking will become hard-wired. As if by second nature, we think negative thoughts, even if there aren't any rational reasons for doing so. All it takes is a trigger, like a parent saying to a child, "just be confident." Or conversely, a child triggering a parent's fear by saying, "I don't know."

LONG-TERM RUT

It's OK to experience apprehension, inertia, irritability and insecurities. It becomes a drag when others have to deal with it over a long period.

Your husband is a good man, but he is stuck in a rut, and you're sick of it.

A few years ago, his employer made him redundant from a thankless, high-pressure job. Rather than look for another job immediately, he took a few weeks off to steady himself, which made sense to you at the time because he had become a bit of an emotional wreck working at that company. Unfortunately, it took him a long time to get back on his feet (eight months all up). The experience was awful. He sent resumes to multiple contacts, all people he thought he could count on. He responded to hundreds of advertisements, jobs he thought he'd be qualified for, only to receive umpteen rejection letters, or worse, not hear at all. Each let-down drained his confidence.

It got to a point where you stopped enquiring about his progress to save him from the humiliation. When he finally did land a role, it was one that was beneath him, but he felt compelled to take it anyway.

It is now approaching three years since he started that job, and unfortunately, he has been stuck in the same role. There has been very little opportunity to grow. His boss keeps overlooking him for promotions, favouring those, apparently, more adept at office politics than actual work. Your husband stays on the lookout for better jobs, but there haven't been many on account of the economy.

You thought your husband was difficult to live with when he was out of a job, but it's even worse now that he's stuck in this job. He is crabby all the time, critical of everything, but does nothing to change anything. He regularly antagonises and belittles you, saying things like: "Are you blind? It's right in front of you!" and "I can't believe you did that again. You really are a slow-learner." You don't let it get to you because it's obviously an inferiority complex. *He'll come out of his rut,* you reassure yourself.

His negative attitude and complacency affect you. You're not going anywhere on weekends like you used to. Having to share a life with him means you spend your entire evening, every evening, being drawn into TV shows you wouldn't otherwise watch, drink more than you normally would, and both of you put on weight.

There is often a cloud over you when he's around due to the inferiority complex. You're sick of being his punching bag.

To get him out of a rut, you leave motivational books scattered around the house. You avoid criticism, and give positive reinforcement, praise any signs of progress, no matter how paltry.

Your husband picks up one of the more cheesy motivation

books. These self-help gurus can be very persuasive. It convinces him that the key to everything is having the right attitude, which in your view isn't the complete picture, but who are you to argue if it brings about change?

One day, in an argument with you, he inadvertently quotes from the book: "You need to break out of a rut, stop being in denial, stop making excuses and blaming others, and take responsibility for your own life."

It's a cliched message, and ironic that it's directed at you and not himself, but again, who are you to argue if there is a chance he applies it? The book inspires him to make many resolutions, much to your relief. He gets into an exercise routine, connects with old friends, and sets himself the challenge of being promoted at work or to find a better job by the end of the year. The book emphasises the importance of finding one's purpose, which your husband decides is "to work in service of others", whatever that means. Encouraged by the book to get in touch with his passions, your husband decides he wants to restore an old sailing boat, apparently a childhood fantasy. You are supportive of anything that gets him out of the house, so together the two of you spend your weekends driving up and down the coast looking at old boats. One day, he comes across a deteriorated wooden ketch, one that is badly in need of love and deep pockets. Your husband falls in love with it at first sight, dreams of reviving it back to its former glory, so you strike a deal with the seller, pay in cash, and tow it home.

The boat takes up three quarters of your backyard. Your husband doesn't start work on it straight away. He says he has a lot of research and planning to do first, plus he doesn't have the right equipment. You often find him standing at the back window, staring at his project, thinking about what work needs to be done, replaying the steps repeatedly in his head, adjusting the sequence, but not doing any actual work. He's afraid of making a start, afraid of making a mistake.

A few months pass. Something bad happens to your husband at work, which really upsets him, so much so that he refuses to talk about it. The episode causes him to revert to his old crabby self: frustrated, angry, critical, anxious and stressed. "I thought my last employer was bad," he says, "but these guys are even worse. I can't believe how badly they treat people."

A week later, your husband proposes to quit his job.

"Have you found another job?" you ask.

"No," he says, "but according to the book I'm reading, I must turn 'should's' into 'must's'."

"What does that mean?"

"Well, I keep saying things like, I *should* follow my dreams, I *should* spend more time with the kids, I *should* support your career, I *should* start work on the boat."

"You should do all those things."

"No, not 'should', 'must'. I *must* follow my dreams, I *must* spend more time with the kids, I *must* support your career, I *must* start work on the boat. The book says I must face my fears, which I've worked out to be: fear of letting you down, the fear of not being a good provider, fear of losing momentum in my career, fear of not being able to get a job again. I need to let go of these fears. They are so called 'limiting thoughts'. The book says I must be open to change, to invest in myself, and look after my mental and physical health."

"That's a lot of self knowledge," you say. "I'm totally supportive of what you want to do. Is this a permanent change? Like, will you become a boat builder slash family man from now on?"

"You're asking me to give you certainty about the future. The book says, 'We must embrace the fear of the unknown...only by letting go of the future can we truly enjoy the present.'"

You feel somewhat relieved. It's unkind to think of it, but you hope your husband might get off your coat tail for the first time in decades. You're excited by the prospect of change, to see him tackle his dreams, find his purpose, unshackle himself from a job that is sucking him dry. And you're quietly excited by the thought of having him pick up the slack at home, deal with the kids, do the grocery shopping, etc.. You even allow yourself to dream, "Wouldn't it be nice to finish work and be surprised by a home-cooked dinner once in a while!"

Your husband hands in his resignation, and, as if to prove a point, takes on his new purpose with fervour. He cooks, he cleans, he is engaged with the kids; he treats you like a queen; and he makes a start on the boat project, buying a whole heap of equipment and supplies. The lawn in the backyard might be brown, but at least it's looking more like a working workshop now.

A couple of months pass. You notice the initial enthusiasm and standards decline, which is understandable: as everybody knows, home duties can be draining when they beckon you all day every day. The satisfaction that comes from cleaning is short-lived when kids undo the work in the blink of an eye. He has discovered that as much as he loves the kids, there is a point at which too much time with them can be too much. You try to create a better balance by taking the kids out, giving him room to work on his boat, or just be in his own mind.

A few weeks on, you notice an uptick in how much time your husband spends staring at screens. He's watching TV, trawling online second-hand stores for boat supplies, trying to create a following on social media, and playing online games. In moderation, you feel that these are harmless ways to relax, connect with friends, learn something new or save some money, but it's clear he's distracted from his purpose. You're not sure what to say because you don't want to sound like his mother. A magnanimous view is that he isn't wasting time, the distraction and hiatus from his purpose is a necessary step towards something greater. A less magnanimous view is that he's hooked on screens. The digital world gives him a sense of progress, the impression that he matters, the illusion that he is connecting with others, and that the savings from shopping at online flea markets are material. In reality, the in-game badges, the social media likes, the bargain deals are hollow rewards: they are inadequate surrogates for activities that would give him genuine fulfilment, such as creating deep bonds with people, making the lives of others better, mastering new skills, creating or fixing things, or engaging in self-care activities such as exercise. What concerns you most is not the waste of time, it's the fear that the distractions do nothing for his confidence and sense of self-worth.

"How's the boat restoration going?" you ask, knowing full well that it isn't going anywhere. "What are you going to work on next?"

"I don't know," he says. He takes a moment to reflect on it, then goes into a ramble about bulkheads, bilges and bulwarks, none of which you understand.

You cut in, "It has been wonderful having you look after the kids, I mean, they're flourishing. I'm also really grateful that you're supporting my career. I can't thank you enough for that."

"But?"

"But I wonder if it's time we support you now? What can *we* do for you?"

"I don't know. I suppose I should...are you trying to say I should go get a proper job?"

"No, that's not what I'm saying. You should do what makes you happy."

"And what do you think that is?"

"I don't know."

He's in a rut, too deep in it to see it, and you're too afraid to point it out for fear of offending him. On the outside, it looks like laziness, at least that's what your father says behind his back, but you know better. It's a lack of confidence. He procrastinates for fear of making bad decisions, avoids action for fear of making mistakes, looks over his shoulder for fear of being judged and cannot back himself for fear of bad things of the past happening again.

The motivation book perpetuates the fallacy, "Being stuck in a rut isn't a physical state or the result of your circumstances. It's a state of mind." Given that your husband has tried and failed to get out of the wrong mindset, he now carries the additional burden, "I must not have enough mental strength" (of course, without saying it out loud or admitting it).

Fear explains the despondency, complacency, and the need to escape into an online world. He's back to his old negative self, often irritable, flying off the handle easily, critical and quick to put everyone down. He seeks refuge in food, alcohol, TV and gaming to make him feel good; he has a gluttonous appetite for sex, demanding submission inside and outside the bedroom, often humiliating. If he can't dominate his mind, then he has to dominate other aspects of his life, including you. All the while, he is indecisive, unsocial, and unproductive. You often take the kids to social events and on road trips without him.

The boat, unloved and decaying, is a giant monument of the state of his ego. Your household lives in its shadow, day and night.

A year on and still no change. Now the two of you fight often. You're sick of making excuses for him. Sick of taking his abuse and being his punching bag. You can't understand why he is content to do nothing, accomplish nothing, be nothing. He doesn't understand why you're always on his back, why you have to put so much pressure on everybody, and why you can't be more content. You're unhappy. He is sapping your energy and being a poor role model for the kids. You feel people should take responsibility for their own lives. He needs to take responsibility for his, and you need to take responsibility for yours. And that's when you make a deeply sad but liberating decision: it's time to cut him loose.

If the husband were to analyse his fears, he might produce a fear matrix like the one to follow.

Most self-help books believe that this is all that is needed: an insight and a new mindset. I don't believe this at all. Even if the husband were to come up with the fear matrix himself, albeit constructive, it's unlikely to be enough to pull him out of the quagmire of a long-term rut, or keep him out of it for very long. So much of his negativity is hard-wired into his attitude and mental processing. It would be like asking a long-term drug user to turn their life around after a weekend retreat – it takes more than an insight and a new mindset. What we're asking people to do is to heal their 'fear-injured' mind. We will cover this in chapters 7 and 8.

Fear Matrix: how do I break out of a rut?

Fears	The Better me
• Making a mistake (thus wasting time and money) • Bad things in the past repeating • Not being good enough • Letting everyone down • Be laughed at or pitied by peers	• Carrot lens: I am already a success (list examples) • Wide-angle lens: my wife leaves me. What do I do? How do I get back on my own two feet and support the children? • Cheat death: I've died and given a second chance in life. Forget the past. What would I do with the remainder of my life? • Stick lens: what am I role modelling for my children?
Acts of Fear	**Fear mastery**
• Avoid pressure situations, procrastinate • Seek comfort in false wins such as getting likes on social media, trawling for bargins online and gaming • Make myself superior by braging and throwing my weight around • Relying on my wife for everything (financial, emotional and decision-making)	• Redefine myself, retrain, target growth sectors, skills and products that are in demand • Break big goals into smaller tasks, and just do. Don't worry about making mistakes. Discovering is fun • Generate a set of wins, one everyday, no matter how small, and ride the momentum • Be a loving and supportive husband, and carry my own weight in terms of domestic duties

NEWS ADDICTION

What do we do when someone we care about falls for conspiracy theories?

You're a board member of a not-for-profit organisation. The president of the organisation has come under heavy criticism lately. In a secret meeting comprising five of the eight board members, the question is put to you, "Would you consider taking over the president role?" It's a great honour, but it puts you in a difficult position because the current president is one of your closest friends.

The two of you met at a fund-raising event over twenty years ago and became instant friends. You've shared an apartment, travelled together, and had children at roughly about the same time. In fact, it was you that nominated your friend to the presidency because at the time the organisation was a failing enterprise.

Over the past decade, under your friend's leadership, the organisation has tripled its membership base, signed high-profile sponsors, increased its relevance to members by offering more member-centric services, and generated a healthy financial surplus.

At this secret meeting, a board member says, "I know we ought to show more loyalty, but it reflects badly on us to have someone in leadership come across as being, well, shall we say, unhinged."

The issue is that the president has been spruiking conspiracy theories lately.

Another board member says, "We're at risk of not being taken seriously by the authorities and losing our influence in policy making."

"We'd be irrelevant," says another board member.

"We risk losing our sponsors," another chimes in.

"The president has ignored our requests to keep the more radical opinions private many times."

"As a board, we set the tone in the organisation. What we tolerate becomes culture. We have to draw the line somewhere."

"We plan to propose a motion to retire the existing president."

You say, "I am conflicted given my personal relationship with the president."

"We must put our personal needs aside and act in the best interest of the organisation."

"I'm going to have to abstain from the vote given my personal relationship with the president," you say, "I will, however, say this for the record: the president has done a lot for this organisation. I'm not making any excuses, but in the end, no harm has been done. Our membership base remains strong, and I'd argue that our sponsors would be upset to see the president go."

The board of directors hasn't exactly been working in harmony in the past few years. As a member-elected volunteer board, there are certain members with a radical agenda for change. They want to see your organisation modernised in terms of its culture and strategy. Other board members want to conserve long-held values and traditions. Not surprisingly, it is the ones seeking change that are capitalising on your friend's questionable behaviour.

Your friend, the incumbent president, is a person who has always held alternate views of the world. It's a strength. His divergent thinking has contributed to making the organisation into what it is now. You admire original thinkers, but what was once a strength now appears to be a weakness.

It was about a year ago that you noticed a subtle change. Conspiracy theories that were a little left field slipped into casual conversation, tentatively, as if they were being tested for social acceptance. In the early days, you didn't think you had the right to judge, so you played along, and even chimed in with a few thoughts of your own that made your friend feel supported.

Over time, conspiracy theories came up in conversation more frequently, delivered with more conviction, and the perspective more far-fetched. In the recent past, your friend said, "You realise we are at war, right?"

"War? With who?" you ask.

"The government, and the people that control the government."

Not feeling accommodating to looney ideas that day, you push back: "Really?"

"The evidence is all around us – you just have to look."

You reply sceptically, "I think you're exaggerating."

"You're guilty of accepting the truth that is presented to you. Have you ever wondered why economic recessions exist?"

"Natural business cycles?"

Your friend says, "That's what we've been told, but it's a lie."

"What is the reason, then?" you ask.

"Economic recessions are instruments to control the masses, to maintain the divide between the rich and the poor. Think about it, don't just dismiss it right away. With so much wealth in this world, there is no justification for why there should be long-term unemployment and families in crippling mortgage debt. It's modern day slavery."

"I wouldn't call it slavery. Most of us in the West live a life of freedom and luxury."

Your friend says, "I'm not surprised that you're blind to the truth. It's hard to see the real world as it is because they hide it from you."

You should have realised that your friend would not be receptive to a rational debate, and backed off, but fear clouded your judgement. Afraid that you were losing a friend, one of your closest friends, you say, "I don't see it that way."

"Just open your eyes, for goodness' sake! The evidence is all around you! Housing inflation, high fructose corn syrup, reality TV – they're all instruments to keep us in line and content with the status quo. Can't you see? Are you really that blind?"

That was the first time that you felt a tremendous distance between you and your friend. You became frustrated. You cut short your engagement with him in the least noticeable way possible, made an excuse, and left.

After this incident, you let the gap between you and your friend grow. From a distance, you watched your friend decline. You heard complaints from fellow board members and mutual friends. There was much gossip and speculation: "Surely he's got some mental condition". You felt powerless to save your friend.

Now, in the secret meeting to oust the president, a board member says, "If you abstain, the four of us will have the majority, so in effect you're agreeing with us."

"Abstaining isn't the same as agreeing," you protest.

"The result is the same," they say.

"But at least my conscience will be clear."

They say, "If we put it to a vote, the president, your friend, will lose, and no doubt suffer humiliation. It will be a massive blow to his ego, don't you think? The alternative is that you talk the president into stepping down. This way, nobody loses face, and you do your friend a favour."

The hairs on the back of your neck bristle at the political manipulation. "You want me to pull the trigger, is this what this is about? You're afraid of making an enemy of the president?"

They say, "This benefits the organisation. We must place the best interests of the organisation above the individual. And, the president gets to save face this way."

You step out of the secret board meeting and wrestle with the dilemma. *Should I do the board's bidding and "help" my friend out? Should I go against the board and warn my friend? Or should I say nothing, play it neutral and hope that my friend never finds out I knew beforehand? What is the right thing to do for the organisation given my friend's state of mind?*

The pivotal question, the question which you wrestle with the most: *will my friend snap out of it, or are the conspiracy theories and the mental funk here to stay?*

You check your calendar and see that your assistant has set up lunch with the president. You ask your assistant how the meeting came about? One of the board members instigated it. You decide to go rather than cancel.

At lunch, after a few awkward pleasantries, your friend talks about lies in food labelling. You've heard it many times. "Did you know that Big Food pays for 90% of the scientific research in nutrition?* Everything we know about what is good for us is a lie."

[*This is a fake statistic, fabricated to illustrate a point]

"Why would they lie?" you ask.

"To increase margins, sell more, keep us hungry even though we're eating more than ever."

"You need to unsubscribe from those blogs," you say sternly. "Stop watching those conspiracy videos. I'm telling you as a long-time friend who cares about you."

"Where is this coming from? You want me to put my blinkers on like everyone else? How will that help?"

"Even if these conspiracy theories are true, what are you actually able to do about it? Meanwhile, your mental health is taking a beating."

"There is nothing wrong with my mind."

"Every time you experience fear, every time you see something that makes you feel like there is something wrong with the world, every time you experience hopelessness, you're taking a hit to your head. It's affecting your well-being, your judgement, your work, your reputation and the organisation."

Your friend says, "So, I see that they've got to you, huh? Are they making you say this?"

"Who, who's making me say this?"

"That's how you're going to play this, huh?" your friend says.

"I'm not playing at anything."

"You think I don't know what's going on, huh? Let's not be cowards and come out of the shadows. There is going to be a vote to oust me and put you in power. I was hoping to count on your support as my long-time friend, but I see now that I've let our friendship blind me to your political greed. You're a fool if you think I'm going to go down without a fight."

"I came here to warn you. I was hoping we could work out a plan together."

"Sure you did. And does that plan involve me stepping down and endorsing you as president? Do you want me to lift my arms up while you slide in the dagger? You're a fool if you think I'm going down without a fight."

Your friend leaves you sitting at the table alone with no opportunity to explain.

Later in the week, the motion passes to sack the president.

Your friend doesn't take it well and accuses you of being the mastermind behind the coup d'état. "You're a backstabber, a coward, a power hungry fraud...the organisation will crumble under you."

The emotional outburst isn't short-lived. The barrage of personal attacks continues for months. They undermine your credibility with members and sponsors, and compromise your effectiveness as a president.

You realise now that you shouldn't have accepted the position. Not only has it damaged your friendship, it is harming your personal and business reputation. Reluctantly, you hand in your resignation to the Board.

You make no effort to mend the relationship with your friend because you feel hurt by your friend's accusations.

Time elapses. It's now a year after the incident. You've grown and learnt from the bitter experience. You're wiser and better at handling people with extreme views that are premised on fear. For example, your father made a racial slur recently: "The Wayans are like weeds because once you let them into your backyard, you'll never get rid of them."

Although you're horrified by what he said, you don't let the words affect you, and instead distract him with a story: "The other day, I lost my purse in a car park. I had all my credit cards, five-hundred dollars in cash, driver's licence, everything. I went into a supermarket nearby and asked one of the shop assistants. The shop assistant had no clue, so he yelled out across the floor to another colleague. A customer, a middle eastern woman, overheard and said that she saw someone find a purse in the car park. Apparently, it was handed into a chemist. The chemist, a latino man, said he handed it in to the police station next door. The police woman, an Asian woman, identified me, and handed me my purse, with all the credit cards, five-hundred dollars, everything. It took a chain of good samaritans to do it, and none of them would accept a cash reward. This country is full of amazing people, don't you think?"

The feel-good story brings a smile to your father's face, and he chimes in with a story of his own. The two of you share a positive experience together. And that is all there is to it. You subdue fear, in this case racism, not by a heated confrontation, which breeds more fear, but by sharing a narrative that creates a positive experience, removing adrenaline and cortisol out of the air, and appealing to his better self.

You wish you could wind back time and better handle the debacle over the presidency position. On the grapevine, you hear that your friend's situation has gotten worse over the past year. You wish that there is something you could do to save your friend from the emotional wreckage, but your friend is not returning your calls.

Your friend continues to slander your name. Your efforts to restore your reputation comes to no avail, no matter how much good you do or how much generosity you demonstrate. Even those who have known you for many years have trouble trusting you. People are so susceptible to fear. Even if they

don't fully believe the rumours, they are enough to leave frag-
ments of doubt swimming around in their mind.

Everywhere you go, you encounter rumours and suspicion
that you're the backstabbing coward, the power hungry fraud
that brought down the best president the organisation has
ever had.

GRIEVING

You lose your father to cancer. Your mother and your siblings are falling apart, which makes you feel the need to stay positive. At the funeral you stay detached, and console everyone with sentiments like: "He lived a long and fulfilled life" and "He's at peace now". A few weeks later, the grief catches up with you.

You experience the Thumping. The pain of loss is heavy on your chest. Every fibre in your being yearns to be with him. At random times, you burst into tears. Guilt burdens you: *I should have done more for him. I shouldn't have argued with him.* The muttering is so loud in your head that you're unable to concentrate or sleep. You find no pleasure in the things you normally enjoy, such as eating or spending time with your children. You don't see the point of doing anything. *What is the meaning?*

You don't want to be this way, so you engage in positive self-talk.

You **frame losses as gains**: *My father lived a good life..it's amazing that he lived as long as he did. He had a good death – it was relatively pain free, everyone had an opportunity to say* *goodbye to him, and in the last days, the people who loved him dearly surrounded him. He was a generous man, and he always believed in me. I am who I am today because of him.*

You **embrace constraints**: *He is gone. I need to accept that. I need to focus on those that are still alive, such as my children – they are the future. They need me to be present.*

You **zoom-in** on your feelings to identify a set of fears:

Fear: *I can never see or talk to my father again.*
Better me: *I will see him in the afterlife. This time apart is just temporary.*

Fear: *I should have done more for my father. I wish I paid more attention to him, seen him more often, listened to him, and gone on more holidays with him. I feel guilty that I dismissed his health complaints, and I feel awful that I didn't do more to encourage him to look after his health.*
Better me: *This is guilt speaking. Some guilt is natural, but too much is toxic. My father had his own mind, and he never took the doctor's advice, let alone my advice. I had so many competing priorities – my job, my children, my friends, my health. If I did more for my father, then I'd pay the price elsewhere. I did a lot for him, more than most children. He was happy.*

Fear of loneliness. *I will never get the chance to put my arms around him, to make him laugh, to have a meal with him, or go for a walk together.*
Better me: *I have many people in my life who are dear to me. I must focus on the future: my partner, my children and my friends.*

Fear of my mortality. *I feel old, and my body feels old. My father's death reminds me of how little time I have left. At forty-six, I'm only nineteen years away from retirement age. I'm saddened by the thought that my best days are behind me. I won't get any stronger or faster. My childhood dreams of becoming a scientist, a painter, or a musician won't be fulfilled. I've had my chance and wasted it.*

Better me: *This is an irrational fear. The life expectancy of my generation is 80-85 years old, and 1 in 4 of us will live to 100. Statistically speaking, I haven't even reached halfway. I still have time to earn four PhDs, paint two thousand portraits and master five musical instruments if I choose to.*

Fear of being a failure in my father's eyes. *He expected big things from me, and I have not met his expectations. I am deeply sad that he will no longer be around to see my future accomplishments. I will never get the chance to make him proud of me again.*

Better me: *All children, young and old, crave for the approval of their parents consciously and subconsciously, even the most successful ones. I must let go of this because it's an insatiable craving. My father was proud of me. He had high expectations of me because he was a big thinker, wanted the best for me, wanted me to rise above my circumstance, and fulfil my greatest potential. He never said I failed him. Quite the contrary, he spoke highly of me to his friends and admired what I've achieved in life.*

Does it work? No, not really, because the Thumping inside is like a house ablaze with fire and smoke, and the See-Switch-

Move mental exercises are as pathetic as water pistols against the raging inferno. The yearning, the pain, and the sense of loss persist. You are teary all the time. In social situations, you pretend there is something in your eye. When you're on your own, you cry out loud with deep misery and self-pity. You spend hours just lying in bed, day and night, doing nothing. You're not in control of how you feel or what your body is doing.

This can't persist — you don't want it to — so you change strategy. As soon as a sad thought arises, you force your mind to switch to another thought; avoid conversations about your father, minimise communication with your younger sister and your mother (because you're bound to think of your father), and get busy with many things, anything just so you don't have to think. You go shopping online and within a few weeks you purchase three new outfits, two pairs of shoes, four different wireless earphones, new t-shirts for every member of the family, two laptops, a guitar, a canoe, a lawnmower, a new vacuum, a stand mixer, tea towels, curtains, and a kitchen knife set. It gives you a sense of progress, like you're being useful. You distract yourself with hours of mindless television, such as food, travel, and lifestyle shows. You keep yourself frantically busy, take on extra responsibilities at work, tackle home and garden chores, and volunteer to help other people with theirs. Your house was never so clean, your garden never so manicured as it is now. You are unaware that these are fear-driven moves.

You bury your emotions deep. You know you're not in an emotionally good place, but at least you're being productive.

By the end of each day, you are completely wasted, physically and mentally. Despite this, you're still sleeping poorly. Here's what a typical night looks like:

You take a long time to drop off. When you do, you wake up

in the middle of the night, often with a nightmare. You try to go back to sleep but you can't. You check the clock, it's 2:30 a.m.. So many thoughts, so many fears, appear in your head. You miss your father. You turn over and adjust your pillow, hoping to find a comfortable position that will be conducive to sleep. You resist looking at your phone, because you know it perpetuates insomnia. As you lie there, you feel the anxiety and tightness in your chest grow. The Thumping in your chest stops you from falling asleep. After a while, who knows how long, you give in, turn on the light, sit up and read a book. At first, it is hard to get into the book on account of all the noise that is in your head, but eventually, you pick up the plot, and the noise subsides. Soon your eyelids feel heavy. You put down the book, turn off the light, hoping to catch a wave of sleep. As you make yourself comfortable, thoughts creep in again. You try to put aside thoughts about your father, but other thoughts flood in. *Should I take the car or the train? Will I get into town on time? What if I can't find a car park? Why did Julie say that in the meeting? I should have said something to defend myself.* And so on, and so forth. You work through the answers to some questions. It's the same answers you've already worked out earlier in the night. Some questions don't have answers, questions related to the future, so you wrestle with them repeatedly, trying to know the unknowable. Rumination was once your strength: it helped you become a more thoughtful person, to solve problems, develop original ideas, be creative, live an examined life, avoid trouble, make better decisions, influence others, optimise, make more money, and make better plans. But now it's your enemy because you can't seem to shut your brain down. The bedside clock says 4:18 a.m. You decide you may as well get out of bed. From recent experience, you know that trying to fall asleep after 4 a.m. has a zero success rate. Getting out of bed and getting busy has the additional benefit of preventing the grief from surfacing. As negative emotions emerge again, you drown it out by putting on a podcast and cleaning the kitchen floor.

Sometimes, when you're working, you weep uncontrollably, and have to stop to mop up the tears with the arms of your sleeves.

They say that time heals all wounds, but you are spiralling downwards, the noise in your head getting louder, the anxiety attacks more frequent, and your self-confidence diminishing day by day. You lose your temper easily. You have a row with your sister:

> Sister: "Don't talk to me like that. I'm not your seven-year-old sister anymore."
> You: "Then stop behaving like a nit-wit because I will not take it."
> Sister: "Fine. How about I never talk to you again?"
> You: "That would make my life so much better."

When your daughter pushes screen-time limits, what starts out as a gentle warning from you escalates into a shouting match. You're aware that you're overreacting, but you can't seem to stop the fury from coming out. You snatch her mobile phone and throw it in the bin. In great pain you let out: "Don't you realise what I am going through? Can't you, for once in your life, think about anyone but yourself?" This incident marks a milestone. Your mind is a wreck. Everyone can see it except you.

People around you, including your friends and your spouse, try to cheer you up by putting a positive spin on things. You've heard them all: "Your father lived a good life", "At least you still have your health" and "You are a good son, you did so much for your father when he was alive." These platitudes mean nothing to you because you're a realist, and you're only interested in the truth. And the truth is, none of this positive thinking rubbish is going to bring him back. You become wary of people who put a positive spin on everything. To you, it's important not to mask your emotions, be it sadness, anger, hate, or jealousy. It is healthy to vent how you feel, to speak your mind and call things as they are. You want to honour the loss of your father, to be true to how you're feeling, and not cover it up with lies. Nobody truly understands what you're going through.

That nobody seems to understand or feel the depths of what you feel is a sign of a fear-injured mind. Certain issues trigger emotional pain, anger, and anxiety easily. You go straight to Def Con 1, armed forces ready to deploy, nuclear missiles engaged, whilst everyone else is loitering in peace mode. It's because you have a wound where others don't. A tiny poke is all it takes because the synapses that deal with these issues are well established and easily fired. It can be over something trivial, like people leaving the lights on, restaurants using too much oil in their cooking, or not being able to find parking. It often relates to matters outside of your control, such as your child refusing to eat what you prepared, global warming, or the direction the Labor Party is taking.

Over time, you fall into a rut. You avoid situations that put you under pressure because you're afraid that your mind might let you down. You lose sight of your purpose. Each day, you go through the motions, eat, work, try to sleep, eat, work, try to sleep. Time with kids, cooking, eating, making love...you're there, but you're not really there. You are numb and terrified at the same time. You are a mess. People talk about you behind your back. In their social circles, you are the benchmark figure for grumpiness and closed-mindedness.

At Christmas lunch, you notice no one has set a place for

your father. You say very little other than bark at the children, who by now are used to your grumpiness and treat you with a mix of apathy and caution. This makes you feel even less effectual. *What is the point of saying anything anymore?*

After lunch, everyone gathers around the TV to watch sports. The outcome of the game doesn't matter to you anymore. You take your seat and feign interest. Across from you is the chair where your father used to sit. The thought of his absence hits you hard. *He's gone. He's never coming back.* You put it out of your head by using the game as a distraction, and avoid crying in front of everyone.

A news update interrupts the televised game. It runs through a list of the usual negative headlines: immigrants cheating the system, self-serving politicians doing nothing, and threats of chaos and mass disobedience at your doorstep. "Tune in at seven for full details."

The news editor's shock tactics push you over the edge. You can't take it anymore. You leave the group, go upstairs, and cry into your pillow.

Downstairs, a second round of dessert, coffee and port is being served. The children are playing with their new toys. Everyone around you is safe, pleasant, and merry. Love and kindness surround you.

Outside, the sun shines, the snow gleams white, the streets empty except for a snowman with a jolly soul, and the sound of Christmas fills the crisp, clean air.

7. KNOW

PART VII

KNOW

A set of essays about the nature of our mind.

FEARLESSNESS VS MASTERY OF FEAR

We must be careful not to conflate the mastery of fear with fearlessness – the two couldn't be more different.

Fearlessness is blind optimism, ignorance of genuine threats, and failure to prepare for the future. Mastery of fear is the opposite: it's eyes-open, mindful, insightful, judicious and anti-fragile.

Having no fear is having no respect for rules that govern normal civil behaviour, thus being a burden on everyone else. Mastery of fear is the ability to transcend rules that govern civil behaviour, so that everyone is better off.

To be fearless is to jump out of an aeroplane without checking your parachute. Mastery of fear is to have the right training, preparation and mindset so that jumping out of an aeroplane is no more risky than crossing a road.

Fearlessness is throwing caution to the wind. Mastery of fear is using the winds of fear to power our sails and propel us.

Our aim is not to be fearless, because in fact, we need fear. It is one of the most important emotions, alongside love and hope. It guides us, motivates us, pushes us through tough times, compels us to do good, drives us to extraordinary heights and keeps us safe.

We can't master fear if there is no fear to master.

WHERE DOES CONFIDENCE COME FROM?

By definition, confidence is the opposite of fear. Given this, how do we be less fearful and more confident? Where does confidence come from? How do we give someone confidence if they don't have it?

Self-help gurus say that it's all about the power of the mind, i.e. believing in oneself. From Michael Jordan to Steve Jobs, from Margaret Thatcher to Oprah Winfrey, we are presented with stories about successful people and told the same truism: when the chips are down, it's their undying self-belief that keeps winners going. This popular notion might sell books and movie rights, but **absolute faith in the mind's power is absolutely dangerous**. What we don't see is the millions of people who had the same self-belief but didn't win. No last-place getter says, "I really believed in myself, but I lost." We never get to hear from them.

Ever said to someone who's failing, "You just have to believe in yourself"? Did they suddenly leap up, stand ten feet taller, and instantly become fearless? Or did they become defensive, "Gee, thanks, if only I thought of that!" Or worse, did they shrivel into a shell because we've just accused them of lacking self-belief?

Confidence comes from three things: self-belief, affirmation *(from those who matter to us), capability (skills and knowledge), and a track record of small wins. I use the acronym S.A.C.S. to remember this, as in, "With SACS, I'll have sacks and sacks of confidence."*

The Confidence Pyramid

As a society, we place too much emphasis on the first two: self-belief and affirmation.

I argue that self-belief is a product of the other three factors. Even the most self-assured amongst us are susceptible to self-doubt if we're missing one of the other factors.

Imagine that I am a seven-year-old child learning to catch a wave at a beach for the first time. As a huge swell emerges, I hesitate, uncertain that I can handle such a big one. My father says to me "You can do it, James, you just have to believe in yourself!" As I perform the infamous manoeuvre called "being tossed around like a rag doll in a washing machine and getting dumped", I'm likely to lose trust in my father and faith in my ability. And as I fish sand out of my crotch, anything he says is going to be received as criticism to my seven-year-old ears. *"You need to paddle harder"* is taken as *"You're not paddling hard enough"*. *"Don't give up, you just need to believe in yourself"* is taken as *"You lack self-belief, that's your problem."*

Who is at fault here? The child who has had no training, or the father with the blind faith in the mind's power?

Winning is to our confidence what fuel is to a fire.

When we see someone brimming with confidence, it is always the case that they have had a lot of wins, if not throughout their life, then a lot recently. If we aspire to be a stand-up comedian, no amount of self-belief (*"I'm funny, I know I am"*), no amount of praise (*"you're funny, you're going to be great"*), and no amount of training and preparation will boost our confidence as much as making a room full of strangers explode with laughter.

If winning is the key to confidence, then how do we experience more wins? Do we limit ourselves to competing against those we know we can beat? No, this just creates false confidence. Should we hold our children back a year so that they have a year's advantage over the other kids at school? Are we to shy away from competition? Do we never put ourselves at risk of failure? This is no way to live.

The key to winning and winning often is to aim small.

To write a book, we shouldn't fret over how many pages we would need to write and how long it would take. A project like a book is too big and daunting. Aim instead for 500 words a day, as author Ernest Hemingway did (or even a hundred a day). Starting at first light, Hemingway often accomplished his goal by midday, thus experiencing a win every day. Author Neil Gaiman wrote in two different coloured pens (e.g. blue one day and brown the next day), *which made it easy to see the gains from a day's toil. To become a long-distance runner, we could set a goal to run a marathon, but this would take us a long time to accomplish if we're starting from scratch. If we aim instead to run fifty metres, on Day 1, and increase this by fifty metres each time we set out for a run, by the time we reach 5kms we'll have experienced 100 wins. If we can run 5 kms, we can run 7kms, and if we can run 7kms, we'd feel more confident about tackling 10kms, and so forth.*

The best teachers, be it at playing piano, swimming or skiing, are those that make us feel like we're winning, not by pitting students against each other, but by setting small, attainable but satisfying challenges along the way. They make us want to learn and get better by enticing us with small wins.

A series of small and recent wins adds more to our confidence than a big win attained a long time ago.

An author with three moderately successful books, published recently, will feel more confident than an author who published one best seller fifteen years ago, even if the best-selling book outsold the three books combined by a factor of ten.

The worst leaders are those that set unrealistic goals, and think this is what leadership is about; abuse people when things don't go as planned; think tough love makes people strong; and belittle their peers, thinking it makes them look good but all the while they're creating a series of losses which drains everyone of confidence.

Wins in one aspect of our lives boost our confidence in other aspects of our lives.

It isn't always possible to break larger challenges into smaller bite-sized challenges. In these circumstances, we can try winning in other aspects of our lives. Want to improve our confidence at work? Try making small gains in our health and fitness every week. Want to feel more confident about public speaking? Try spending time with people who make us feel good about ourselves. Want to put aside our anxieties about our children? Try experiencing a series of successes ourselves rather than focusing on them.

Who we choose to spend time with defines us.

As social creatures, we thrive on the affirmation of others. We want people to laugh at our jokes, nod and endorse what we say, think that we can walk on water, and so forth. We are shy about asking for affirmation, and rarely do it out loud, even though we crave it, because it makes us sound needy and insecure. How then do we get it if it isn't forthcoming? And worse, what if we don't like what we hear? The answer: spend more time with the right people, those that lift you up, and less with the wrong people, those who put you down. While affirmation fuels confidence, it's opposite, disapproval, disappointment, put-downs and public shaming are toxic to confidence. A single show of disappointment undoes the benefit of ten praises. [1]

Here's a brief story that brings these ideas together.

Jo is a lawyer who is up for promotion to Senior Associate in six months' time. She has to present her case to a committee comprising senior partners. She's nervous; afraid that her peers are more accomplished; worried that there are gaps in her knowledge; aware that she'll fail if she does anything less than exude confidence at her presentation. No amount of positive self-talk seems to ease her nerves. She tries several mind tricks to quell her fears, such as "zooming-in". Although she learns her fears are irrational (i.e. "I am as qualified as the other candidates, and it isn't expected that I have deep knowledge across all areas"), she remains apprehensive and unsure. She can't explain it, it's just how she feels emotionally. Rather than focus on mindset alone, she addresses the other three factors that underpin confidence:

- *Ability: She identifies her knowledge gaps and creates a reading list. She sets up one-on-one coaching sessions with senior lawyers to practice mock cases.*
- *Small wins: She defines a series of small goals to be tackled over the next few months. This includes personal goals, such as fitness goals, as well as workplace goals, such as volunteering to facilitate training for junior lawyers. Each time she has a win, she celebrates with a reward, and tells others about it. The sense of accomplishment, the track record of wins, gives her a natural boost in confidence.*
- *Affirmation: She fills her social calendar with people she enjoys spending time with. They're interested in her ideas and laugh at her jokes. She seeks feedback from senior lawyers that she trusts on her strengths and improvement opportunities. She works on her weaknesses, and reports back to the senior lawyers. They admire her work ethic. Gains on the health front gives her a natural boost. Positive feedback from junior lawyers who attended her training makes her feel valued.*

By the time Jo presents her promotion case to the committee of senior partners, she might still be nervous, but she's confident. Had she relied on self-talk alone (i.e. mindset), her confidence would be fragile, and the panel of interviewers would see through her false bravado.

THE AGE OF FEAR-MONGERING

Fear-mongering is used to capture and hold our attention. It's how newspapers and social media make money, how politicians rally support, and how social disruptors build apathy against important issues.

Consider the headlines in today's tabloid newspaper[1] and note the corresponding fear they arouse (in brackets):

"Police hospitalised in violent protest."[2]
(fear of social chaos and disorder)

"Mystery case forces 22 people to isolate."
(fear of unknown, fear of death);

"Big banks may not pass on [home loan rate] cuts for weeks."[3]
(fear of being taken advantage of by faceless corporations, fear of injustice);

"Dead and numb: accuser tells her story."

(fear of crime getting out of control, fear of personal harm, fear of social degradation)

"Big consequences: China warning."
(fear of China, fear of harm to our economic future, fear of conflict).

Fear-mongering isn't new. Headlines of tabloid news of the 1980s were as provocative as they are today. What's different now is the intensity, frequency and vividness in which we are exposed to messages of fear. Whilst our devices and the internet make it easier than ever to access information, it is easier than ever for fear mongers to reach us. Social media triggers us, bombards us and engages us at a deeper level than any other media. Silicon Valley author, Nir Eyal, says that an investment by users in a platform increases the odds that we will be hooked.[4] *When we post political content, assert a political opinion, subscribe or follow certain influencers, share inflammatory material, save material in our library, customise our preferences, we inadvertently make an investment, and therefore feel more buy-in.*

Stories that shock capture more attention and travel with greater velocity on social media.

With so much exposure to fear-mongering, it's no wonder that we feel more on edge and hostile when we encounter opposing ideas.

Author Steven Pinker wrote:

"...heavy newswatchers can become miscalibrated. They worry more about crime, even when rates are falling, and sometimes they part company with reality altogether: a 2016 poll found that a large majority of Americans follow news about Isis closely, and 77% agreed that "Islamic militants operating in Syria and Iraq pose a serious threat to the existence or survival of the United States," a belief that is nothing short of delusional.... Consumers

of negative news, not surprisingly, become glum: a recent litera-
ture review cited "misperception of risk, anxiety, lower mood
levels, learned helplessness, contempt and hostility towards
others..."[5]

If we have a bias against government intervention, partly it
would be because we only hear of cases of government failure and
mismanagement. Successes, such as projects delivered on time and
on budget, or delivery of world-class standard of service, never make
it on the news or ever go viral on social media.

If we distrust corporations, it is in part because we are
constantly hearing about employee misconduct and corporate greed.
First Big Mining, then Big Pharma and now Big Food and Tech.
Many of us proactively choose the little guy. We'd rather support
small businesses, one that has no statutory obligation to report their
dealings, than give our business to listed companies that face scru-
tiny from a litany of health, environmental and securities agencies.
Do managers at large organisations sit around a table all day
coming up with schemes to bully, cheat and screw employees and
customers? Or are there just as many good folk in big companies as
there are in small businesses? My intention here is not to favour
large businesses over small, but to flag the skewed impression we can
get depending on what is headlined in the media. To get a more
balanced view, shouldn't we hear the positives, not just the nega-
tives? Such as breakthroughs in corporate innovation, reduction in
waste (thus falling prices), and improvements in employment
conditions?

If we distrust science, medicine and technology, it's partly
because it's easy to portray anything that is new and complicated as
being unstable, untested, unnatural, dangerous, and deadly. They
stoke our fear of the unknown, fear of change, and undermine our
sense of control.

If we distrust economists, it's partly because we report them as *being heartless bureaucrats that seek to take away our livelihood and disrupt our way of life. We hear more about job losses, rising taxes, inflation, social degradation and compromises to our freedom caused by economic policy, and by comparison, rarely hear about the benefits from the biggest ideas in economics, those that we take for granted, such as free-trade, carbon-trading and fiscal policy. Media and politicians alike misrepresent brilliant ideas in economics because it helps them gain attention and votes.*

I make the claim that the Information Age has given birth to the Age of Fear-Mongering. This itself is a hyperbole, the words chosen to capture your attention. Ultimately, we get to decide if it is or isn't. We control what comes into our lives, how much sewage they pump through our TVs into our living rooms and our minds. The only reality that matters is what is in our minds, and ultimately we get to control that. A less solipsistic view is that all it takes for the fear-mongers, politicians, journalists and influencers to be less effectual is for more of us to be unaffected by them.

FIVE INTERESTING QUIRKS IN OUR BRAIN

It's a conundrum that conspiracy theories persist in an information age. There is more data than ever, and we have greater access and visibility into government dealings and corporate behaviour than ever before in human history. And yet trust in government, corporate institutions and mainstream media is at an all-time low in the free world.[1]

There are roughly 6.6 billion smartphones[2] *around the globe: that's roughly 44 recording devices per square kilometre on the earth's land surface (albeit spread unevenly).*[3] *How can people buy into false claims of widespread election tampering and Illuminati paedophile rings run by people in office when a camera is never too far away to seize visual evidence of wrongdoing?*

We can fact-check and verify sources, from nearly anywhere in the world, 24/7, often within a few clicks. And yet, more and more people are buying into ludicrous beliefs like the Flat-Earth Theory.

We are turning our back on advances in human intelligence in the fields of science, nutrition, medicine and economics. We are just as likely to heed unsubstantiated opinions of influencers, shock-jocks and celebrities over research institutions and the smartest people on earth.

No one is immune. It's affecting the intelligent, the educated, the wealthy, the famous and the wise because intelligence, education, money, fame and wisdom have nothing to do with it. Ever tried to correct someone with facts and data and end up escalating into an argument?

We think of ourselves as being good at discerning truth from lies. Ask a room full of people to put their hand up if they are good at detecting false and over-sensationalised claims and it's almost a certainty that everyone will have their hands up.

Why then do so many of us buy into illogical, exaggerated, and blatantly false claims (or lose our original conviction about the truth)? How do conspiracies get us?

Conspiracy theories work because they are fueled by the most abundant resource on planet earth: fear. This sounds crazy, because how can fear cause normal intelligent people like us to shun facts with insurmountable evidence and logical reasoning?

To understand why, we must first understand how our brain works. Consider the following five concepts from psychology and brain science:

1. We have two brains.

*What we know about the human brain is that our behaviour is driven by the interplay between two modalities of our brain. Let's refer to them here as the **Animal Brain** and the **Thinking Brain**. This is not an original idea: the concept is abundant throughout human history in literature, philosophy and psychology.*[4]

The Animal Brain handles just about everything that keeps us alive. It's where our intuition comes from, and why we experience emotion, pain, hunger, lust and fear. The Thinking Brain handles logic, deduction, rational thinking, self-control, and regulation of our emotions.

Whilst our Thinking Brain makes New Year's Resolutions, it's our Animal Brain that persuades the Thinking Brain that having a second helping of chocolate cake fits within our goal's parameters. Our Thinking Brain reads parenting books so that we can role model equanimity to our kids, but when the kids spill paint all over the carpet, it's our Animal Brain that causes us to lose it and yell at them. Whilst our Thinking Brain tells us we should always practice safe sex, in the heat of the moment, the Animal Brain weakens our resolve, and says "what the heck, it'll be alright just this once".

2. The Animal Brain is a dictator and a manipulator.

Nobel Prize laureate, Daniel Kahneman, says our Animal Brain makes most of our decisions, even the most important ones.[5] It shares its decision-making powers with the Thinking brain only when it is feeling happy, calm, well-fed and safe. When we are in a "hot-state" (e.g. hungry, angry, horny, tired, scared, or sensing opportunity), our Thinking Brain loses its powers of deduction and rationality. The Animal Brain takes charge, overshadowing the Thinking Brain.

Who's in control?

Animal brain
Where actions and
decisions are automated,
based on gut instinct, or
driven by hunger, fear,
arousal etc.

Thinking brain
Where we make
conscious and
effortful decisions

Illusion of control
Where we believe Thinking brain is in
the driver's seat, but actually Animal
brain is ruling our thoughts and actions

The problem is, in a hot-state, we have the illusion that we're in the driver's seat, making rational choices, but we're not at all. The Animal Brain has dominance over the Thinking Brain, often manipulating it to justify its decisions.

For example, imagine we are planning to buy a car, and the choice is between a petrol family wagon and a sexy electric sports vehicle, but we're keen on the electric vehicle. Our heart is set on it. Our Thinking Brain comes up with a selection criteria, such as safety and fuel economy, gathers facts, and puts them into a spreadsheet. What we are not fully aware of is the manipulation of our Animal Brain. It sneaks biases into the process. Our Thinking Brain unknowingly gives more weight to certain criteria and is selective about what data goes into the analysis, giving the sexy electric sports car an unfair advantage. And even if the biased analysis proves the family wagon to be the more sensible choice, our Animal Brain might hijack the entire process, change the rules, or throw it out altogether. "What the heck, life is short, I should just buy the car I want!"

Let's flip the scenario to cement the point. Assume now that our Animal Brain favours the petrol family wagon because we're anxious about running out of battery, the safety of unproven technology, and that electric vehicles don't carry a spare tyre. "What happens if we get stuck in the middle of nowhere late at night?" Our Thinking Brain won't get much of a say. We'll dismiss facts and rational reasoning in favour of security and certainty.

3. The Animal Brain is brilliant at recording and storing data.

Our Animal Brain is switched on and working all the time. We record sights, smells, faces, threats and other information without any conscious effort. Advertisers know this. It's why they ubiquitously surround us with ads, online, on TV and in the streets. We believe we are good at ignoring advertisements such as banner ads, we think logos plastered all over sports stadiums and jerseys are harmless, but our brains are phenomenally good at noticing, absorbing, and storing everything into memory. Why else would advertisers spend so much money?

The Animal Brain absorbs everything: sounds and images,
truths and lies. The data manifests in our gut as 'feelings'.

4. We approximate the truth based on gut feel or how easy it is to recall something.

Consider this question: "Is the current leader of your country doing a good job?" To come up with a robust answer, we ought to develop criteria set, gather facts, validate the sources, perform analyses comparing the current leader against, say, past presidents and leaders of other countries. Most people won't do any of this. Most of us will come up with a gut opinion based on recent headlines that are easy to recall from memory, what the president looked like in recent appearances on TV, what a friend or a neighbour said, etc.. [6]

We apply this approximation, this mental short-cut, to everyday decisions. It governs how we feel about most things. Toyota or Volkswagen – which is more reliable? Should we buy more life insurance? Is vaccination safe? Should we invest in real estate or buy shares in the stock market? Does eating red meat improve your virility? Is privatisation good for society? Does America do more harm than good? To answer these questions, did we perform a thorough analysis and fact-check our sources, or did we use our gut, basing it off what we can recall from memory?

These approximations happen so much that by accumulation it affects our outlook and mental well-being. Is it safe to leave the back door unlocked if we're popping out for fifteen minutes? Are Wayans taking over this country? Is the world getting too crowded? Should we build a wall to protect us? Should we carry guns just in case? Is the air we breathe and the water we drink polluted with toxins? Are corporations spying on us? Is the world going mad?

5. The Animal Brain doesn't qualify information as being true or false, real or unreal.

This statement implies that we can construe anything as being true, even if we know it to be false. Surely we are smarter than that?

Picture this: we are standing in front of the aftermath of an accident between a large petrol truck and a small red car. There are two scorched dead bodies on the road, and one of them is a child. The bodies are so charred they are beyond recognition. Thanks to our Thinking Brain, we know that the horrifying image we've just pictured in our head isn't real. However, our Animal Brain doesn't think in terms of whether it is real or imagined. It records the image of scorched dead bodies, fire and smoke, mangled car parts, and the associated feelings we felt, be it dread, revulsion, or horror. It swims around in our brain, ready to be called upon by us when we make gut decisions. Our Animal Brain doesn't test the truck accident scenario for validity, it simply records it.

This quirk in how our brain functions explains why when we watch an intense horror film, our Thinking Brain might tell us that the blood and gore aren't real, but we'll still have trouble sleeping afterwards. Knowing that something is false doesn't stop us from being affected by it.

Putting the five doctrines together gives us an insight into how conspiracy theories recruit us. Here's what a typical journey looks like:

> **Stage 1: Curious.** *We come across a news article that casts doubt on fluoride. "Does Fluoride Cause Cancer?*" We know the answer is "No", because fluoride has been in use for decades to prevent tooth decay, it's in our toothpaste and our water. We read the article anyway because we believe in staying open-minded.*
>
> *The article conjures the 'feeling' that we're being lied to by the government, that there is a strong link between fluoride and cancer. "Everywhere there is fluoride, there is cancer." Notice that I've used the word 'feeling' here. Our Thinking Brain continues to doubt the credibility of the claims, but our Animal Brain, always on, always sensing, always recording, can't help but 'feel' something.*
>
> **Stage 2 Cautious.** *Over the next few months, similar articles and videos appear on our social media feed. "New Research Reveals Shocking Truth About Drinking Water." We can't resist looking at them because we feel compelled to know more about potential threats. The side-effect of this is that our Thinking Brain now has less conviction than it did about the benefits and safety of fluoride. This is because our gut instinct, our Animal Brain, senses something isn't right. We're not yet convinced that fluoride causes cancer, because our Thinking Brain won't let us go that far, but we feel that there might be some truth to it. What we know and what we feel are in conflict.*
>
> *As time goes by, we give more attention to inflammatory content because the issue is something we've become anxious about. "Medical Abomination Revealed." Social media makes it easy for us to come across this material, but we can't blame social media entirely. Their algorithm isn't trying to manipulate us, it*

just gives us what we seem to be interested in. We're the ones doing the swiping and tapping.

We buy fluoride-free toothpaste and install a filter, just in case. "Why take the risk?"

Stage 3 Convinced. *One day, late at night, feeling restless, we go down a fluoride rabbit hole, searching for and consuming articles and videos written by zealots against fluoride. Don't judge us, we're doing it out of good conscience: to protect our society and the people we love. All the same, it's a fear driven act: we're terrified that something so insidious can be so widespread. "How can no one be doing anything about it?" The fear causes us to find out as much as we can. The problem is, our Animal Brain, always recording, always sensing, is being exposed to more and more scary images and terrifying implications. Shocking pictures of mouth cancer, a sad story of a single-mother of three children with only three months left to live, a long list of ailments, from bone leaching to migraines, and diagrams showing the direct link between cancer and fluoride.*

We warn others of the danger.

Stage 4 Committed. *After a while, our Animal Brain is genuinely afraid, and in an actual state of alarm. With so much fear on board, the Animal Brain inevitably recruits the Thinking Brain. We embrace evidence that supports how we feel without the usual sanity checks because they make us feel we are in the right. "Fluoride is killing 40,000 healthy children every month. Share this post to help save our children." The Thinking Brain, the one that earned us a university degree says, "40,000 sounds high, but it doesn't matter what the exact number is, it must be high." We dismiss evidence that isn't aligned with how we feel. We feel frustration and anger, and have no patience for those who disagree with us (especially those that are close to us).*

By this stage, it is very hard to change our mind, not without erasing the fear that our Animal Brain feels. And this is very difficult to do because there is no delete button: our social media feed continues to stoke our fears, and our Thinking Brain rejects evidence that contradicts us. We have expressed our position to the world irrevocably, and had heated arguments about the topic to the point that we would humiliate ourselves if we were to change our minds now. Evidence that 'proves' we are right is comforting.

[*Please note that it is not my intention to discredit fluoride as a public health measure. I have fabricated these headlines and numbers for the purpose of illustrating how easy it is for sound scientific waters to be muddied.]

It doesn't matter what the issue is. We could be against fluoride, free trade or fairy floss: if our emotions are on a constant simmer, if we get upset easily when people challenge us, if we are against the wisdom of the crowd, if our minds are fear-injured, there is a chance that we have arrived at our position through a similar journey. We may be right, our hunches may be proven correct, but for now, we are unbalanced, unhappy and potentially closed-minded because of our fears.

How do we protect ourselves from this kind of fear-mongering? We can't ignore the news or become apathetic to it because that's how evil prevails. How do we keep up to date with what is going on in the world, stay abreast of threats, perform our civic duty, keep governments honest, without taking hits to our Animal Brain? How do we discern fear-mongering lies from genuine threats when both are laced with fear?

There are no straightforward answers, no safety goggles or prophylactic we can use before we consume media. We have to accept that we're going to be infected by some level of fear because it's absolutely necessary for the health of our society that we stay informed and open-minded.

So, to avoid losing our sense of proportion, we can regularly ask ourselves:

- **What does my information diet look like?** *News that inflames rather than informs us is to our information diet what fatty fast-food is to our body. Consider placing limits on how much of this type of news we consume. If we feel anxious, rather than check the news multiple times a day, we might quell our minds by reading a novel or a history book.*
- **Is this news or is it more of the same fear-mongering message (or no message at all)?** *Am I learning anything new or am I seeking this information out of fear and anxiety? If we can avoid seeing the same inflammatory content, we'll avoid multiple hits to the head.*
- **What fears or emotions am I feeling when I consume this?** *Do this for two reasons. If it is highly emotive, then we can become conscious that our Animal Brain will give the information more weight than it deserves. Second, it helps us remain mindful of the emotional toll, the feelings that our Animal Brain is experiencing, and therefore the state of our overall well-being. Are there sources of news that are less emotive? Would we be just as well informed by reading monthly journals that adopt a more objective voice?*
- **Have I had enough?** *Have I overestimated my ability to think rationally and decipher the truth given my fear load? Should I treat myself to a week free of news and social media? Think of it as a retreat rather than abstinence. Make a conscious trade: will a book, time in nature or a chat with an old friend do me more good than keeping up with the headlines?*

If we have become tarnished by overly emotive information, we can settle our fearful minds by doing the things we normally do that return us to equanimity, such as meditation, going for a walk, playing with children and positive self-talk.

In describing the laws of propaganda, Nazi Joseph Goebbels said, "Repeat a lie often enough, and it becomes the truth". We know this isn't quite right because our Thinking Brains aren't that gullible. We will not swim in a pool of sharks, no matter how many times we're told that sharks are safe. I believe what he meant was: "Repeat a fear often enough, and it becomes real."

HEALING A FEAR-INJURED MIND

American philosopher and psychologist, William James, said, "The greatest weapon against stress is our ability to choose one thought over another". But what if fearful thoughts pound our mind every minute of the day? What if we are so filled with dread, grief and the Thumping that we can hardly breathe or lie still without pain in our chest? How can we heal our fear-injured mind if our mind is impaired in the first place?

The See-Switch-Move framework may not be enough to help our minds when we're in an injured state. The negative thought patterns are so deeply entrenched in our minds that change becomes difficult.

Neuroscience science offers us hope.

Our brains have a tendency to fabricate details to fill in the missing details. The rub of it is that we do this unwittingly. For example, ask me who came to my 16th birthday party, and I struggle because it took place over three decades ago. If pushed, I'd say Brad, Garth and Mario. I believe I am recalling this from memory, but my creative brain has lent a hand. A study by neuroscientists, Bridge and Paller, shows that we store newly concocted versions into our memory as if they were the original, so that when we later recall it, we're recalling the concocted version and not the original.[1] Ask me in a month who attended my 16th birthday party, and I'll say with greater confidence, Brad, Garth and Mario. And if my creative brain added another person, say Andy, then my memory will be altered again, and I'll unwittingly add Andy to my 16th birthday guest list as if it happened in reality. It explains why witnesses can have different accounts of a bank robbery or a car accident.

Something that has happened a long time ago (say, over ten years), has the risk of being inaccurate because it has had the opportunity to be rewritten many times over. It explains why adult siblings can have different recollections of "unforgettable" events in their childhood.

Another important feature of memory is that we have a tendency to skew our memory to suit our disposition. It explains why divorcees almost always have conflicting versions of the past.

Loss and grief have a tendency to lessen in intensity over time as our memory of them fades. The exception is if we constantly re-enforce it. Every time we recall a sad or traumatic event, or carry a fearful thought, we are strengthening the synapses associated with these negative memories and thought patterns.

Every time we carry a fearful thought we are
strengthening the synapses associated with it.

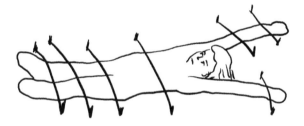

We can free
ourselves by
interrupting
negative mental
loops and mending
the narrative.

This feature of the human brain can cause a downward spiral. Those of us in a fear-injured state are more likely to relive bad memories, think negative thoughts, and succumb to fear, which further entrenches the negative thought pattern. Rather than recover over time, it's easy to see how this can actually become worse.

The good news is that it also works the other way. With conscious effort and practice we can rewire these brain patterns, and free ourselves from being easily triggered by negativity, healing our fear-injured minds.

How? Introducing: the Flow-Mend Cycle.

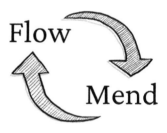

Start with Mend

Mend is the combination of See and Switch. To recap:

See *our fears, acknowledge them, understand how they make us feel, and avoid making harsh judgements about ourselves. We might accomplish this through meditation, journaling, or using a friend as a sounding board.*

Switch *out of the excessively negative mindset by looking through one of the four lenses:*

- *Carrot (identify the gains from losses, reframe constraints as advantages)*
- *Stick (countering one fear with another fear)*
- *Microscopic (break a fear into smaller fears and analyse them more closely to discern if the fears are rational) and/or*
- *Wide-angle (see the bigger picture by time-travelling into the future or 'cheating death').*

This gives our brains the best chance of locking into memory a more accurate and balanced view of the world, rather than reinforcing negative narratives.

Mend into Flow

In a fear-injured state, Mend isn't enough to quell our fears. The Thumping is too intense, the noise in our heads is too loud to shut down, and our fears don't seem to go away even when we apply the perspective-switching techniques. The solution is to give the fear-injured brain some respite, a moment's rest from the negative chatter. We can do this by getting into Flow i.e., lose ourselves in an activity.

The aim is to stay in Flow for as long as we can, to experience the contentment that comes from being in Flow, and along the way gain a few small wins. The Flow state may last ten minutes or ten hours.

The best way to get into Flow is to make a start on a task or a project. Just do, don't think. Avoid second-guessing ourselves, worrying about whether we are going in the right direction, whether the tasks are in the right sequence, whether there is a more efficient way, whether we are doing it right, or what others will think. Just do. We might spend a small amount of time planning at the start, e.g. break bigger tasks into smaller ones, but this should take little time (e.g. 30 seconds to 15 minutes). The more thinking we do, the more likely we are to fall into an unproductive mental loop, trying to know the unknowable, and falling prey to our fears. The right mindset is, "It's OK to make mistakes, I can always fix it later – what's more important is that I put one foot in front of the other."

To stay in Flow, it may be necessary to suppress and bury negative emotions and thoughts. Remember that we're talking about 10 minutes or 10 hours in duration only, a fleeting moment of rest.

Flow with purpose

When we're feeling miserable, it can be tempting to lose ourselves in activities that give us short-term boosts such as gambling, binge-watching TV and online shopping. These may be necessary distractions in the short term, depending on the crisis we're facing, but if we can manage it, it's better to opt for one of The Seven Purposes that are better for us over the long run.

The Seven Purposes

...for ageing gracefully

Do Good

Help the poor, save the planet, stand up for the disadvantaged, enforce fairness etc.

Master

Learn something new, hone skills, self-improve, master a domain, explore, gain knowledge etc.

Give

Better the lives of others, give care, feed, nurture, entertain, inform, teach, fix, heal etc.

Create

Produce original work, invent, build, solve unique problems, discover what was previously unknown, decode etc.

Invest

Acquire income generating assets (as opposed to spending), grow reputation, join community etc.

Bond

Deepen relationships, spend quality time with family, have shared experiences and adventures, work collaboratively etc.

Care for Self

Exercise, relax, eat well, meditate, do taxes on time, create a clean environment, spend time in nature etc.

Out of Flow and into Mend

At some point, we need to come out of Flow. For those of us experiencing the Thumping, this is when we're hit with a barrage of anxiety about the future and grief about the past. It's time to force our mind into Mend mode. Often, all that is required is to re-visit the set of fears and resolutions that we previously listed and repeat them in our heads.

And repeat

After Mend, we get back into Flow, give our mind a rest, then out of Flow and into Mend, force our mind to change our narratives, and so forth.

The roots of Flow-Mend cycle is as old as religion, and it is widely used today in sports, psychology and business.

In the beginning, it will feel like no progress is being made. Grief remains painful and fearful thoughts persist, frequently and loudly. And that is OK. We can't suppress a negative memory, and we shouldn't try to. The Animal Brain is in too much pain and is too dominant to be muffled. The aim of the Flow-Mend cycle isn't to suppress, it's about creating periods of rest, avoiding regurgitation and hence re-enforcement of fear and pain, and taking advantage of the quirk in our memory by saving concocted, more desirable versions of our narrative. It works because of the "use it or lose it" principle in neuroscience. If we stop firing up the synapses associated with fear and negativity, then the brain slowly and, over time, repurposes these synapses to serve other functions.

By repeating the Flow-Mend cycle over time, perhaps months, years or decades, we give ourselves the best chance of healing our fear-injured mind. I will provide an example of how we can apply the Flow-Mend practice in the next chapter.

At some point in our lives we will suffer tragic loss. The pain can be so great that it feels like it will never pass. The best thing we can do is to be kind to ourselves i.e., not judge ourselves harshly for having negative feelings. This said, we can't afford to be complacent for too long because we'd put ourselves at risk of deepening the wound and spending the rest of our lives fixated on the loss. We can aspire to survivors of the holocaust who experienced unimaginable loss and human atrocity, yet still emerged strong and resilient. A holocaust survivor said: "It is a very cruel and difficult part of my life. Sometimes I wonder...when I visited the camp with my son, wife, and grandson, how could anyone escape from that place? Yet, I escaped! I feel like I am very strong health-wise, mentally. Strong willed in my life. I can think even with fear of death."

What sets these amazing people apart isn't genetics or luck, it's mental practice. Irrational fear is to our brain what weeds are to a garden. Without constant pruning and shaping, we risk making space for irrational fears to thrive and crowd out everything we cherish.

PART VIII

QUELL

FEAR OF IMPERMANENCE

There is a cylindrical wheel in China that is enormous, over two-storey tall, to encircle it's circumference, we'd need seven to eight adults holding hands. Made of carved wood and solid stone, it would most definitely crush you in an instant if it fell on you.

I discovered it by accident when travelling with a friend through China. If memory serves me right, it sits on the top of a hill, in a desolate and forgotten location.

Curious about what it does, we looked for a sign to inform us of its purpose, but there weren't any. We noticed handles, six poles protruding outwards from the base of the wheel. We correctly guessed that the poles were used to turn the wheel, so the two of us grabbed hold at opposite ends and pushed like mules, huffing and grunting until we were red. Despite our best effort, the wheel didn't budge a millimetre, in either direction.

A short while later, three women showed up, tourists by the look of them. We persuaded them to help us.

We wondered what would happen if we turned the wheel. Would it produce music? Would a trap door open to a secret ancient *passageway or water flow from a fountain? Perhaps a fountain of youth?*

With five of us, the wheel turned slowly, but nothing happened. I thought perhaps we weren't going fast enough and urged everyone to go faster. Yet still nothing happened.

We were over three thousand metres above sea level, so it didn't take long for the thin air to exhaust us.

In letting go, I had hoped that we could stand back and admire the wheel spin for a while. It wasn't like I had high expectations — I wasn't expecting it to be a perpetual motion machine, but to my great disappointment, the wheel ground to a halt as soon as we stopped pushing.

At the time, I thought the machine was a dismal failure of engineering. Its deeper meaning was lost on me then.

I understand now that the wheel is a symbol of impermanence — a reminder that nothing lasts forever.

I bring it up now because mastering fear is exactly like that. We only get to stay on top of our fears so long as we practice, in the same way the benefits of exercise fade if we stop putting in the effort. Even Michael Jordan, at the height of his career, had to practice free throws. No matter what level of fear mastery we achieve, we will always remain vulnerable to succumbing to our fears in careless moments, at the snap of a finger.

Readers might find this disappointing, but to stay disappointed for too long is to be taken by the fear of impermanence. It would be like thinking: "My husband loves me now, but will it last forever?" Those of us who seek permanence do so with folly and futility.

What we can do is put into place habits and systems that will help us stay on top of our fears. For example, we can make meditating, journaling and self-analysis a daily practice. We can recruit others, those who know us best, to remind us, look for signs that we've ventured off course, help us stay sane, and act as sounding boards. And we can practice, practice, practice until seeing fear, switching mindsets, quelling anxieties and making the right moves becomes second nature.

Conversely, if we are in the habit of letting fear and worry rule our minds, then that's exactly what our brains will be good at in the future.

It follows that what we do now, how we handle our fears in this decade, defines not just who we are now, but the person we will be in the next decade.

MOVING MOUNTAINS

You work for a large tech company designing software solutions for clients. You've been doing it for over seven years. The next step up in your career involves generating sales, but you're neither interested in, nor good at selling. The thought of cold calling, schmoozing, and using 'closing tactics' makes you break out in a sweat. It would be like being a dentist who cringes at the sight of teeth and gums. You're happy where you are, so why consider a promotion at all? Why not just stay where you are?

It's what they expect of you. It's what everybody does, to work four or five years building technical expertise, then move up to senior roles where sales targets kick in. You could stay where you are, but it looks bad. It looks like you're going nowhere in your career, and you're afraid of what others might think. Aside from more pay, people who can sell curry more favours and wield more clout in the organisation. They sit at desks with views, have an expense budget, and frequently travel to conferences and company-sponsored events. For once you'd like to show off at lunch with associates, pull out your corporate credit card and say, "I'll get this bill", knowing that you're not paying out of your own pocket. At the moment, you pretend to have an expense account, "it's OK, my budget will cover this," you say, and later regret the lie. *Why the hell did I do that?*

You've fallen behind in your career compared to your peers. Some people who previously reported to you are now more senior than you are. One of them is Sasha, or Cap, as they call her, short for Captain America, on account of her rapid rise in the organisation. She is nice, but you think she is naïve and too young to deserve her last two promotions.

One day, at lunch with your boss Vincent, you say, "I'd like to put my hand up for a promotion this year."

"Sure, if that is what you want," he says.

"You have reservations?" you ask.

"No, no reservations. We can put your name forward to the committee, I'll support you, absolutely. I just want to be sure we do what is right for you. For example, are you comfortable with having a sales target?"

"Sure, why not," you reply.

"Well, you once said, and I quote, 'I am neither interested in, nor good at sales'."

"Sasha seems to do alright. I have twice her knowledge and experience."

"That's true. I'm not saying you can't do it." He pauses. "Let's look at it this way, if Sasha is our Captain America, which superhero best describes you as a professional?"

"I don't know," you say.

"What about Batman?" offers Vincent, your boss. "You're good at the technical stuff. You get things done with no fame and glory, whereas Captain America is covered in stars and stripes, all fanfare and showmanship."

"I can be Captain America if the situation demands it," you say.

"I know you can. We ought to be true to our stripes, though, ought we not? Are you a self-promoter? The person who likes the sound of their own name? When you walk into the room, do you feel you need to dominate the room? When you're at a conference, do you work the floor charming everyone or do you hide in a corner waiting for people to say hello to you? Are you well connected? Do you have an old boys' network you're happy to call on? Have you got the 'gift of the gab'? Would you be happy to sit in sales meetings after sales meetings, in your expensive Italian suit, talking about forecasts? Do you have the poker face to listen to clients, even when they are talking rubbish?"

"So you have just a few reservations, then? Am I doomed to work in the shadows like a mushroom?"

Vincent continues, "Sure, it's nice to have an expense account and a desk by the window, but along with that comes sales pressure, cold calling, and hundreds of rejections. Are you prepared to call your contacts for a favour and risk being ghosted? Are you prepared to be pushy even when clients say no? Do you have what it takes to pressure clients to sign on the dotted line?"

"I don't know."

"Nothing stops you from dabbling in sales this year, of course. In your current role, I mean. Try to get a few leads and close a deal – get a taste of it to see if you like it before you commit."

You reach the realisation that it's pointless to continue talking: *he's made his position clear. Now he is trying to get me to do two jobs without the promotion.*

"That makes sense," you say. "Let me think about it."

He says, "You do that. In the meantime, let *me* get the bill." He takes out his shiny platinum corporate card.

Vincent manipulated you by tapping into your fears. He has a conflict of interest in that if he promotes you, he'd lose an important member of his technical team, a gap he'd have to fill, a new person he'd have to train, a period of employee inexperience he'd have to tolerate, and he'd have to find more money to cover your salary increase, which is difficult when managers are being asked to tighten their budgets.

You are sick of working in the shadows. Yet, you have so many fears to deal with. As a technical expert, you're in a position of power. People need you, value your time and listen to your advice. As a salesperson, people resist you, avoid you, don't follow through on what they say, don't return calls and ignore emails. As a technical expert, you can point to tangible outputs every day: designs, reports, solutions, process maps, problems solved, customers you've helped, etc.. In sales, you might work for weeks and have nothing to show for it. It's no wonder that a lot of technical people look down at sales jobs. It's fear not arrogance: fear of loss of relationship power, risk of damage to their reputation, apprehension over not being in control, fear of wasting time, and fear of rejection.

You say to yourself: *Standing still is going backwards if everyone else is going forwards.* With this thought, you muster the courage to ignore your fears. You put your name forward to the committee for promotion.

A week later, you get a call. "Congratulations", Vincent says, "I knew you had it in you." You wince. It's not his insincere approval that bothers you so much but the dread of getting what you wished for. In an instant, all the benefits you coveted, the window seat, the expense account and the status doesn't seem such a big deal anymore.

Vincent assigns you an enormous sales target. You push

back: "You're asking me to move mountains here – it's my first year. Shouldn't there be a smaller target?"

"The CEO is pushing everyone harder this year. We need to hit a growth target in order to continue to prosper as a company," says Vincent.

It feels unfair. Worse, you're assigned a set of lame accounts. They're dud accounts because your company isn't well known or regarded at these accounts, the relationships are weak or non-existent, and your competitors are well entrenched in these organisations. By comparison, your peers are playing on plum wickets: all they have to do is show up in a suit, smile and be helpful, and the requests for quotes will come rolling in.

You soldier on, swallowing your fears. In the first week, you develop a plan. It involves a lot of guesswork, plucking sales numbers out of the air, making up sales forecasts for each account. You take a guess at the issues the clients are facing, and define a set of strategies and tactics. The guesswork makes you feel uncomfortable because of the fear of being wrong and not knowing what you're doing.

In the second week, you craft a few emails and send them out to thirty contacts. You don't hear back immediately. You decide to give them a week before following-up.

In the third week, you send follow-up emails. By this point, it feels like your wheels are spinning. You feel the pressure to evidence that you are working, so you set up meetings with people who know you well, but you know deep down this isn't necessarily a good use of time because they're not people who are involved in making buying decisions. At these meetings, you feel uncomfortable prying into their business, nor do you ask for their business. You're afraid of coming across as needy, losing their respect, using up favours, putting friends in an awkward position, and burning these relationships.

At the end of week three, much to your dread, there isn't much to show for the work that you've done. You tell yourself: *This is sales. I need to be patient. If Captain America can do it, so can I.*

In the fourth week, you update your sales plan, and stay "busy" by updating customer records. You volunteer for menial work in the office so that you can feel useful to others, which you don't realise is an act of fear[1]. You get a few meetings, but again, they're not with the right people, and you don't have the guts to push for what you want, so nothing comes of them.

One day, Sasha (aka Captain America) comes to your desk and inquires, "How's everything going?".

Normal people in normal discourse say things like, "fine thanks," but you say, "swimmingly great!" She holds eye contact with you, saying nothing, inviting you to fill the awkward silence. You don't.

"Well, I just thought I'd reach out. You're much more experienced than I am around here, but sales can be tough in the beginning."

"Is it?" you say, feigning nonchalance, your best impression of Kate Moss on a runway. "Well, I'm doing swimmingly great." There it is again, those overly positive words. You want to make it on your own, prove you've got what it takes, prove she is not better than you. The need for validation is an obstacle to your best interests.

In week eight, you land a meeting with a potentially important client. You do more talking than you should because you're overly eager to seize this rare opportunity and make the client fully grasp all your product's features and benefits. It's a fear-driven act, because you are imposing your needs on others as opposed to ascertaining their needs first. You're conscious of this, but you can't help yourself because you're afraid that you might not get a chance to meet this client again.

The clients express no interest. You don't get a chance to meet them again.

In the open-plan office, you overhear Vincent say, "Some folks are just not cut out for sales. Doesn't it make you cringe to watch them struggle like a mouse in a bucket of water?" The colleagues around him laugh smugly at the analogy.

In week eleven, you land a promising meeting, and hope it will be the opportunity to make Vincent eat his words. The client is very upbeat and asks if you could send him more information. They agreed to meet again later. You send them materials, wait a week before making contact, but don't hear from them. You make contact two weeks later, and again you don't hear back. The clients were too polite to say no to your face. It's much easier to ghost you.

You want to ask for help, but your pride says, "It's too late, I should have asked earlier." You're afraid of showing weakness, afraid to admit that you are not as good as other employees with half your knowledge and experience.

News of Sasha bringing in the biggest deal to date exacerbates your fears. You say to yourself: *I'll be OK, I just need to stick with it. If she can do it, I can do it. How hard can it be? I just need to be patient.* The self-talk isn't helpful because it's blind optimism (i.e., you're burying your fears and not doing anything materially different to improve your odds of success).

With each passing week, the dread grows heavier. The mountain that is your sales target seems more and more insurmountable. You regurgitate your fears often, force it back down, becoming progressively more insecure.

Four months into the role, after putting yourself through the grind, you secure a promising lead worth half your sales target. It gets you a lot of attention in the organisation. You're mentioned in the CEO's address to the team, who describes your lead as a "strategic opportunity". You respond to several requests for information from the client, create customised designs, presentations, project plans and business cases for them. Content creation is the stuff you're good at, unfortunately more than the stakeholder management side. You haven't been able to meet several key stakeholders, especially the sponsoring executive.

You've never worked harder, investing huge amounts of your time. Having been a sceptic of the deal, your boss Vincent was unsupportive of you putting all your eggs in one basket, but now that the deal shows promising signs, he is muscling in on the action. Everyone in the office is. You keep them all, especially Vincent, in the dark and at a distance. You say: *I can do this myself.* This is a fear-driven act because you're afraid others will steal your credit. Obstructing others, going it alone and not utilising the experience of others diminishes your chances of success.[2]

Finally, you get to meet the sponsoring executive, but at the very outset of the meeting, things don't go well. She seems to have already decided because she is hostile, and questions the validity of everything you say.

After the meeting, your contact says, "something came up and we have had to put this project off for a while."

What does she have against me? Is she upset? Why did they lead me on for so long if they never intended to buy? These are the wrong questions. The questions you should ask are: *What were her objection, and can we address them sincerely? What offer can we come back with, if not now, then in six months? I have developed good relationships with a few stakeholders, what other opportunities can I leverage? What can I learn from this experience? How could I have engaged senior decision-makers like her earlier in the buying process?*

But at this point, you're not in the headspace to ask constructive questions like these. By now, you are a bit of a mental train-wreck because of the constant pressure, worry, self-doubt, losses, disappointments and ongoing fear of failure. You experience panic attacks and regular headaches. You push the account to the bottom of your priorities because it's a source of frustration and embarrassment.

Deprived of a sense of control in one aspect of our lives, we try to gain a sense of control in another area. Some of us are harsher than usual towards our families, some turn to alcohol and drink excessively, some overeat, some go shopping, some gamble, and some micromanage. You set ambitious goals to get fit. You sign up for a triathlon. Every time you achieve a milestone, you feel better about yourself because you feel more in control of your life. You become obsessed with getting the right equipment because the feeling you get from researching, finding and buying the right bicycle or accessory gives you a sense of control and progress. The trouble is, you're not dealing directly with the source of what is making you feel out of control.

One day, on a hill climb, you tear your achilles. Your physio says you'll need at least eight weeks of rest, possibly more. You ignore the advice, believing it's all in the mind, and get back on the bike after four restless weeks. It's the same dogged optimism that got you into hot water at work. You exacerbate the injury. After weeks of pain and no sign of recovery, you throw in the towel, and give up on the dream of competing in a triathlon. Your body has failed you, and this makes you feel even more out of control.

At work, you're waiting for the day you get discovered as an imposter. It could be any day now. You develop a deep resentment for your job, your company, your boss. You complain about the economy, your company's product, the CRM system, the marketing department, the coffee making facilities in the kitchen...

You discover others in the same circumstance. The lot of you huddle together, drink coffee, debrief and whine. This makes you feel better. At least you're not alone. Too bad that it doesn't actually help you deal with your fears.

One day, you bump into Sasha. "How's everything going?" she enquires.

"I'm swimming great!" you say.

She says nothing, giving you room to elaborate. You don't.

"Well, I was clearing out my files, and I came across this training folder that I thought you might find useful. I imagine you've done plenty of sales training over the years, have you come across this one before?"

"Don't know," you say.

"Would you like to borrow it?"

"I'll be fine," you say.

"Do you want to borrow it, anyway?" she asks.

"No, really, I am fine,' pushing back.

Part of the reason for not accepting the help is your sense of hopelessness. You've been thinking about throwing in the towel, resigning, finding another job, and getting back to solution design, away from sales. You have little faith that you will learn anything you don't already know, confirming your suspicions that you are just inherently bad at sales. The sales training you've come across so far has been full of 'power of the mind', pseudo-science, babble.

One night, after a particularly downcast day, you find yourself alone in the office. You'd spent the afternoon looking at job classified ads and bicycle equipment, and hadn't noticed that everyone had left the office. All alone, for no particular reason, you sit at someone else's desk. Look at their things. It's not the sort of thing you usually do, but you allow yourself the thrill of voyeurism because it feels like your days here are over. Your neighbour's desk isn't particularly interesting: piles of paper, award certificates, computer codes, reminders.... You move to another desk, Malcolm's. There's a rotten mandarin, green with mould in his drawer. At Cindy's desk, you help yourself to her stash of chocolates (just one). You swipe a protein bar from an intern's desk. Discover a hip flask in Geoff's locked cupboard (everyone knows where he hides the key), take a swig, feel the burn in your throat, and put it back. You rearrange a collection of trolls on Mary's desk. You switch people's chairs around. It entertains you to imagine the look of confusion on their faces in the morning when they sit down.

Too much exposure to fear can make us act this way. Tired of being afraid, we say, "what the heck", throw caution to the wind, behave foolishly and fearlessly and momentarily out of character. Someone might be in the office, or there could be a security camera, you can't be 100% certain.

At Vincent's desk, in his drawer, you find a selfie photo of him with a semi-naked woman, his wife, you presume. You look closer and see that it's not his wife, it's Cindy, the lady with the stash of chocolates you stole from. She's asleep, one of her breasts showing. He's looking smug. You slip the photo into your pocket for safekeeping. You think to yourself: *it could come in handy.*

Sasha's desk is relatively boring, so you pry deeper, looking through folders and papers. *What's her secret?* You come across the training folder she offered you before. You scan the titles, as you suspected, it's full of truisms like, "Address the fear, not the words." At the back of the folder there is a worksheet filled out in what looks like Sasha's handwriting:

1. My Fears

- Failing, looking bad and wasting time

- Not being a "natural" salesperson
- The uncertainty associated with selling, not being in control, getting rejected, prying into other people's affairs, risk of harming my reputation and damaging relationships
- Doing things I don't feel comfortable with.

2. The better me

- Zoom in: It's ok to fail, I can always go back to my old job (or another job); my old colleagues are likely to welcome me back rather than judge me
- I might not be a natural salesperson, but plenty of people like me have had success. We have our advantages e.g. I will come across as being more genuine and less pushy
- I lack capability because I am a novice, but I won't always be a novice
- Frame losses as gains: I get the chance to develop an important skill, one that will be necessary to get to the next executive level
- With sales experience, I'd be more attractive to future employers and be more in control of my future career
- I must reframe my challenge: from "selling" to "creating value and helping others"; from "prying" to "showing interest in others"; from "pushing" to "problem solving"; and from "closing" to "project managing towards a result that is a win for everyone".

3. Acts of fear

- Not asking for help, not sharing the burden, constantly looking for validation and acting like a lone wolf
- Keeping busy without creating value, e.g. playing internal politics to prove my worth rather than doing actual work
- Doing what is easy rather than what is valuable, e.g. meeting anyone who will take a meeting as opposed to prioritising and qualifying my leads
- Maintaining false optimism, not reading the signs, not changing tack based on what is actually going on
- Spamming a broad set of targets with emails that are not specific to them
- Being pushy. i.e. ramming information down a client's throat as opposed to listening
- Acting in my self-interest, and applying "closing tactics" that make clients feel pressured and jeopardises the long-term relationship

4. Fear Mastery

- Ask for help, e.g. sign-up for training, do joint sales visits with mentors to learn, seek advice to overcome obstacles
- Prioritise top prospects and conduct deep research to find out the issues they are facing, who the decision makers are etc. (as opposed to a 'scattergun' approach)

- I shouldn't be afraid to ask questions about a client's situation (people are happy to help me so long as they understand why and what is in it for them). Demonstrating interest isn't prying if I'm genuinely trying to help.
- Be in the moment at meetings. The aim is to understand their needs, facilitate and help solve problems, not push my products and pressure people to close deals.

The most striking thing about what you see is how alike the two of you are. You've assumed that Sasha is a natural at sales, but she isn't. The two of you share the same fears.

I need to stop being a puppet to my fears.

There are a lot of ideas under "The Better Me" to take in. You understand them cognitively, but not entirely, unsure you're able to embody the mindset change required. This said, you feel for the first time a sense of hope.

You return the folder back to its place.

You rearrange the office chairs that you moved earlier to their original owners; return the trolls to their previous positions; put five dollars in the intern's drawer to compensate for the protein bar you stole; make a mental note to buy Geoff a drink for the sip of his hip flask; retrieve Malcolm's mouldy mandarin out of his drawer and dump it in the kitchen bin; and write yourself a reminder to replace the chocolate you stole from Cindy.

The next day, you say hello to Sasha, and ask if you can borrow the folder.

"Sure," she says.

"After I study it, can I buy you a coffee so we can talk about it?" you ask.

"It'll cost you a lot more than a coffee."

"Oh?"

"I have a sales meeting later today, and it would be great to have someone with technical knowledge in the room to answer questions I might not be comfortable with. Would you have time to come along?"

"Sure".

At the meeting, much to your surprise, Sasha doesn't do any product advocating at all. Instead, she asks questions that get clients talking, more like a skilled interviewer than a salesperson. She mines for relevant information, and when she gets it, she'll play back her understanding before asking an even more pertinent question.

The client, having expressed their needs, and gained the feeling that the two of you understand them well, asks a set of technical questions. Sasha doesn't pretend to know the answer and defers them to you. You furnish them with well-practised answers, but unlike before when it felt like you were pushing information at people, this time your audience is genuinely interested. You feel respected for your expertise.

A week later, the client awards Sasha the contract, to which she gives you 50% credit. It's your first sale!

"I did nothing," you protest.

"Are you kidding me?" Sasha says. "You handled the toughest part of the sales meeting. They like us because of your expertise."

"Yeah, but it's you they trust."

"It's us they trust."

In the weeks ahead, you adopt Sasha's information-mining style; buddy with others to learn from them; and qualify leads to avoid wasting time.

Sales is not for the fainthearted. You often go into mental loops, worry about the same problem repeatedly, and experience episodes of anxiety. You refer to Sasha's fear matrix often to get out of your own head and restore a more balanced state of mind, but it doesn't always work. In a competitive office environment, under a boss like Vincent, who believes that an insecure employee is one that will try harder, you never quite feel on top of your game.

You take a long time before you score a second win; you are unsure of when the next one will come, and it's unlikely you will make your sales target this year.

It's OK to fail. I am learning, building relationships, and nurturing my career.

You feel in control, as opposed to blindly optimistic, because you know what you have to do. You're comforted by what Sasha said once: *"It's an unrelenting struggle, isn't it?"* If someone like her feels this way, then maybe there is nothing wrong with you.

And what happened to the incriminating selfie photo of Vincent – the one with Cindy, semi-naked in the background? Did you put it back where you found it? Did you make copies of it? Do you still have it, hidden somewhere to be used as leverage in future? That night, the night you stole chocolates and rearranged chairs, you placed it in an envelope, addressed it to Cindy anonymously, and put it in Cindy's drawer.

It's none of my business, but she has a right to know.

SWIM WITH CROCODILES

You are in a team meeting. A spritely new team member introduces herself to everyone. She is from Baltimore. You once went on a road trip with your late father to Baltimore – the two of you had a terrible row that gave you reason to never take him on a holiday again. At the team meeting you become teary. You try, but you can't hold it back. Your father died of cancer, suddenly last year. You turn your head to hide your face. *I wish I had done more for him when he was alive.* You pretend there is something in your eye. *He was mean to me.* It's likely that others can see that you're off-colour, but no one is saying anything for fear of embarrassing you.

For the rest of the day, you are off-kilter, unable to concentrate, mind racing, suffer pangs of guilt and loss, and experience the Thumping. People ask if you're OK, so you lie and tell them you're fine.

It has been more than a year since your father died. You wish you had a better relationship with him, but he was a difficult man to love. At his best, he was as charming and magnanimous as Nelson Mandela, but he was an alcoholic. When he drank, he became self-absorbed and abusive, as if everyone owed him something. In his last years, he became a mean and angry man. He regularly scolded you for being ungrateful. It hurt you then, and it haunts you now – an echo that gets louder and louder in his absence.

The trip to Baltimore, the one that took place over two decades ago, was a generous act on your part because you found it suffocating to spend long periods of time with him. A condition of the trip was that it was to be alcohol-free. On the third day, at the end of a long day's drive, he wanted to order a beer to go with his dinner, but you tried to stop him because you knew from experience that he cannot stop at one drink. You threatened to leave. "I just want us to have a pleasant memory together, is that OK?" He yields.

You order two whole lobsters in garlic butter. "Let's do it Dad, it's my treat, let's have a night to remember!"

After you placed the order, your father excused himself and was absent for quite a while. When he returned, you asked, "Is everything OK?"

"No problem," he said with a smile.

During entrees, he excused himself again.

"You were gone a long time," you said upon his return.

"I went to the loo, and got a phone call from an old friend," he said.

"Who?" you ask.

"Johnny, you know Johnny, the fisherman? He wants to know if I'm free next year for a trip to the Cape."

You sense he is lying.

Before the main course, your father excused himself again. After a small absence, you left the table to look for him. You found him sitting at the bar of the restaurant with a beer in hand. "I see you don't really need me to enjoy your night. I'll go then, enjoy your dinner." You left him to eat two lobsters by himself.

That night, you booked yourself a separate hotel room. You didn't answer his phone calls, and you ignored the messages he left on your voicemail.

To anyone else, this seems like an overreaction. What they don't see is the trauma from the drunken abuse you suffered as a child. The yelling and bullying. To an outsider, a sip of alcohol is harmless. To you, it's the mark of the beginning of torment and dark times.

The next morning, he didn't offer an apology. You didn't offer him one either because he was the one who lied and ruined the evening. You behaved civilly and spoke to him as if the events of the previous night had never taken place. He didn't bring it up either, presumably feeling ashamed.

The trip was a turning point in your adult relationship with your alcoholic father. Up to this point, your father had power over you, as if he had invisible reins that controlled how you felt. In your professional circles, you have the reputation for being steady, composed and good under pressure. With a tug of these reins, your father could turn you into your five-year-old self – tempestuous, entitled and disempowered, all at once. After the trip, you became immune to his emotional blackmail by hardening yourself against it. You distanced yourself. You no longer felt obliged to take him on a holiday with you. *He doesn't deserve it. I gave him a chance, and he blew it.* You kept contact to a bare minimum, more than he deserved, in your view. You watched his health decline from afar, all the while pushing out the pang of guilt in your heart.

That was two decades ago. He's gone now.

There's a photo of the two of you in a drawer. You are only two years old in that photo, and he's a lanky twenty-something year-old with all his hopes and dreams ahead of him.

He's carrying you in his arms, looking at you the way new fathers look at their child. The photo pains you now because of the way he is looking at you, how he must have adored you, yet you showed little gratitude late in his life. You nurse a cocktail of grief, remorse, guilt, loss and anger. You hate him but know you shouldn't, so you hate yourself for hating him.

You think of that trip to Baltimore, and you wish now that you had been nicer to him, to have let him have what he wanted, and to have gone on more holidays with him.

You picture him sitting somewhere, by himself, forever out of your reach. This image causes you so much heartache.

At night, you have a nightmare about your father. He is swimming in a river, and you are standing on a bridge a fair distance away. Suddenly a bask of crocodiles surface behind him and swim towards him. You yell at the top of your voice to warn him of the danger, but to no avail. He can't seem to hear you. You try to get help, but no one seems to care. He is too far away for you to reach by foot, the crocodiles are closing in too fast, but you run towards him, anyway. Despite putting in the big strides, you don't seem to cover much ground, so you run even faster, but it doesn't matter how fast you run, you don't get closer. The crocodiles are now on him. They drag him under the water without a sound. There is no trace of him bar a few bubbles on the surface. You are still a fair distance away, and everyone seems oblivious to the tragedy. Your father never surfaces again.

You wake up from this nightmare and feel the Thumping, an ache in your chest. Your Thinking Brain says, "It's not real, it's just a silly dream," but your Animal Brain can't differentiate reality from fantasy (it is after all the Animal Brain that conjured this dream). The stress hormones flood your bloodstream, causing you to experience more grief. You cannot return to sleep, and the more you try, the deeper the stress drags you into the depths of the Thumping. You sit up, attempt a ten-minute meditation, but there is so much noise in your head that you can't seem to find any peace.

It's 2:00 am. You get out of bed, slip on some socks, and make yourself a herbal tea. At the kitchen bench, out of desperation, you force your mind to rewrite the dream:

The crocodiles are not live crocodiles, they're crocodile-shaped inflatable rafts – the ones kids play with in swimming pools.

He isn't swimming in a river, he's at a resort, where there are colourful umbrellas and sun lounges.

You close your eyes and try to create this visual image in your head, and in doing so, crowd out the horrible image of the crocodiles. You add more details: the inflatable crocodile has a broad, friendly smile, and there is a bucket of beer sitting on its head. Your father is keeping himself afloat by holding the inflatable friendly croc in a headlock with one arm. With his free arm, he grabs a cold beer from the bucket, takes a big swig, looks up at you, smiles and winks. He is relaxing and having the time of his life. *(This is the "Mend" stage of the Flow-Mend cycle.)*

It may be a contrived thought exercise, but you're sick of being tormented by guilt and hatred. The Thumping subsides a little. Your Animal Brain is still unhappy and anxious, but at least you're not dealing with the grief-stricken, panicky feeling that you felt a moment ago.

Wary that you're still on edge, and that the Thumping may return the moment you return to bed, you take out some drawing materials to create a sketch. You lose yourself in the work, get into Flow, and this seems to further calm your Animal mind. You draw an owl. Stress hormones ebb away. Sketch background leaves. The noise in your head lessens. Draw mountains in the background. The Thumping in your chest settles. Twenty-five minutes later, images of your father being taken by crocodiles long forgotten, you return to bed, begin a meditation routine, focus on your breath, and soon, without notice, fall asleep.

The next day, the nightmare appears in your mind again. It causes your heart to thump. You force it out of your mind by re-creating the cheerful scene: inflatable crocs, colourful umbrellas, sun lounges, your father smiling with a drink in hand. The same thing happens several times a day over the next few days. You can't control what thoughts come into your mind, but you can replace the scary version with the happy version. Over time, it happens less and less, and in time, the happy version becomes the only one that remains.

At work, every time you encounter the new team member from Baltimore, feelings of guilt and sadness surfaces, causing you to seize up, say less and become closed-minded.

Recognising the pattern, you set your mind to break this cycle of behaviour because it's affecting your work. *I miss my father, and that's OK. I took a stand against him on that trip, and it upset him, but I did it in his best interest. After that incident, I gained his respect, and our relationship improved.* This is the Thinking Brain rationalising. It does nothing to address the anxious Animal Brain.

I ought to look at all the good things that happened on that trip, not just focus narrowly on that incident. Baltimore was not the only place we visited. We crossed the extraordinary Chesapeake Bay Bridge-Tunnel.

"This is incredible," he said. "It's like we're driving over the ocean."

You picture him in the car next to you, the wind in his hair, the bay waters in the background, the salt in the air, the look of contentment on his face. You lock this happy image into your head. Every time you meet the team member from Baltimore, you make an effort to bring this scene and this feeling into your mind. You are calming and rewriting the memory stored by your Animal Brain.

Life goes on. Mend: *my father is proud of me.* Flow: get lost in the process of painting. Mend: share your father's wisdom with your children. Flow: listen to music. Mend: *I shouldn't blame my father for his alcoholism. He was a product of his time and circumstances, just like the rest of us.*

Will it work? Will I be able to create a bridge from where I am now, a vulnerable, grief-stricken place, to where I need to be for my children? Not necessarily a sunny, happily ever-after disposition: all I am asking for is to be in control of my mind again. To be balanced and strong.

You don't know. Nobody knows.

A song triggers you to choke up with tears. Mend: m*y father was a great man. He built a business from nothing to give us a better future. I am proud of him, as much as he is proud of me.* Flow: play a board game with the children and lose yourself in the banter and competition.

Every now and then, memories of his drunken abuse comes back to haunt you. Mend: recall happy memories, like how he backed you when everyone else didn't. Flow: go for a long run, along the river, past the old grain silo, through the park, over the fence, across the grassy hill, into the forest, and finish at a cafe.

My father was a flawed man, and he was proud of me. He always spoke highly of me, and walked tall in my company. He loved me as much as I loved him.

My father lives on in my work. All that is him is now me.
Thank you, Dad.

THE END

I wish you all the best in the ups and downs of your journey to mastery.

James Lau

Mend

Flow

Mend

Flow

Mend

Flow

Mend

Flow

Mend

Flow

Mend

NOTES

The hidden force that holds us back

1. The sunk cost trap happens when we continue to stand by poor decisions of the past despite evidence to the contrary. It is a fear of admitting to ourselves and to others that we've made a bad decision.

   We fall for the sunk cost trap when we make investment decisions. For example, we are reluctant to sell assets at a loss, aiming to at least break-even if we can, ignoring the risk of losing more money. We ignore the fact that we might be better off admitting we were wrong and cutting our losses (i.e. selling up and investing in better performing assets).

   We fall for the sunk cost trap in relationships, sticking with partners with whom we no longer get along, or share common values.

   It affects our everyday decisions: we finish movies we don't enjoy; finish food we have ordered at a restaurant even if we don't like it; hang on to clothes that we've never worn; keep exercise equipment we don't use; and add ingredients to a curry-gone-wrong, hoping to rescue it.

   Large organisations aren't immune to falling for the sunk cost trap either, despite having sophisticated governance processes. This is because fear is present at every stage of the decision-making process: it influences what data we gather, what data we leave out, how we communicate the data, who we choose to communicate to, how we interpret the data, and who we feel we owe our allegiance to.

   Once a business leader has made a commitment to a course of action, such as investing in a project, they are more likely to stick to the same course of action, even if the evidence suggests they shouldn't. It explains blow-outs in capital projects. It's hard to cut and run because of we're afraid of admitting that we made a mistake to our employees and bosses. We don't want to tarnish our reputation and be seen as a flip-flop who has wasted company money.

   For the same reason, once a political leader has taken a position, such as being tough on immigrants, it's hard for them to reverse their position.

2. Or is it driven by fear? Fear of being the kind of person to give up easily. What looks like tenacity is actually a fear-driven act.

The wake-up call

1. King, S.. 2000. On Writing: A Memoir of the Craft.
2. Albom, M.. 2003. The Five People You Meet in Heaven.

What progressives and conservatives have in common

1. These are made up statistics that have no basis of truth in them, created by me to illustrate a point.

Why we overwork, overeat and overexercise

1. I know this from firsthand experience. I avoided running for years because of a basketball accident in my early twenties. I discovered in my mid-forties that proper running form heals and strengthens my achilles.

What lurks behind every buying decision

1. Sue Hewitt, "Premium petrol a waste of money, RACV research reveals." 25 November 2019. https://www.racv.com.au/royalauto/moving/news-information/premium-petrol-guzzling-cash.html

Discerning rational from irrational fear

1. This is a rough approximation. Ontario sample data from 1993 indicates 1.44 out of 100,000 children die from bicycle accidents, compared to US 2018 data that indicates 5.21 children die from motor accidents. Spence, J., Dykes, E., Bohn, D., Wesson, D.. 1993. "Fatal bicycle accidents in children: a plea for prevention", Journal of Pediatric Surgery. Feb;28(2):214-6. https://pubmed.ncbi.nlm.nih.gov/8437084/. Cunningham, R., Walton, A., Carter, P.. 2018. "The Major Causes of Death in Children and Adolescents in the United States", N Engl J Med 379:2468-2475 https://www.nejm.org/doi/full/10.1056/nejmsr1804754.

Behind every conflict, every argument, and every grudge lies...guess what?

1. United States Parachute Association. 2021 data. https://uspa.org/Discover/FAQs/Safety
2. Insurance Information Institute, based on National Center for Health Statistics and the National Safety Council. 2020 data. https://www.iii.org/fact-statistic/facts-statistics-mortality-risk

The epiphany

1. A reference to a line in the film *"Jerry Macguire"*.

The four lenses

1. Promotions depend on who else is in the running, how the company is performing, how decision makers feel about you relative to others, what luck you experienced during the year, what political games people are playing etc.. Much of this is outside of our control.

Racism

1. The U.S. unauthorised immigrant population stood at 12.2 million in 2007, declining to 10.5 million in 2017. The number of unauthorised Mexican immigrants in the US was ~7 million in 2007, declining to ~5 million in 2017 (2/7 = ~30%), Lopez, M.H., Passel, J.S. and Cohn, D.. 2021. "Key facts about the changing U.S. unauthorised immigrant population." Pew Research Center.
2. In my endeavour to tackle racism, I leave out-of-scope racism that is driven by resource scarcity, religious extremism, and inter-generational conflict. Neither am I looking to solve unconscious stereotyping, such as discrimination in recruitment and non-psychological or systems based racism, such as those driven by credit score algorithms. I am not an expert in political correctness, and I don't pretend to speak for oppressed minorities. A lot of racism is driven not by the colour of our skin but by other factors such as jealousy and tribalism. Although they can be explained by fear, a full and proper treatment of them needs to factor in political, social, economic and legacy issues, which is beyond the scope of this book.

Cheating death and time travelling

1. Some of the fears include: fear of loss of status, loss of influence in the organisation, going backwards in your career, letting people down, not being able to protect your people, and loss of autonomy.
2. Fear of bureaucracy, loss of autonomy, loss of past privileges, and having to answer to people beneath you.
3. Fear of authority, being a burden, and making a mistake that could have bad career repercussions.
4. Fear of not knowing what to do, having to give bad news to people in your tribe, losing the faith in the people in your team, not following corporate orders, looking weak against your peers, your career going down the gurgler, that you'll lose everything you've built, and being forced to take action against your will.
5. Customers subconsciously choose brands they recognise, conflating familiarity with trustworthiness or value. Unfamiliar brands arouse fears such as fear of buying products that are unsafe, untested, don't work, or are of poor quality. The other trepidations are fear of looking cheap, that you're compromising your family's well being, and fear of being ripped off.
6. Using fear of unknown generic brands and fear of inferior products to overcome fear of wasting money.

V. MOVE

1. Moore, L.. 2000. Self Help.

Gaming addiction

1. Your fears include: fear of being wrong, realising you've been a poor parent, losing an argument, being taken in by populist dogma, and fear of being a sheep.
2. The fear matrix doesn't have to be organised as a 2 x 2 table, it can be written out as a list as a list – as is often the case in my journal.

Oppression

1. Sorry to spoil your victory, but had you considered your nephew's fears, rather than assume he's a spoiled child, you might have had more success with him. Like many fussy eaters, he has had unpleasant experiences with foreign food, foreign meaning anything he isn't familiar with. His fear is that he'd be forced to eat something distasteful and repeat the awful experiences of the past.

The End

1. *I'd like to say that I felt I owed this to my readers, but in truth it was a fear driven act. I was afraid of producing something that doesn't resonate or doesn't help anyone.*

Where does confidence come from?

1. Explained by the "headwind-tailwinds effect": a human bias that gives more weight to negativity over positivity. Davidai, S., Gilovich, T.. 2016. The headwinds/tailwinds asymmetry: An availability bias in assessments of barriers and blessings. J Pers Soc Psychol. 111(6): 835-851pp.

The age of fear-mongering

1. The Daily Telegraph 4 Nov 2020
2. The original headlines used the slang term "cop" instead of "police".
3. The central bank has cut official interest rates. The implication of this article is that greedy banks may not pass on rate cuts to mortgage owners.
4. Eyal, Nir. "Hooked: How to Build Habit-Forming Products". 2014. Penguin.
5. Pinker, S.. 2018 Enlightenment Now: The Case For Science, Humanism and Progress. Cited from The Guardian "The media exaggerates negative news. This distortion has consequences." https://www.theguardian.com/commentisfree/2018/feb/17/steven-pinker-media-negative-news

Five interesting quirks in our brain

1. Examples: USA: https://www.pewresearch.org/politics/2022/06/06/public-trust-in-government-1958-2022/; UK: https://www.ippr.org/news-and-media/press-releases/revealed-trust-in-politicians-at-lowest-level-on-record/; and Australia: https://www.anu.edu.au/news/all-news/trust-in-government-hits-all-time-low
2. Statistica. Feb 2022. Number of smartphone subscriptions worldwide from 2016 to 2027. https://www.statista.com/statistics/330695/number-of-smartphone-users-worldwide/
3. 6,567,000,000 smartphones divided by 148,900,000 km2 (Earth's total land area) = 44.1 smartphones per square km.
4. Referred elsewhere as the rational vs emotional brain (Plato, 428-348 BCE), conscious vs unconscious (Sigmund Freud), neocortex vs limbic (Paul MacLean, Yale Medical School), Elephant vs Rider (Jonathan Haidt, Professor at NYU, and Richard Thaler, Nobel Prize Laureate), and System 1 vs System 2 (made famous by Daniel Kahneman Nobel Prize laureate).

5. This is because using the Thinking Brain taxes our mental resources, so we avoid it in the same way we avoid a flight of stairs if there is an elevator alongside. It's not a matter of laziness, it's a matter of survival because the Thinking Brain cannot cope with the plethora of actions and decisions we need to execute everyday. For example, when we eat, much of what we do/decide is automated thanks to our Animal Brain. Imagine if it weren't, imagine the effort to complete simple tasks like eating: "Do I use a fork or spoon? Do I start with a piece of chicken, or would it be optimal to have a mouthful of rice first?" Do we need our Thinking Brain to analyse these decisions? Thanks to our Animal Brain, we know to test for temperature before putting hot food in our mouth, we can chew without effortful thought, and we know when we have had enough to eat. Daniel Kahneman illustrates the interplay between the two brains with two questions. Question 1: "What is the capital of France?" The answer "Paris" pops into our head automatically, involuntarily, thanks to our Animal Brain. Question 2: "What is 17 x 24?" To come up with an answer, it's likely that we'd have to engage our Thinking Brain, and in doing so, stop everything else we are doing (for example, if we're walking and someone asks us what is 17 x 24, it's likely that we would pause mid-step to work out the answer). Source: Kahneman, D., 2011. Thinking Fast and Slow, pp. 20-21.
6. Kahneman, D.. 2011. Thinking Fast and Slow.

Healing a fear-injured mind

1. D.J. Bridge and K.A. Paller. 2012. Neural Correlates of Reactivation and Retrieval-Induced Distortion. Journal of Neuroscience 29 August 2012, 32 (35) 12144-12151. https://www.jneurosci.org/content/32/35/12144

Moving mountains

1. It's an act of fear because you're doing things to keep busy as opposed to doing things that contribute towards your goal.
2. It's not entirely the fault of the salesperson. Many companies foster a competitive culture and incentive system which rewards lone wolf behaviour.

ACKNOWLEDGMENTS

I am grateful for the love, support and encouragement from Dr Jocelyn Rikard-Bell, my muse, sounding board and editor. It's hard to know how much of the thinking originated from her, in truth, quite possibly all of it, or at least ninety-one percent.

There is no me without my family. I am grateful for my father's fear mastery, who backed me even when my primary school grades showed little promise. I admire my mother's tenacity and work ethic, the woman who made countless sacrifices for us. My sister's love and nurture means everything to me, without which I'd be a much lesser person.

A book is an output of a collective rather than that of a single individual. I'm grateful to Megan Rikard-Bell whose equanimity and people skills are my role model for giving people a sense of control; and Dr Hal Rikard-Bell whose fear mastery, particularly the discipline of pre-decisioning (making decisions ahead of moments of truth) is the premise of the business I created (xempli.com) as well as the Fear Matrix (Chapter 5). I'd like to thank Mike Nield for the coaching sessions on character development and story writing; Jane Weir for her contribution to the "seven purposes for ageing gracefully"; Jermir Punthakey and Benjamin Lau for their incredible eye for detail and superior grammar; Marisol Ortega — the wonderful artist who came up with the idea of a spiral staircase for the book cover (marisolortega.com); Samuel Lau with whom I collaborated to come up with ideas for the illustrations; Johanna Penn, whose podcast encouraged me to self-publish; Sidney Minassian, my business mentor who advised me to "concentrate on the product"; Sue Heath, Burkhardt Schuett, Haris Preljevic, Penelope Terry, Elizabeth Lau (no relation), Jaeho Sim, Claire Talbot, Amy Collins and Sebastian Bather for their support — thanks for spurring me on. And finally, thanks to Roman Sisa, whose friendship makes me feel I can take on the world.

ABOUT THE AUTHOR

J.S. Lau is a management consultant, entrepreneur and coach. He has advised senior executives at some of the largest companies in the world, solving problems related to profitability, supply chain and change. As an entrepreneur, James created xempli.com, an organisation change program powered by behavioural science. James lives in Bathurst, in rural Australia, with his partner and two children.

Printed in Great Britain
by Amazon